of
Saint
Alphonsus
Liguori

The Way of Saint Alphonsus Liguori

SELECTED WRITINGS ON THE SPIRITUAL LIFE

Edited With An Introduction By
BARRY ULANOV

LIGUORI/TRIUMPH
LIGUORI, MISSOURI

Published by Liguori/Triumph
An Imprint of Liguori Publications
Liguori, Missouri
http://www.liguori.org

This edition is a revised version of *The Way of St. Alphonsus Liguori*, copyright 1961 by P. J. Kenedy & Sons, New York, compiled by Barry Ulanov.

Library of Congress Cataloging-in-Publication Data

Liguori, Alfonso Maria de', Saint, 1696–1787.
[Selections. English. 1999]
The way of Saint Alphonsus Liguori : selected writings on the spiritual life / edited with an introduction by Barry Ulanov. — Rev. ed.
p. cm.
ISBN 0-7648-0382-4
1. Spiritual life—Catholic Church. I. Ulanov, Barry. II. Title.
BX2350.2.L48413 1999
248.4'82—dc21 98–47863

Printed in the United States of America
03 02 01 00 99 5 4 3 2 1

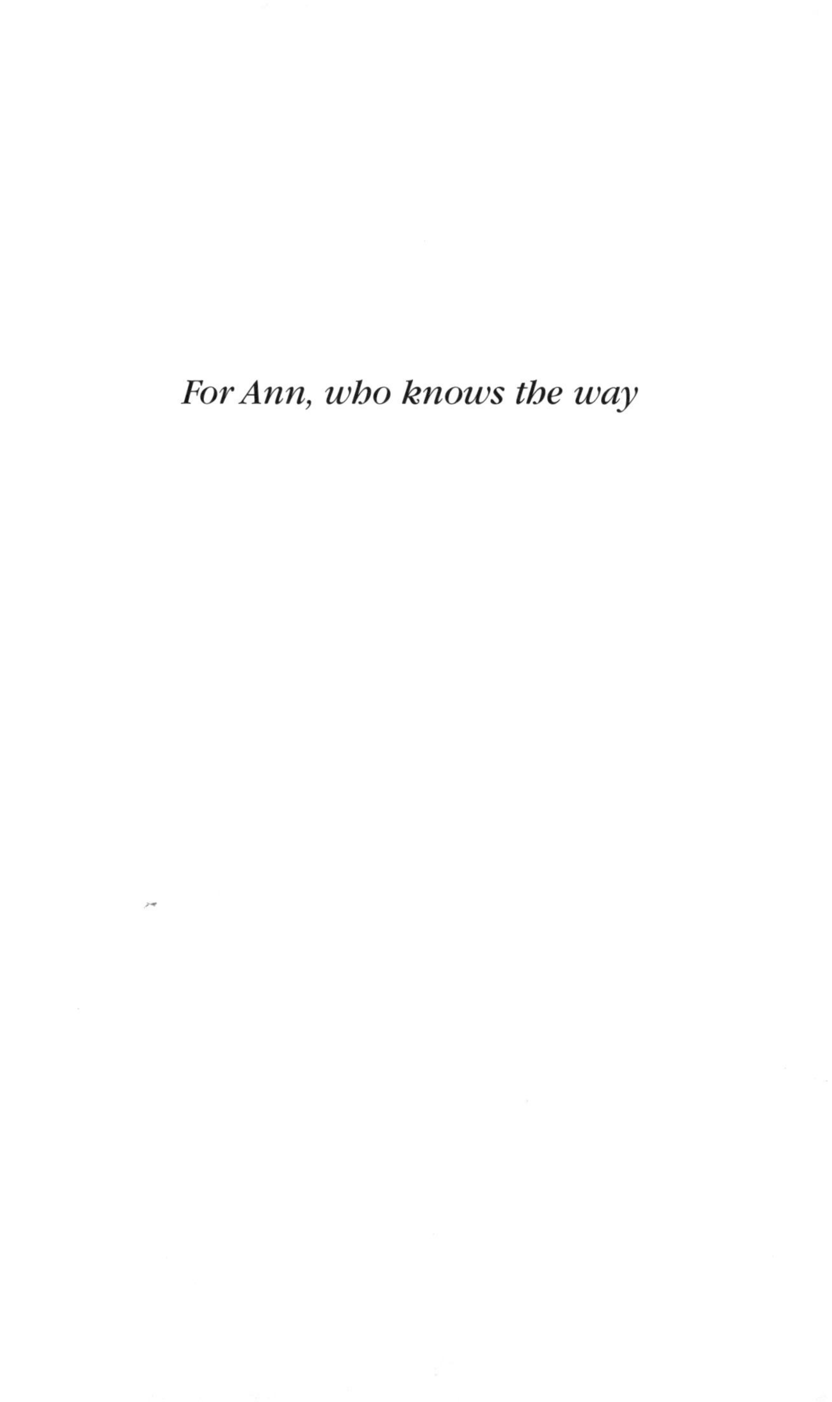

For Ann, who knows the way

Contents

Meditations On the Blessed Sacrament 26

Novena of the Holy Spirit: Meditations for Each Day of the Novena 44

The Glories of Mary 55

On the Love of God, and the Means to Acquire It 93

The Practice of the Love of Jesus Christ 108

A Christian's Way of Life 167

A Reading Plan for the Church Year

Christmas Cycle

Advent

Meditations on the Incarnation: pages 1–12.
Novena of the Holy Spirit: Meditations 1, 6–7 (pages 45–46, 49–51).
The Practice of the Love of Jesus Christ: Sections on the patience and forbearance of Charity (pages 116–120, 145–147).

Christmas

Meditations on the Incarnation: pages 5–7, 9–10, 12–13.
Meditations on the Blessed Sacrament: pages 26–30.

Epiphany

Meditations on the Incarnation: pages 13–17.
On the Love of God and the Means to Acquire It: pages 93–107.

Lenten Cycle

Pre-Lenten preparation

The Practice of the Love of Jesus Christ: Sections on how Jesus Christ deserves our love and how we are obliged to love him (pages 108–116).

Meditations on the Blessed Sacrament: pages 30–43.

Lent

A Christian's Way of Life: pages 167–204.

Counsels From Which a Soul May Derive Comfort and Confidence: pages 254–279.

Passiontide

Meditations on the Incarnation: pages 18–25.

The Practice of the Love of Jesus Christ: pages 108–114.

Meditations on the Blessed Sacrament: pages 26–43.

Easter Cycle

Eastertide

The Practice of the Love of Jesus Christ: pages 108–166.

Pentecost Cycle

From the vigil of Pentecost to Trinity Sunday, read the Novena of the Holy Spirit on pages 44–54.

From Trinity Sunday to the feast of the Transfiguration, read On Prayer: Parts I and II on pages 205–253; A Christian's Way of Life: Part I on the means of preserving God's grace on pages 167–171.

From feast of the Transfiguration to the feast of the Seven Sorrows of Mary, read The Glories of Mary on pages 55–92.

From the feast of the Seven Sorrows of Mary to the First Sunday of Advent, read On Conformity to the Will of God on pages 280–297.

A Note On Style

This set of selections from the work of Saint Alphonsus Liguori is based on the translations of Father Robert A. Coffin and others of the English Redemptorist community of the middle of the nineteenth century. I have condensed some sentences and paragraphs and made some changes to fit modern usage. The changes were made to clarify Saint Alphonsus's meaning, not to alter his style. Though he sometimes says things, especially unpleasant things, with a shattering force, his writing shows him to be a man of great sweetness and filled with a love of souls. Such sweetness and love should be allowed full flow, I believe, even when they involve certain baroque extravagances of style. For if the words are occasionally immoderate, so is the love behind them.

B. U.

Introduction: On Saint Alphonsus Liguori

The saints are the footnotes of Saint Alphonsus Liguori's writings. They make their way through his discourses as they did through his life, acting as teachers, judges, intercessors. They reject foolishness. They confirm wisdom. They plead the cases of the morally crippled, the inept, the timid, the tormented. And they almost certainly win every case they plead simply by pleading it. They are advocates of grace so confirmed in grace that they have merely to ask something to have it granted, all of them, but especially the highest of them, the Mother of God.

If this central belief of Saint Alphonsus's were all of his belief, it would be enough to show him a good man, a pious man, a trusting man, but not much more. What makes his reading of the saints so startling is the translation he makes of their works into the lives of ordinary men. The advocacy of the saints becomes in his spirituality the advocacy of anybody, of everybody. The confirmation in grace which supports the pleas of the saints with such certainty does as much again for every person. Saint Alphonsus sees everything in Scripture, everything in the history of the Church, everything in the mysteries of the faith pointing to this rescuing gift. It had rescued him, it had rescued others, it could rescue all. One had merely to ask—as an abundance of scriptural incidents and quotations assures one—to receive. If grace was proffered, one had to correspond with it. If it was not clearly presented, one had to solicit it. To that harmony of agreement and supplication, Alphonsus dedicated his life and works, his writings, his prayers. He founded the Congregation of the Most Holy Redeemer, the Redemptorists, to conduct missions to make that point. He suffered the tortures of the elect to make that point.

Alphonsus began his career of advocacy as his family's great hope. Born in 1696, he was the oldest of seven children and was expected to lift an old and once well-connected and not ignoble family from the shabbiness of genteel poverty in Marinella, near Naples. Toward that end he was outfitted with eight Christian names, among them a pair of martyrs (Cosmas and Damian), an angel (Michael), the saintly rescuer of lost objects (Antony), the beloved disciple (John), and the Virgin Mary. He was trained in riding, fencing, the harpsichord; he was tutored in the liberal arts. And in 1713 at the age of sixteen, four years younger than the statutory age, he received the degree of doctor of laws from the University of Naples.

Alphonsus was a small man, so small that when he first appeared in court he shuffled forward in a doctor's gown that covered him like a tent, a figure out of slapstick comedy, and drew a spontaneous laugh. It was not intentional. He was not a clown by taste or skill. He was an advocate, a serious man, a brilliant pleader who had explored the logic of the law in theory and in practice. For eight years his explorations were successful—and more. He had the making of a legend in his pleas, that of an almost undefeatable advocate before the bar. Then came a shattering moment of melodrama. He was in court. He had just delivered his opening speech, as usual a virtuoso performance, when he was handed a document he had read over and over again—and each time entirely differently from the way he now saw it. He turned color, shivered, and conceded the case. He fled from the court, from the law, from the world. Once more he had been made a clown, this time from a cause not quite so innocent as the first.

Alphonsus was disgusted with himself and with his profession. It was not just a wound to his vanity. He was frightened that a simple truth, not far beneath the surface of the evidence, should have eluded him as it had. He was fearful that in the desire to win a case he would himself turn from the truth. For three days after the experience in court, he refused any consolation, even that of food. When some months afterward in the course of a visit to a hospital he saw what seemed to him a supernatural light and heard some sort of voice inside him asking him firmly to withdraw from the world, he responded eagerly. He went to a church with a significant name for him, the Redemption of Captives, and there resolved to become a religious.

The Oratorians were Alphonsus's first choice but his father would have none of them. The elder Liguori had done much to give his son a solid religious foundation, but not looking forward to a career in religion for him. The law was for Alphonsus. When Alphonsus insisted, and with good reason, that he was not for the law, his father was willing to accept a compromise. He could become a priest, if he would live at home. Alphonsus left the Oratory, returned home, and after a year of preparation joined a group of secular priests called the Neapolitan Propaganda. Their work was preaching missions; they did not live in community. Alphonsus's father was delighted. At the age of thirty his son was ordained a priest.

A lawyer's training and a missionary's are both grounded in rhetoric. Alphonsus was well prepared to make his appeals across the dirt and despair of Naples to the poor and the sick and the miserable, and especially to the beggars, the *Lazzaroni*, whom he gathered in great number into an Association of the Chapels, a thriving confraternity which was the foundation of Alphonsus's life as an organizer. What followed were visions, prophecies, a clamorous insistence for a new congregation of Sisters—not his but those of Sister Maria Celeste, member of a community of religious near Amalfi. Sister Maria Celeste had a piercing foresight. She even came up with a rule, of which Alphonsus became a solemn advocate. His advocacy won the local bishop's support and in 1731 Sister Maria Celeste's community adopted the new rule and a new habit. Quickly enough, new visions came to the prophetic Sister, this time of a community of male religious.

The precise part played by the visionary Sister in Alphonsus's life is not clear. Certainly his faith was not too sophisticated to accept such promptings. And equally certainly, he was more moved by her suggestions than by the pessimistic predictions of his priest friends, wise men some of them, courageous men many of them, but none of them very clear about the structure of Alphonsus's work. On November 9, 1732, he founded the Congregation of the Most Holy Savior, the Redemptorists to be, with the Bishop of Castellamare as superior.

There were all sorts of difficulties in the new community, disagreements about its purposes, about the rule, about the way of conducting missions, about the frequency of such evangelizing and its place in the life of the Congregation. In spite of the breadth of his preparation as a priest, as a lawyer, and as a man, Alphonsus had no range of ambitions as a founder, or later as superior general. He did not want to found schools or colleges; he was not interested in the subtleties and many levels of activity of a far-flung community life. He was a missionary priest, founder of a congregation of missionaries. He survived the defection of all but two religious of the original community and with just the two men rebuilt the missionary organization he had founded. He survived the almost insane harassment of the prime minister of Naples, the Marchese Tanucci, who for decades refused royal recognition to the community. He even survived thirteen years as Bishop of Sant' Agata de' Goti, a town near Naples with about thirty thousand people and every possible indisposition to the Christian life.

Alphonsus had successfully turned down the urgent request of the King of Naples to become Archbishop of Palermo in 1747, but in 1762 he was required under obedience to the Pope to take the hat, the miter, and Sant' Agata. Religious instruction there was at a kindergarten level. The clergy were either indifferent, fascinated with the sound of their own voices, or in a hurry to get through Mass, to get through the Office, to get through all their religious duties. Alphonsus applied his missionary principles to the reorganization of sermons, of seminary teaching, of convent and church life. The poor, the sick, and the ignorant came first. Feeding, clothing, shelter, and instruction were the central works of mercy, the last, as always with Alphonsus, first in importance if not in sequence. And as always, Alphonsus felt inadequate to his work: for as many years as he was Bishop of Sant' Agata he sent word to the Pope—whoever was Pope—asking to be relieved of his duties.

Finally, in 1775, Pius VI allowed Alphonsus to resign. He returned to one of the houses of his Congregation, of which there were now nine, for what looked to be peaceful retirement from the world. He was almost eighty and half paralyzed with the arthritis from which he had suffered since a thirteen-month bout with rheumatic fever that had begun in his seventy-second year. There were a few years of comparative quiet and then began the special torment which religious reserve for their founders.

A decree of 1779 permitted the Redemptorists to erect a novitiate, a house of studies, and a proper structure of superiors. Whereupon, almost immediately, a thorough rewriting of the rule was accomplished, with the help of the vicar general of the Congregation, Alphonsus's own confessor. His friends generally conspired against his ideas, against the traditions he had created over decades, against his devout practice, against himself. They persuaded Alphonsus, failing in his senses, deaf and almost blind, to sign a revision he could barely see, weakening the rule in every way and forming the Congregation into a loose society without even vows to stiffen it. Alphonsus signed away almost everything he believed in. He signed away his religious life. The King of Naples approved. The ordinary members of the Congregation, the rank-and-file religious, were shocked, miserable, and helpless. The Pope, however, was reduced to none of these conditions. He lifted the Redemptorists out of their Neapolitan swamp and placed them in the Papal States under direct obedience to him. Then, after suitable if incomplete inquiry, Alphonsus was expelled from his own community by Pius VI, the same Pope who in 1798 declared him venerable and admitted that he had persecuted a saint.

Any description of the last years of Alphonsus is bound to seem exaggerated, for it all came at once to the saint in his late eighties—physical exhaustion but not death, a dark night that omitted none of the terrors of despair, every sort of temptation, every sort of scruple, every sort of hallucination. The consolations of earlier years, the mystical graces, the miraculous cures that some people still talked about—these were sketchy memories, and usually other people's, rarely Alphonsus's. When a degree of tranquillity came to him in his last two years, he welcomed it with a kind of numbed silence, and in that state he died in 1787, two months before his ninety-first birthday. Six years later the original rule was at last given state recognition in Naples, the Redemptorists of Naples and the Papal States were brought together again under one superior, and Alphonsus's original Congregation was fully restored. Eleven years later he was declared venerable. He was beatified in 1816, canonized in 1839, and in 1871 named a Doctor of the Church.

Alphonsus did a great deal of writing in the second half of his life, but wrote nothing other than some poems until he was almost fifty. His *Moral Theology*, published in 1748, was a spectacular success, printed with the support of Pope Benedict XIV and quickly popular with priests in the confessional because of its mixture of legal precisions and that flexible position generally called "probabilism" or "equiprobabilism." For Alphonsus, evidence was as much to be weighed in the confessional as in the law court. Conscience took primacy over moral theology, particularly in those cases where there were such doubts about the lawfulness of a moral act that one could follow any of several good opinions, no matter how contradictory. Any one of these opinions could be considered probable and accepted when an action had to be taken and no certain opinion was available. There are degrees in the moral life, Alphonsus was saying, outside of those areas in which the theology is definitive and moral choice absolutely clear. Neither the harshness of a severe reading of moral doctrine nor the softness of a lax one could serve as a guide either to confessor or penitent. There is more need in the confessional for the discernment of spirits than for the rote application of textbook rules.

Alphonsus respected the rules enough to examine them in great detail, using his skills as a lawyer to make every possible distinction that would encourage the development of the life of the spirit. If there is a bias in his reading of canon law and its reflection of doctrine and dogma, it is for the resources of human interiority. There, where personhood is defined, redemption begins as a movement to correspond with grace. There, a wavering faith, sin, every moral confusion may find an answering hope, if nothing more. With hope comes the impetus to understand and to believe. It is an impetus that must always be followed. But there are forces, even in the religious life, that often make the effort to understand and to believe dispiriting.

Alphonsus is not so much concerned here with the great

dramas of evil as with the small hindrances. It is not the sudden swooping down of the devil that is so fearful in the life of the spirit, but the intrusions of scrupulosity that make us doubtful of the possibility of any good act, of any spiritual impulse, of any unflawed move in the service of faith. Thus it is that he counsels so winningly against the weakenings of tepidity, that corrosion of the will which so insistently counsels self-doubt. And thus it is that he makes so persuasive his analysis of the ravages of desolation in the life of a religious and the counter movements against what he was prescient enough to call depression, more than a century before the term found urgent currency in depth psychology and psychiatry.

The moral life, in Alphonsus's construction, is a life of freedom. There are constraints, of course, but even these when viewed through the lenses of grace become enabling rather than disabling. They do so, these redemptive limitations, when they hold us down just long enough to permit us to view the freeing purpose of all spiritual discipline, the coming together with the Spirit that lives in each of us.

The ambition that Alphonsus holds for each of us, and not simply for those who are professed religious, is to become a saint. His audacity here is matched only by the certainty of his conviction. In the life of freedom which the life of the spirit ordains, the contemplation of sanctity is an inevitable exercise, and a joyous one. As few theologians, working in the precincts of moral theology or elsewhere, Alphonsus responded to the promptings of the heart and in answering them did his utmost to lead others to heed their own loving inclinations.

In his own distinct way, Alphonsus Liguori was a balladeer of the Passion, of Mary, of the love proclaimed in The Song of Songs. It is in his constant attention to music, whether in the composing of hymns or in writing about it in his letters. It is the governing texture of his fervent poems. We do not need to read his poetry with some care to discover how keenly he feels whatever part his own failings may have contributed to the burdens of Jesus on the Cross, to see how even a great figure so remote from the ruminations of Christians as Alexander the Great may occasion in a few lines a deepened understanding of repentance and the much more than formulaic advice, "Who gives his heart to God alone is wise."

In the service of Mary, he produces an arrestingly original rhetoric of love: "Sweet loving Robber! Seize your prey...." In addressing his beloved Teresa of Ávila, he does not hesitate to use the language of the Sông:

To see her loving Spouse
So fierce is her desire,
That evermore she burns,
Consuming in its fire.

We can understand in such poetry the extraordinary graces of love that make Alphonsus so thoughtful an examiner of the complications of the sexual life in marriage. Peter Gardella in *Innocent Ecstasy*, his book on the Christian sources of the American "Ethic of Sexual Pleasure," is properly impressed by Alphonsus's insistence on the rights of women to experience orgasm, and his recognition of the spiritual significance of the marital act. None of this or any of his other recognitions of the reality of human sexuality should be construed as an untoward permissiveness, however remarkable for its time, but rather of Alphonsus's high respect for the inclinations toward love which the body shows in its housing of the Spirit.

In the nineteenth century the moral theology of Saint Alphonsus was used by anti-Catholics to beat John Henry Newman over the head. It was used crudely, highly selectively, stupidly really, to demonstrate the laxity of the Catholic moral conscience. One could just as easily read Alphonsus as a rigorist, especially in his counselings on the spiritual life, on prayer, and on approaching the sacraments, if one reads half sentences, parts of paragraphs, even large sections of his treatises. One must read any argument of his through to the end, to see it as the balanced, fair, and compassionate thing it is. He was, as all who know his work well must realize, a remarkably compassionate man, determined to make as attractive and as persuasive as possible the life of the spirit. But he would not falsify. He could not. Since his last experience in court, it had become an obsession with him to present ideas, doctrines, the whole way of life of Christians, with a fullness that could not be faulted. He offered his own ideas with conviction but not without some diffidence. There were more powerful advocates, more certain ones—Scripture, the saints and Doctors of the Church, theologians of indisputable authority. Nothing he said would go unsupported. For every statement by Alphonsus Liguori there would be two, three, a dozen by others more eminent, at least from his point of view.

In this collection of his spiritual writings, it has been my concern to arbitrate among the authorities, to offer as much of Alphonsus Liguori as possible, selecting among his pages of supporting testimony only those passages that seemed essential. What emerges is, I think, an accurate representation of the spirituality of Saint Alphonsus, its comfort, its comprehensiveness, its inspiration. It is, as even the briefest sampling of these pages will show, a spirituality that rests upon prayer. No matter where one goes with Alphonsus, or for what reason, one goes with prayer. Salvation depends upon it. Damnation can be defined as its privation. Desolation can be combated by prayer. Through it one can be sure of the fullest participation in the Church year, daily and on feast days, and the deepest approach to the mysteries. But prayer is not merely doctrinal or ideological with Alphonsus. It is a way of life with a logic and a psychology all its own.

The wholeness of the Christian life as seen by Saint Alphonsus Liguori is what the following pages have been gathered to demonstrate, gathered chiefly from his volumes on the Christian virtues, on the mysteries of faith (the Incarnation, the Redemption, the Eucharist), and on what he calls with celebrated precision of phrase "the glories of Mary." It is a unity not to be gathered all at once or from any one selection. It is compounded of meditation and petition, mental prayer and novena, acts of faith, love, and contrition and treatises on conformity to the will of God and the love of Jesus Christ that can take one to the heights of contemplation. I echo Alphonsus when I suggest that the reader note well the words "take one to the heights of contemplation." Alphonsus is a man of method; he will "take one," if one will go with him step by step, following his injunctions, positive and negative, performing his acts, offering his prayers. I say "his" injunctions, "his" acts, "his" prayers. He would decline the pronoun. He would say that the rules and words and attitudes were too long consecrated by the recommendation and practice of others to be ascribed to him. But the fact is that the words are his own and of an unmistakable freshness and vitality which are his own. The organization of duties and the reorganization of distressed lives are his own. The passion and compassion are his own.

Finally, it should be said that no one with a particular bias in favor of one kind of spirituality or another, or against one or another, should allow that to stand in the way of a close examination of the materials and methods of Saint Alphonsus. His work is not directed to any one level, the highest or the lowest or any degree in between. As in his moral theology, he allows for every sort of person and for every kind of approach and procedure. He is as tender of the worship of those who must for one reason or another rest content with set prayers as he is of the devotions of those who are totally dedicated in action and affection to the life of the spirit. Only those who have no use at all for prayer will find Saint Alphonsus useless. For he is as good as his word, he does as he promises he will do: he admonishes, he exclaims, he repeats again and again, "Pray, pray, never cease to pray...." But he does more than repeat it. He shows us how to pray, as if our life depended on it, for he is sure that it does.

BARRY ULANOV

The Way of Saint Alphonsus Liguori

Meditations On the Incarnation

In the Fullness of Time, God Sent His Son

Consider how God allowed four thousand years to pass after the transgression of Adam before he sent his Son on earth to redeem the world. And in the meantime, what fatal darkness reigned on the earth! The true God was not known or adored, except in one small corner of the world. Idolatry reigned everywhere; so that devils and beasts and stones were adored as gods. But let us admire in this the divine wisdom: He deferred the coming of the Redeemer in order to render his advent more welcome to man, in order that the malice of sin might be better known, as well as the necessity of a remedy and the grace of the Savior. If Jesus Christ had come into the world immediately after the fall of Adam, the greatness of this favor would have been but slightly appreciated. Let us therefore thank the goodness of God for having sent us into the world after the great work of redemption was accomplished.

Behold the happy time is come which was called the fullness of time: "When the fullness of time was come, God sent his Son…that he might redeem them who were under the law." It is called fullness, because of the fullness of grace which the Son of God came to communicate to men by the redemption of the world. Behold the angel who is sent as ambassador into the town of Nazareth to announce to the Virgin Mary the coming of the Word, who desires to become incarnate in her womb. The angel salutes her, calls her full of grace and blessed among women. The humble virgin, chosen to be the mother of the Son of God, is troubled at these praises, because of her great humility: but the angel encourages her, and tells her that she has found grace with God, the grace which brought peace between God and man and the reparation of the ruin caused by sin. He then tells her that she must give her Son the name of Savior—"You shall call his name Jesus"—and that this her Son is the very Son of God, who is to redeem the world, and thus to reign over the hearts of all people. Behold, at last Mary consents to be the mother of such a Son: "Be it done unto me according to your word." And the eternal Word takes flesh and becomes man: "And the Word was made flesh."

Let us thank this Son, and let us also thank his mother, who, in consenting to be mother of such a Son, consented also to be mother of our salvation, and mother also of sorrows, accepting at that time the deep abyss of sorrows that it would cost her to be the mother of a Son who was to come into the world to suffer and die for us humans.

His Son Took the Form of a Servant

The eternal Word descends on earth to save humankind; and from where does he descend? "His going out is from the end of heaven" (Ps 18:7). He descends from the bosom of his divine Father, where from eternity he was begotten in the brightness of sanctity. He descends into the womb of a virgin, a child of Adam, which in comparison with the bosom of God is an object of horror; wherefore the Church sings, "You did not abhor the Virgin's womb." Yes, because the Word being in the bosom of the Father is God, like the Father, is immense, omnipotent, most blessed, and supreme Lord, and equal in everything to the Father. But in the womb of Mary he is a creature, small, weak, afflicted, a servant inferior to the Father, "taking the form of a servant."

It is related as a great prodigy of humility in Saint Alexis, that although he was the son of a Roman gentleman, he chose to live as a servant in his father's house. But how is the humility of this saint to be compared to the humility of Jesus Christ? Between the son and the servant of the father of Saint Alexis there was, it is true, some difference; but between God and the servant of God there is an infinite difference. Besides, this Son of God, having become the servant of his Father, in obedience to him, made himself also the servant of his creatures, that is to say, of Mary and Joseph: "And [He] was subject to them" (Lk 2:51).

Moreover he made himself even a servant of Pilate, who condemned him to death, and he was obedient to him and accepted it; he became a servant to the executioners, who scourged him, crowned him with thorns and crucified him; and he humbly obeyed them all, and yielded himself into their hands. And shall we, after this, refuse to submit ourselves to the service of so loving a Savior, who, to save us, has subjected himself to such painful and degrading slavery?

Christ Has Delivered Himself for Us

Consider that the eternal Word is that God who is so infinitely happy in himself that his happiness cannot be greater than it is, nor could the salvation of all humankind have added anything to it or have diminished it: and yet he has done and suffered so much to save us miserable worms, that if his happiness (as Saint Thomas says) had depended on that of human beings, he could not have done or suffered more: "As if without him He could not be happy." And indeed, if Jesus Christ could not have been happy without redeeming us, how could he have humbled himself more than he has done, in taking upon himself our infirmities, the miseries of infancy, the troubles of human life, and a death so barbarous and ignominious? None but God was capable of loving to such an excess such wretched sinners as we are, so unworthy of being loved. A devout author says: If Jesus Christ had permitted us to ask him to give us the greatest proof of his love, who would have ventured to ask of him that he should become a child like unto us, that he should clothe himself with all our miseries, and make himself of all men the most poor, the most despised, and the most ill-treated, even to being put to death by the hands of executioners, and in the greatest torments upon an infamous gibbet, cursed and forsaken by all, even by his own Father, who abandoned his Son that he might not abandon us in our ruin? But that which we should not have had the boldness even to think of, the Son of God has thought of and accomplished. Even from his childhood he has sacrificed himself for us to sufferings, to opprobrium, and to death. He has loved us, and out of love has given us himself, in order that we, by offering him as a victim to the Father in satisfaction for our debts, might through his merits obtain from the divine goodness all the graces that we desire; a victim dearer to the Father than if we had offered him the lives of all men and of all the angels. Let us therefore continually offer to God the merits of Jesus Christ, and through them let us seek and hope for every good.

A Man of Sorrows

The prophet Isaiah designates our Lord Jesus Christ as "a man of sorrows" because this man was created on purpose to suffer, and from his infancy began to endure the greatest sorrows that any person ever suffered. The first man, Adam, enjoyed for some time upon this earth the delights of the earthly paradise; but the second Adam, Jesus Christ, did not pass a moment of his life without sorrows and anguish; for even from his childhood he was afflicted by the foresight of all the sufferings and ignominy that he would have to endure during his life, and especially at his death, when he was to close that life, as David had predicted: "I am come into the depth of the sea: and a tempest has overwhelmed me" (Ps 68:3). Even from the womb of Mary, Jesus Christ accepted obediently the sacrifice which his Father had desired him to make, even his passion and death, "Becoming obedient unto death" (Phil 2:8). So that even from the womb of Mary he foresaw the scourges and presented to them his flesh; he foresaw the thorns, and presented to them his head; he foresaw the blows, and presented to them his cheeks; he foresaw the nails, and presented to them his hands and his feet; he foresaw the cross, and offered his life. Hence it is true that even from his earliest infancy our blessed Redeemer every moment of his life suffered a continual martyrdom, and he offered it every moment for us to his eternal Father. But what afflicted him most was the sight of the sins which men would commit even after this painful redemption. By his divine light he well knew the malice of every sin, and therefore did he come into the world to do away with all sins; but when he saw the immense number which would be committed, the sorrow that the heart of Jesus felt was greater than all the sorrows that all men ever suffered or ever will suffer upon earth.

The Infant Lord Is Laid in a Manger

Holy Church, in contemplating this great mystery and prodigy of a God being born in a stable, exclaims, full of admiration, "Oh, great mystery! Oh, wonderful sacrament! for animals to behold the Lord lying in a manger." In order to contemplate with tenderness and love the birth of Jesus, we must pray the Lord to give us a lively faith. If without faith we enter into the grotto of Bethlehem, we shall have nothing but a feeling of compassion at seeing an infant reduced to such a state of poverty that, being born in the depth of winter, he is laid in a manger of beasts, without fire, and in the midst of a cold cavern.

But if we enter with faith, and consider what an excess of bounty and love it was in a God to humble himself to appear like a little child, wrapped in swaddling clothes, placed on straw, crying and shivering with cold, unable to move, depending for subsistence on his mother's milk, how is it possible that we should not feel ourselves gently constrained to give all our affections to this Infant God, who has reduced himself to this state to make us love him! Saint Luke says that the shepherds, after having visited Jesus in the manger, "returned, glorifying and praising God, for all the things they had heard and seen" (Lk 2:20). And yet what had they seen? Nothing more than a poor child trembling with cold on a little straw; but being enlightened by faith, they recognized in this child the excess of divine love. Inflamed by this love they went on their way glorifying God, that they had had the happiness to behold a God "who had emptied himself" and annihilated himself for the love of men.

The Sun of Justice Shall Arise

Your Physician will come, says the prophet, to cure the infirm; and he will come swiftly like the bird that flies, and like the sun which, on rising from the horizon, instantly sends its light to the other pole. But behold him, he is already come. Let us console ourselves, and return thanks to him. Saint Augustine says, "He descends to the bed of the sick," that is to say, even to taking upon him our flesh, for our bodies are the beds of our infirm souls. Other physicians, if they love their patients, do indeed use all their efforts to cure them; but what physician, in order to cure the sick, ever took upon himself his disease? Jesus Christ has been that physician, who charged himself with our infirmities in order to cure them. Neither would he content himself with sending another in his place, but he chose to come himself to fulfill this charitable office, in order to gain for himself all our love: "He has borne our infirmities and carried our sorrows" (Isa 53:4). He chose to heal our wounds with his own blood, and by his death to deliver us from eternal death, which we had deserved. In short, he chose to swallow the bitter draught of a life of continual sufferings and a painful death, to obtain for us life, and deliver us from our many evils: "The chalice which my Father has given me, shall I not drink it?" he said to Saint Peter (Jn 18:11). It was necessary, then, that Jesus Christ should suffer so many ignominies to heal our pride; that he should embrace such a life of poverty to cure our covetousness; that he should be overwhelmed in a sea of troubles, and even die of pure sorrow, to cure our eagerness for sensual pleasures.

God Spared Not Even His Own Son

Consider that since the eternal Father has given us his own Son to be our mediator and advocate with him, and the victim in satisfaction for our sins, we cannot despair of obtaining from God whatever favor we ask of him, if we avail ourselves of the help of such a Redeemer. "How has he not also, with him, given us all things?" adds the Apostle. What can God deny us when he has not denied us his Son? None of our prayers deserves to be heard or granted by the Lord, for we do not deserve graces, but punishment for our sins; but Jesus Christ, who intercedes for us, and offers for us all the sufferings of his life, his blood, and his death, does indeed deserve to be heard. The Father cannot refuse anything to so dear a Son, who offers him a price of infinite value. He is innocent; all that he pays to divine justice is to satisfy our debts; and the satisfaction he offers is infinitely greater than all the sins of men. It would not be just that a sinner should perish who repents of his sins, and offers to God the merits of Jesus Christ, who has already superabundantly atoned for him. Let us therefore thank God, and hope for all things from the merits of Jesus Christ.

Sacrifice and Oblation Is the Son's Lot

Consider the great bitterness with which the heart of the infant Jesus must have felt itself afflicted and oppressed in Mary's womb at the first moment when his Father proposed to his consideration all the series of contempt, sorrow, and agonies which he was to suffer during his life, to deliver men from their miseries: "In the morning he wakens my ear…and I do not resist…I have given my body to the strikers" (Isa 50:4–6). Thus did Jesus speak by the mouth of the prophet: "In the morning he wakens my ear," that is to say, from the first moment of my conception my Father made me feel that it was his will that I should lead a life of sorrows, and in the end should be sacrificed on the cross: "And I do not resist…I have given my body to the strikers." And all this I accepted for your salvation, oh, you souls of men, and from that time onward I gave up my body to the scourges, to the nails, and to the death on the cross. Consider that whatever Jesus Christ suffered in his life and in his passion, was all placed before him while he was still in the womb of Mary, and he accepted everything that was proposed to him with delight; but in accepting all this, and in overcoming the natural repugnance of sense, oh, what anguish and oppression did not the innocent heart of Jesus suffer! Well did he understand what he was first of all to endure, shut up for nine months in the dark prison of Mary's womb; in suffering the shame and the sorrows of his birth, being born in a cold grotto that was a stable for beasts; in having afterward to lead for thirty years a humble life in the shop of an artisan; in considering that he was to be treated by men as ignorant, as a slave, as a seducer, and as one guilty of death, of the most infamous and painful death ever allotted to the most worthless of criminals. All this did our dearest Redeemer accept every moment, but each moment that he accepted it he suffered at once all the pains and humiliations that he would afterward have to endure even unto death. The very knowledge of his divine dignity made him feel still more the injuries he would have to receive from men: "All the day long my shame is before me" (Ps 43:16). He had continually before his eyes his shame, especially that confusion which he should one day feel at seeing himself stripped naked, scourged, and suspended by three iron nails; and so to end his life in the midst of the insults and curses of those very men for whom he was to die, "becoming obedient unto death, even to the death of the cross" (Phil 2:8). And for what? To save us miserable and ungrateful sinners.

A Child Is Born To Us

Consider that after so many centuries, after so many prayers and sighs, the Messiah, whom the holy patriarchs and prophets were not worthy to see, whom the nations sighed for, "the desire of the everlasting hills," our Savior, has come; he is already born, and has given himself entirely to us: "A child is born to us, and a son is given to us." The Son of God has made himself little, in order to make us great. He has given himself to us, in order that we may give ourselves to him. He has come to show us his love, in order that we may respond to it by giving him ours. Let us, therefore, receive him with affection. Let us love him, and have recourse to him in all our necessities. "A child gives easily," says

Saint Bernard; children readily give anything that is asked of them. Jesus came into the world a child in order to show himself ready and willing to give us all good gifts: "The Father has given all things into his hands." If we wish for light, he has come on purpose to enlighten us. If we wish for strength to resist our enemies, he has come to give us comfort. If we wish for pardon and salvation, he has come to pardon and save us. If, in short, we desire the sovereign gift of divine love, he has come to inflame our hearts with it; and, above all, for this very purpose, he has become a child, and has chosen to show himself to us worthy of our love, in proportion as he was poor and humble, in order to take away from us all fear, and to gain our affections. "So," said Saint Peter Chrysologus, "should he come who willed to drive away fear, and seek for love." And Jesus has chosen to come as a little child to make us love him, not only with an appreciative but even a tender love. All infants attract the tender affection of those who behold them; but who will not love, with all the tenderness of which they are capable, a God whom they behold as a little child, in need of milk to nourish him, trembling with cold, poor, abased, and forsaken, weeping and crying in a manger, and lying on straw? It was this that made the loving Saint Francis exclaim: "Let us love the child of Bethlehem, let us love the child of Bethlehem. Come, souls, and love a God who has become a child, and poor, who is so lovable, and who has come down from heaven to give himself entirely to you."

He Was Offered of His Own Will

The divine Word, from the first instant that he was made man and an infant in Mary's womb, offered himself of his own accord to suffer and die as the ransom of the world: "He was offered because it was his own will." He knew that all the sacrifices of goats and bulls offered to God in times past had not been able to satisfy for the sins of men, but that it required a divine Person to pay the price of their redemption; wherefore he said, as the Apostle tells us, "When he comes into the world, he says sacrifice and oblation you would not: but a body you have fitted to me. ...Then said I: Behold, I come" (Heb 10:5,7). "My Father," said Jesus, "all  the victims hitherto offered to you have not sufficed, nor could they suffice, to satisfy your justice; you have given me this passible body, in order that by shedding my blood I might appease you and save men: Behold, I come; here I am ready, I accept everything, and I submit myself in everything to your will." The inferior part felt repugnance, for it naturally was averse to this life and death, so full of sufferings and shame; but the rational part, which was entirely subordinate to the will of his Father, conquered and accepted everything; and Jesus began from that moment to suffer all the anguish and sorrows that he would have to suffer during all the years of his life. Thus did our Redeemer act from the very first moment of his entrance into the world. But, oh, God, how have we conducted ourselves toward Jesus since we began as adults to know by the light of faith the sacred mysteries of Redemption? What thoughts, what designs, what goods have we loved! Pleasures, amusements, vengeance, sensuality—these are the goods that have engrossed the affections of our hearts. But if we have faith, we must at last change our life and our affections. Let us love a God who has suffered so much for us. Let us represent to ourselves the sufferings which the heart of Jesus endured for us, even from his infancy; for then we shall not be able to love anything else but that heart which has loved us so much.

OPEN

The Grace of God Appeared To All

"The grace of God our Savior has appeared to all men; Instructing us, that we should live godly in this world, looking for the blessed hope and coming of the glory of the great God and our Savior Jesus Christ" (Titus 2:11–13).

Consider that by the grace which is said here to have appeared is meant the tender love of Jesus Christ toward men, a love that we have not merited, which therefore is called "grace." This love was always the same in God, but it was not always apparent. It was at first promised in many prophecies, and foreshadowed by many figures; but at the birth of the Redeemer this divine love indeed appeared, and manifested itself by the eternal Word showing himself as an infant, lying on straw, crying, and shivering with cold; beginning in this way to make satisfaction for us for the penalties we have deserved, and so making known to us the affection which he bore us, by giving up his life for us: "In this we have known the charity of God, because he has laid down his life for us" (1 Jn 3:16). Therefore the love of our God appeared to all. But why is it, then, that all men have not known it, and that even to this day so many are ignorant of it? This is the reason: "The light is come into the world, and men loved darkness rather than the light" (Jn 3:19). They have not known him, and they do not know him, because they do not wish to know him, loving rather the darkness of sin than the light of grace. But let us try not to be of the number of these unhappy souls. If in the past we have shut our eyes to the light, thinking little of the love of Jesus Christ, let us try, during the days that may remain to us in this life, to have ever before our eyes the sufferings and death of our Redeemer, in order to love him who has loved us so much: "Looking for the blessed hope and coming of the glory of the great God and our Savior Jesus Christ." Thus may we justly expect, according to the divine promises, that paradise which Jesus Christ has acquired for us by his blood. At his first coming Jesus appeared as an infant, poor and humble, and showed himself on earth born in a stable, covered with miserable rags, and lying on straw; but at his second coming he will come on a throne of majesty: "They shall see the Son of Man coming in the clouds of heaven with much power and majesty" (Mt 24:30). Blessed then will they be who have loved him, and miserable those who have not loved him.

On the Dwelling of Jesus in Nazareth

Saint Joseph, on his return to Palestine, heard that Archelaus reigned in Judea instead of his father Herod. Therefore he was afraid to go and live there. Being warned in a dream, he went to live in Nazareth, a city of Galilee, and there in a poor little cottage he fixed his dwelling. Oh, blessed house of Nazareth, I salute and venerate you! There will come a time when you will be visited by the great ones of the earth. When the pilgrims find themselves inside your poor walls, they will never be satisfied with shedding tears of tenderness at the thought that within them the King of Paradise passed nearly all his life. In this house, the Incarnate Word lived during the remainder of his infancy and youth. And how did he live? Poor and despised by men, performing the offices of a common working boy, and obeying Joseph and Mary: "and [he] was subject to them" (Lk 2:51). Oh, God, how touching it is to think that in this poor house the Son of God lives as a servant! Now he goes to fetch water. Then he opens or shuts the shop. Now he sweeps the room. Now he collects the shavings for the fire. Now he labors in assisting Joseph at his trade. Oh, wonder, to see a God sweeping! A God serving as a boy! A thought that ought to make us all burn with holy love for our Redeemer, who has reduced himself to such humiliations in order to gain our love. Let us adore all these servile actions of Jesus, which were all divine. Let us adore, above all, the hidden and neglected life that Jesus Christ led in the house of Nazareth. Oh, proud men, how can you desire to make yourselves seen and honored, when you behold your God, who spends thirty years of his life in poverty, hidden and unknown, to teach us the love of retirement and of a humble and hidden life!

On the Loss of Jesus in the Temple

Saint Luke relates (chapter 2) that Mary and Joseph went every year to Jerusalem on the Feast of the Passover, and took the infant Jesus with them. It was the custom, says the Venerable Bede, for the Jews to make this journey to the Temple, or at least on their return home, the men separated from the women; and the children went at their pleasure, either with their fathers or their mothers. Our Redeemer, who was then twelve years old, remained during this solemnity for the three days in Jerusalem. Mary thought he was with Joseph, and Joseph that he was with Mary. The holy child employed all these three days in honoring his eternal Father by fasts, vigils, and prayers, and in assisting at the sacrifices, which were all figures of his own great sacrifice on the cross. If he took a little food, says Saint Bernard, he must have procured it by begging, and if he took any rest, he could have had no other bed but the bare ground. When Mary and Joseph arrived in the evening at their home, they did not find Jesus, so, full of sorrow, they began to look for him among their relations and friends. At last, returning to Jerusalem, the third day they found him in the Temple, disputing with the doctors who, full of astonishment, admired the questions and answers of this wonderful child. On seeing him, Mary said, "Son, why have you done so to us? Behold your father and I have sought you sorrowing." There is not upon earth a sorrow like that which is felt by a soul that loves Jesus, when she fears that Jesus Christ has withdrawn himself from her through some fault of hers. This was the sorrow of Mary and Joseph, which afflicted them so much during these days; for they perhaps feared, through their humility, as says the devout Lanspergius, that they had rendered themselves unworthy of the care of such a treasure. That is why Mary said to him, in order to express this sorrow to him: "Son, why have you done so to us? Behold your father and I have sought you sorrowing." Jesus answered, "Did you not know that I must be about my Father's business?" Let us learn from this mystery two lessons; the first, that we must leave all our friends and relations when the glory of God is in question. The second, that God easily makes himself found by those who seek him: "The Lord is good to the soul that seeks him" (Lam 3:25).

For the Feast of the Epiphany

The Son of God is born humble and poor in a stable; there indeed the angels of heaven acknowledge him, singing, "Glory to God in the highest." But the inhabitants of the earth, for whose salvation Jesus was born, leave him neglected; only a few shepherds come and acknowledge him, and confess him to be their Savior. But our loving Redeemer desired from the very beginning to communicate to us the grace of redemption, and therefore he begins to make himself known even to the gentiles, who neither knew him nor expected him. For this purpose he sends the star to give notice to the holy Magi, enlightening them at the same time with internal light, in order that they might come and acknowledge and adore him as their Redeemer. This was the first and sovereign grace bestowed upon us: our calling to the true faith. Oh, Savior of the world, what would have become of us if you had not come to enlighten us? We should be like our forefathers, who worshiped as gods animals, stones, and wood, and consequently we should have been all damned. I give you thanks today on the part of all men.

Behold, the Magi without delay set out on their journey: and by means of the star they arrive at the place where the holy infant is lying: "they found the child with Mary his mother" (Mt 2:11). They find there only a poor maiden and a poor infant wrapped in poor swaddling clothes. On entering into that abode, which was a stable for beasts, they feel an interior joy, and their hearts are drawn toward this sweet infant. That straw, that poverty, those cries of their infant Savior, are all darts of love and tire to their enlightened hearts. Yes, my infant Jesus, the more humbled and poor I behold you, the more do you inflame me with your love.

The infant looks upon these holy pilgrims with a joyful countenance, and thus shows that he accepts these first fruits of his redemption. The divine mother is also silent, but by her smiling looks welcomes them, and thanks them for the homage done to her Son. They adore him also in silence, and acknowledge him for their Savior and their God, offering him gifts of gold, frankincense, and myrrh. Oh, Jesus, my infant king, I also adore you, and offer you my miserable heart. Accept of it and change it. Make it wholly thine own, so that it may love nothing but you. My sweet Savior, save me, and let my salvation be to love you always and without reserve. Oh, Mary, most holy Virgin, I hope for this grace from you.

Jesus Came To Cast the Fire of Love on the Earth

The Jews solemnized a day called by them *dies ignis*, the day of fire with which Nehemias consumed the sacrifice, upon his return with his countrymen from the captivity of Babylon. Even so, and indeed with more reason, should Christmas Day be called the day of fire, on which a God came as a little child to cast the fire of love into the hearts of men. "I came to cast fire on the earth." So spoke Jesus Christ, and truly so it was. Before the coming of the Messiah, who loved God upon earth? Hardly was he known in a nook of the world, that is, in Judea; and even there how very few loved him when he came. As to the rest of the world, some worshiped the sun, some the brutes, some the very stones, and others again even viler creatures still. But after the coming of Jesus Christ, the name of God became everywhere known, and was loved by many.

It is a custom with many Christians to anticipate the arrival of Christmas a considerable time beforehand by fitting up in their homes a crib to represent the birth of Jesus Christ; but there are few who think of preparing their hearts, so that the infant Jesus may be born in them, and there find his repose. Among these few, however, we would be reckoned, in order that we too may be made worthy to burn with that happy flame which gives contentment to souls on this earth, and bliss in heaven. Let us consider on this first day how the eternal Word had no other end in becoming man than to inflame us with his divine love. Let us ask light of Jesus Christ and of his most holy mother, and so let us begin.

The Love of God

Anyone who loves has no other end in loving but to be loved again: God, then, having so dearly loved us, seeks nothing else from us, as Saint Bernard remarks, but our love. Therefore, he goes on with this admonition to each one of us: "He has made known his love, so that he may experience yours." Oh, whoever you are, you have seen the love which God has borne you in becoming man, in suffering and dying for you. How long shall it be before God knows by experience and by deeds the love you bear him? Every person at the sight of a God clothed in flesh, and choosing to lead a life of such hardship, and to suffer a death of such ignominy, ought to be enkindled with love toward a God so loving. "O that you would rend the heavens, and would come down: the mountains would melt away at your presence…the waters would burn with fire" (Isa 64:1,2). Oh, that you would deign, my God (thus the prophet cried out before the arrival of the divine Word on earth), to leave the heavens, and descend here to become man among us! On seeing you like one of themselves, the mountains would melt away, men would surmount all obstacles, all difficulties, in observing your laws and your counsels, the waters would burn with fire. You would enkindle such a furnace in the human heart that even the most frozen souls must catch the flame of your blessed love. And, in fact, after the Incarnation of the Son of God, how brilliantly has the fire of divine love shone to many loving souls! And it may be indeed asserted, without fear of contradiction, God was more beloved in one century after the coming of Jesus Christ than in the entire forty preceding centuries. How many youths, how many of the nobly born, how many monarchs even, have left wealth, honors, and their very kingdoms to seek the desert or the cloister that there, in poverty and obscure seclusion, they might the more unreservedly give themselves up to the love of this their Savior! How many martyrs have gone rejoicing and making merry on their way to torments and to death! How many tender young virgins have refused the proffered hands of the great ones of this world, in order to go and die for Jesus Christ, and so repay in some measure the affection of a God who stooped down to become incarnate, and to die for love of them!

Saint Augustine says that God, in order to captivate the love of men, has cast several darts of love into their hearts: "God knows how to take aim at love; he draws the arrow that he may make a lover." What are these arrows? They are all the creatures that we see around us; for God has created them all so that man might love him. Hence, the same saint says, "Heaven and earth and all things tell me to love you." It seemed to the saint that the sun, the moon, the stars, the mountains, the plains, the seas, and the rivers spoke to him and said: Augustine, love God, because God has created us for you, so that you might love him. When Saint Mary Magdalene of Pazzi held in her hand a beautiful fruit or flower, she declared that that fruit or flower was like a dart to her heart, which wounded her with the love of God, thinking as she did how from all eternity God had deigned to create that flower that she might discover his love, and love him in return. Saint Teresa said that all the fair things which we see—the lakes, the rivers, the flowers, the fruits, the birds—all upbraid us with our ingratitude to God, for all are tokens of the love God bears us. It is related likewise of a pious hermit that, walking in the country and beholding the herbs and the flowers, he fancied they reproached him with his ingratitude, so that as he went along he struck them gently with his staff, saying to them: Hush, be silent, I understand you. No more! You upbraid me with my ingratitude, because God has created you in such beauty for my sake, that I might love him, and I do not love him. Oh, be silent,

I hear you. Enough, enough! And thus the good man pursued his way, giving vent to the ardors of love which he felt consuming his heart for God at the sight of those fair creatures.

Saint Peter Chrysologus says that our Redeemer took many and various forms to attract the love of man. God, who is unchangeable, appears now as a child in a stable, now as a boy in a workshop, now as a criminal on a scaffold, and now as bread upon the altar. In these varying guises Jesus chose to exhibit himself to us; but whatever character he assumed, it was always the character of a lover. Tell me, my Lord, is there anything else left for you to devise in order to make yourself loved? "Make his works known," cried out Isaiah (12:4). Go, redeemed souls, said the prophet, go and publish everywhere the loving devices of this loving God, which he has thought out and executed to make himself loved by man; for after lavishing so many of his gifts upon them, he was pleased to bestow himself, and to bestow himself in so many ways: "If you desire a cure for your wound," says Saint Ambrose, "he is a physician." If you are infirm, and would be healed, look at Jesus, who heals you by his blood. "If you are parched up with fever, he is a fountain." If the impure flame of worldly affections troubles you, behold the fountain to refresh you with his consolation. "If you fear death, he is life; if you long for heaven, he is the way; in short, if you do not wish to die, he is the life; if you wish heaven, he is the way."

The Will of God

If we have not the strength to desire and seek for sufferings, let us at least try to accept with patience those tribulations which God sends us for our good.

"Where there is patience, there is God," says Tertullian. Where is God? Give me a soul that suffers with resignation, there assuredly is God: "The Lord is nigh unto them that are of a contrite heart" (Ps 33:19). The Lord takes delight in being near those who are afflicted. But what kind of afflicted people? It must be those who suffer in peace and are resigned to the divine will. To such as these God gives true peace, which consists, as Saint Leo says, in uniting our will to the will of God. Saint Bonaventure tells us that the divine will is like honey, which makes even bitter things sweet and pleasant. The reason is this, that he who obtains all he wishes has nothing left to desire: "Blessed is he who has everything he desires," says Saint Augustine. Therefore he who wills nothing but what God wills is always happy; for, as everything happens by the will of God, the soul has always that which it wills.

And when God sends us crosses, not only let us be resigned, but let us also thank him, since it is a sign that he means to pardon our sins and save us from hell, which we have deserved. He who has offended God must be punished; and therefore we ought always to beg of him to chastise us in this world, and not in the next. That sinner is to be pitied who does not receive his chastisement in this life but, on the contrary, is prosperous. May God preserve us from that mercy of which Isaiah speaks: "Let us have pity on the wicked" (Isa 26:10). "I do not want this mercy," says Saint Bernard; "such pity is worse than any anger." The prayer of the saint was: Lord, I do not desire this mercy; for it is more terrible than any chastisement. When God does not punish a sinner in this life, it is a sign that He waits to punish him in eternity, where the punishment will have no end.

The Ministry of Jesus

After thirty years of hidden life, finally the time came that our Savior was to appear in public to preach his heavenly doctrines, which he had come from heaven to teach us. Therefore it was necessary that he should make himself known as the true Son of God. But, how many were there who acknowledged and honored him as he deserved? Besides the few disciples who followed him, all the rest, instead of honoring him, despised him as a vile man and an impostor. Then was verified in the fullest manner the prophecy of Simeon: "This child is set…for a sign which shall be contradicted" (Lk 2:34). Jesus Christ was contradicted and despised by all. He was despised in his doctrine; for when he declared that he was the only-begotten Son of God, he was called a blasphemer, and as such was condemned to death—as the wicked Caiaphas said, "He has blasphemed! He deserves death" (Mt 26:65,66). He was despised in his wisdom, for he was esteemed a fool without sense: "He hath a devil, and is mad: why hear you him?" (Jn 10:20). His morals were reproached as being scandalous—they called him a glutton, a drunkard, and the friend of wicked people—"Behold a man that is a glutton and a drinker of wine, a friend of publicans and sinners" (Lk 7:34). He was accused of being a sorcerer and of having commerce with devils—"By the prince of the devils he casts out devils" (Mt 9:34). He was called a heretic and one possessed by the devil—"Do not we say well that you are a Samaritan, and have a devil?" (Jn 8:48). A seducer—"What that seducer said," etc. (Mt 27:63). In short, Jesus Christ was considered by all the people so wicked a man that there was no need of a tribunal to condemn him to be crucified—"If he were not a malefactor, we would not have delivered him up to you" (Jn 18:30).

The Passion of Jesus

At last the Savior came to the end of his life and to his Passion, and, oh, God, what contempt and ill-treatment did he not receive in his Passion! He was betrayed and sold by one of his own disciples for thirty pieces of money, less than would be given for a beast. By another disciple he was denied. He was dragged through the streets of Jerusalem bound like a thief, abandoned by all, even by his few remaining disciples. He was treated shamefully as a slave, when he was scourged. He was struck on the face in public. He was treated as a fool, when Herod had a white garment put on him, that he might be thought a foolish person without any sense: "He despised him as ignorant," says Saint Bonaventure, "because he did not answer a word; as foolish, because he did not defend himself." He was treated as a mock king, when they put into his hand a piece of reed instead of a scepter, a tattered red garment upon his shoulders instead of the purple, and a chaplet of thorns on his head for a crown. After thus deriding him, they saluted him: "Hail, king of the Jews" (Mt 27:29). And then they covered him with spitting and blows, "and spitting upon him" (Mt 27:30); "and they gave him blows" (Jn 19:3). Finally, Jesus Christ willed to die; but by what death? By the most ignominious death, which was the death of the cross: "He humbled himself, becoming obedient unto death, even to the death of the cross" (Phil 2:8). Anyone who suffered the death of the cross at that time was considered the vilest and most wicked of criminals: "Cursed is every one that hangs on a tree" (Gal 3:13). Therefore, the names of those who were crucified were always held as cursed and infamous, so that the Apostle wrote that Christ is made "a curse for us" (Gal 3:13). Saint Athanasius, commenting on this passage, says: "He is called a curse, because he bore the curse for us." Jesus took upon himself this curse that he might save us from an eternal curse. But where, Lord, exclaims Saint Thomas of Villanova, where is your beauty, where is your majesty in the midst of so much ignominy? And he answers: "Ask not, God has gone out of himself." The saint's meaning was this: that we should not seek for glory and majesty in Jesus Christ, since he had come to give us an example of humility, and make manifest the love that he bears toward men, and that this love had made him, as it were, go out of himself.

In the fables of the pagans, it is related that the god Hercules, because of the love which he bore for the King Augea, undertook to tame his horses, and that the god Apollo, out of love for Admetus, kept his flocks for him. These are inventions of the imagination, but it is of faith that Jesus Christ, the true Son of God, for the love of men, humbled himself to be born in a stable, and to lead a contemptible life, and in the end to die by the hands of executioners on an infamous gibbet. "Oh, grace! Oh, power of love!" exclaims Saint Bernard. "You, the most high, became the lowest of all!" Oh, the strength of divine love! The greatest of all has made himself the lowest of all!

"Who did this?" rejoins Saint Bernard. "It was love, regardless of its dignity. Love triumphs over God." Love does not consider dignity, when there is question of gaining for itself the person it loves. God, who can never be conquered by anyone, has been conquered by love; for it was that love which compelled him to make himself man, and to sacrifice himself for the love of human beings in an ocean of sorrows and contempt. "He emptied himself," concludes the holy abbot, "in order that you may know that it was through love that the highest made himself equal to you." The divine Word, who is majesty itself, humbled himself so far as to annihilate himself, so that humankind might know how much he loved them. Yes, says Saint Gregory Nazianzen, because in no other way could he better show forth the divine love than by abasing himself, and taking upon himself the greatest misery and ignominy that men ever suffer on this earth. Richard of Saint Victor adds that, human beings having had the boldness to offend the majesty of God, in order to expiate his guilt the intervention of the most excessive humiliation was necessary. Saint Bernard says, "The lower he showed himself to be in human nature, the greater did he declare himself in goodness."

Meditations On the Blessed Sacrament

The Company of Our Lord Is Not Tedious

Friends on earth find such pleasure in being together that they lose entire days in each other's company. With Jesus in the Blessed Sacrament, those who love him do not get weary.

To every soul who visits Jesus in the Blessed Sacrament, he addresses the words which he said to the sacred spouse: "Arise, make haste, my love, my dove, my beautiful one, and come" (Song 2:10). Soul which visits me, "arise" from your miseries; I am here to enrich you with graces. "Make haste," approach, come near me; fear not my majesty, which has humbled itself in this sacrament, in order to take away your fear, and to give you confidence. "My beloved," you are no longer my enemy, but my friend; since you love me and I love you. "My beautiful one," my grace has made you fair. "And come," draw near and cast yourself into my arms, and ask me with the greatest confidence for whatever you want.

Saint Teresa says that this great King of Glory has disguised himself in the sacrament under the species of bread, and that he has concealed his majesty, to encourage us to approach his divine heart with greater confidence. Let us, then, draw near to Jesus with great confidence and affection; let us unite ourselves to him, and let us ask him for graces. Oh, eternal Word made man, and present for my sake in this sacrament, what joy should be mine now that I stand in your presence, who art my God, who art infinite majesty and infinite goodness, and who has so tender an affection for my soul!

O Lord of Hosts, You Are My God

"The sparrow has found herself a house, and the turtle a nest for herself where she may lay her young ones: Your altars, O Lord of hosts, my king and my God" (Ps 83:4). The sparrow, says David, finds a dwelling in houses, turtledoves in nests, but you, my King and my God, has made yourself a nest and found a dwelling on earth on our altars, that we might find you, and that you might dwell among us. Lord, we can only say that you are too much enamored of men; you no longer know what to do to gain their love. But do, my most amiable Jesus, give us the grace that we also may be passionately enamored of you. It would indeed be unreasonable if we were cold in our love toward a God who loves us with such affection. Draw us to you by the sweet attractions of your love; make us understand the endearing claims which you have on our love.

Oh, infinite majesty and infinite goodness, you love men so much, you have done so much in order to be loved by men. How is it, then, that among men there are so few who love you? I will no longer be as I have hitherto been, among the unhappy number of those ungrateful creatures. I am resolved to love you as much as I can, and to love no other than you. You deserve it; You command me with so much earnestness to do so, I am resolved to satisfy you. Grant, oh God of my soul, that I may fully satisfy you. I entreat you to grant me this favor by the merits of your Passion, and I confidently hope for it. Bestow the goods of the earth on those who desire them; I desire and seek the great treasure of your love alone. I love you, my Jesus; I love you, infinite goodness. You are all my riches, my whole satisfaction, my entire love.

Foolish ones of the world, says Saint Augustine, miserable creatures, where are you going to satisfy your hearts? Come to

Jesus; for by him alone can that pleasure which you seek be bestowed. "Unhappy creatures, where are you going? The good you seek for comes from him." My soul, be not among the number of these foolish ones; seek God alone: "seek for that one good in which are all good things." And if you desire to find him soon, look, he is close to you; tell him what you desire, because it is for this end that he is in the ciborium, to console you, and to grant your prayer. Saint Teresa says that all are not allowed to speak to their king; the most that can be hoped for is to communicate with him through a third person. To converse with you, oh King of Glory, no third person is needed; you are always ready in the sacrament of the altar to give audience to all. All who desire you always find you there, and converse with you face to face. And even if anyone at length succeeds in speaking with a king, how many difficulties has he had to overcome before he can do so! Kings grant audiences only a few times in the year; but you, in this sacrament, grant audience to all, night and day and whenever we please.

If men always had recourse to the most Blessed Sacrament to seek from it the remedy for their ills, they certainly would not be as miserable as they are. The prophet Jeremiah, lamenting, exclaimed: "Is there no balm in Gilead? or is there no physician there?" (Jer 8:22). Gilead, a mountain of Arabia, rich in aromatical spices, according to the Venerable Bede, is a figure of Jesus Christ, who in this sacrament keeps in readiness all the remedies for our woes. Why, then, our Redeemer seems to ask, do you complain of your misfortunes, sons of Adam, when you have the Physician and the remedy for them all in this sacrament? "Come to me…and I will refresh you" (Mt 11:28). I will, then, address you in the words of the sisters of Lazarus, "behold, he whom you love is sick" (Jn 11:3). Lord, I am that miserable creature whom you love; my soul is all wounded by the sins which I have committed:

my divine Physician, I come to you, that you may heal me; if you will, you can cure me: "heal my soul, for I have sinned against you" (Ps 40:5). Draw me wholly to yourself, my most sweet Jesus, by the all-winning attractions of your love. I would much rather be bound to you than become the lord of the whole earth. I desire nothing else in the world but to love you. I have little to give you; but if I could gain possession of all the kingdoms of the world, I would do so, in order that I might renounce them all for your love. For you, then, I renounce what I can; I give up all relations, all comforts, all pleasures, and even spiritual consolations. For you I renounce my liberty and my will. On you I desire to bestow all my love. I love you, infinite goodness, I love you more than myself, and I hope to love you for all eternity.

It is sweet to everyone to be in the company of a dear friend. Shall we not find it sweet, in this valley of tears, to remain in the company of the best friend we have, who can do us every kind of good, who loves us with the most tender affection and therefore dwells always with us? Behold, in the Blessed Sacrament we can converse at pleasure with Jesus, we can open our hearts to him, we can lay our wants before him, and we can ask him for his graces. In a word, in this sacrament we can treat with the king of heaven, in all confidence and without restraint. Joseph was only too happy when, as Scripture tells us, God descended by his grace into his prison to comfort him: "She went down with him into the pit, and in bonds she left him not" (Wis 10:13–14). But we are still more highly favored; for we have always with us in this land of miseries our God made man, who, by his real presence, is with us all the days of our life, and comforts and helps us with the greatest affection and compassion. What a consolation it is to a poor prisoner to have an affectionate friend, who keeps him company, consoles him, gives him hope, succors him, and thinks of relieving him in his misery! Behold our good friend Jesus Christ, who in this sacrament encourages us, saying: "Behold, I am with you all days."

Where the Body Is, There Will Be the Eagles

The saints generally understand by this body that of Jesus Christ; and by the eagles, souls who, being detached from creatures, rise above the things of the earth and fly toward heaven, after which they always sigh in thought and affection, and where they constantly dwell. These eagles also find their paradise on earth wherever they find Jesus in the Blessed Sacrament; so much so, indeed, that they seem never to tire hovering around him. If eagles, says Saint Jerome, on scenting a dead body go from afar to seek it, how much more should we run and fly to Jesus in the Blessed Sacrament, as to the most delicious food of our hearts! Hence saints in this valley of tears have always as parched hearts run to this fountain of paradise. Father Balthasar Alvarez, of the Society of Jesus, in whatever occupation he was engaged, used often to cast his eyes toward the place in which he knew that the Blessed Sacrament was; he often visited it, and even spent entire nights before it. He used to weep when he saw the palaces of the great ones of this world filled with people, who courted those from whom they hoped for some miserable earthly good, and the churches so abandoned, in which the supreme sovereign of the world dwells, and remains with us as on a throne of love, rich in immense and eternal treasures. He used also to say that religious persons were indeed fortunate, because in the very houses in which they reside, they can, whenever they please, either night or day, visit this great Lord in the Blessed Sacrament, and this lay people cannot do.

Many Christians submit to great fatigue, and expose themselves to many dangers, to visit the places in the Holy Land where our most loving Savior was born, suffered, and died. We need not undertake so long a journey, or expose ourselves to so many dangers; the same Lord is near us, and dwells in the church, only a few steps distant from our houses. If pilgrims, says Saint Paulinus, consider it a great thing to bring back a little dust from the crib, or from the holy sepulcher in which Jesus was buried, with what ardor should we not visit the most Blessed Sacrament, where the same Jesus is in person, and where we can go without encountering so much fatigue and so many dangers!

You Are a Hidden God

In no other work of divine love are these words so fully verified as in this adorable mystery of the most holy Sacrament, where our God is entirely hidden. When the eternal Word took flesh, he hid his divinity, and appeared as a man on earth; but remaining with us in this sacrament, he hides even his humanity, and, as Saint Bernard remarks, appears only under the form of bread, to show thereby the tenderness of the love which he bears us: "The divinity is hidden, the humanity is hidden; the bowels of charity alone appear."

And did you not know to how much contempt this loving design of yours would expose you? I see, and before me you did see it very well yourself, that the greater part of men adore you not, neither will they acknowledge you for what you are in this sacrament. I know that these very men have gone so far as to trample on the consecrated hosts.

Oh, could I, my most sweet Savior, but wash with my tears, or even with my blood, those unhappy places in which, in this sacrament, your love and your enamored heart have been so greatly outraged! But if so much is not granted me, I desire at least, my Lord, and determine, to visit you often, in order to adore you as I now adore you, and this in compensation for the insults which you receive in this most divine mystery.

Saint Paul praises the obedience of Jesus Christ, saying that he obeyed his eternal Father even to death (Phil 2:8). But in this sacrament he has gone still further. For here he has been pleased to become obedient, not only to his eternal Father, but also to human beings; and not only to death, but as long as the world shall last, so that we can say: "He has become obedient even unto the consummation of the world." He, the king of heaven, comes down from heaven in obedience, and then seems to dwell and converse there, in order to obey men: "And I do not resist" (Isa 50:5). He allows himself to be placed where men wish, whether for exposition in the monstrance, or to be enclosed in the tabernacle. He allows himself to be carried wherever he is borne, into houses or through the streets. He allows himself to be given in Communion to whomever he is administered, be they just or sinners. Saint Luke says that while he dwelt on earth he obeyed the Blessed Virgin and Saint Joseph; but in this sacrament he obeys as many creatures as there are priests on earth: "And I do not resist."

Why Hide Your Face?

Job feared when he saw that God hid his face. But to know that Jesus Christ veils his majesty in the Blessed Sacrament should not inspire us with fear, but rather with greater love and confidence, since it is precisely to increase our confidence, and with greater evidence to manifest his love, that he remains on our altars concealed under the appearance of bread. Novarinus says "that while God hides his face in this sacrament, he discloses his love." And who would ever dare approach him with confidence, and lay bare before him his affections and desires, did this king of heaven appear on our altars in the splendor of his glory?

Oh, how beautiful a sight it was to behold our sweet Redeemer on that day when, fatigued by his journey, he sat down, all engaging and loving, beside the well to await the Samaritan woman, that he might convert and save her (Jn 4:6). It is precisely thus that this same Lord seems sweetly to dwell with us all the day long, having come down from heaven upon our altars as upon so many fountains of graces, where he awaits and invites souls to keep him company, at least for a while, that he may thus draw them to his perfect love. From every altar on which Jesus remains in the sacrament he seems to speak and address all, saying: Men! why do you fly my presence? Why do you not come and draw near to me, who love you so much, and who remain thus annihilated for your sakes? Why do you fear? I am not now come on earth to judge; but I have hidden myself in this sacrament of love only to do good, and to save all who have recourse to me: "I came not to judge the world, but to save the world" (Jn 12:47).

Let us, then, understand, that as Jesus Christ in heaven is "always living to make intercession for us" (Heb 7:25), so in the sacrament of the altar he is continually, both night and day, exercising the compassionate office of our advocate, offering himself as a victim for us to the eternal Father, to obtain for us his mercies and innumerable graces. Therefore, the devout Thomas à Kempis says, we ought to approach and converse with Jesus in the Blessed Sacrament without the fear of chastisement, and unrestrained, as to a beloved friend.

Prayer Before the Blessed Sacrament

I recommend to you, oh Lord, the Sovereign Pontiff and all bishops and priests; grant them the Spirit of their state, so that they may sanctify the world. I recommend to you infidels, heretics, and all sinners; grant them light and strength to renounce sin, so that they may live only to love you, the sovereign good. I recommend to you all who are in their last agony, my relations, benefactors, and friends. I also recommend my enemies to you in a special manner, because such is your command: make them happy and saints. I recommend the holy souls in purgatory to you; relieve them in their sufferings, and shorten the time of their exile, that they may soon go to enjoy you in heaven.

And now, oh Jesus, hidden in the Blessed Sacrament, I pray to you for myself. From the throne of love on which you are on this altar, grant me by your merits great sorrow for my sins, and forgiveness for all the offenses which I have committed against you. Grant me holy humility and meekness, that I may bear all insults and persecutions with patience. Grant me the grace to mortify myself in everything which is displeasing to you. Grant me perfect resignation to your holy will, so that I may with interior peace embrace all crosses which come to me from your hands. Grant me light to know and strength to execute your holy will. Grant me great confidence in your most holy Passion, and in the patronage of your most holy mother Mary. Grant me the supreme gift of your holy love, together with a great desire to love and please you, so that from now on I may always repeat the words which I now address to you, "My God, you alone do I desire, and nothing more." Grant me perseverance until death in your love, so that I may never again have the misfortune to lose your holy grace. Above all, I beseech you to help me always to seek for this holy perseverance from you, by always recommending myself to you and to your holy mother, more especially when I am tempted to offend you, saying, "Jesus and Mary, Jesus and Mary, help me!" Eternal Father, for the love of Jesus your Son, grant me all these graces.

A Spiritual Communion

My Jesus, I love you with my whole heart, and I wish to live always united to you. As I cannot now receive you sacramentally, I receive you in spirit. Come, then, into my soul. I embrace you, and I unite my entire self to you, and I beseech you never more to allow me to be separated from you.

The Litany of the Blessed Virgin can now be recited, followed by the hymn, Pange Lingua

Sing, my tongue, the Savior's glory,
Of his flesh the mystery sing;
Of the blood, all price exceeding,
Shed by our immortal King,
Destined, for the world's redemption,
From a noble womb to spring.

Down in adoration falling,
Lo, the Sacred Host we hail;
Lo, o'er ancient forms departing
Newer rites of grace prevail;
Faith for all defects supplying,
Where the feeble senses fail.

V. You gave them bread from heaven.
R. Containing in itself every delight.

Let us pray.

Oh God, who, under a wonderful sacrament, hast left us a memorial of your Passion; grant us, we beseech you, so to venerate the sacred mysteries of your body and blood, that we may ever feel within us the fruit of your redemption, who lives and reigns world without end. Amen.

Acts Before Communion

Acts of Faith. "Behold he comes leaping upon the mountains, skipping over the hills" (Song 2:8). My most amiable Savior, over how many, what rough and craggy mountains have you had to pass in order to come and unite yourself to me by the means of this most holy Sacrament! You, from being God, had to become man; from being immense, to become a baby; from being Lord, to become a servant. You had to pass from the bosom of your eternal Father to the womb of a virgin; from heaven into a stable; from a throne of glory to the gallows of a criminal. And on this very morning you will come from your seat in heaven to dwell in my bosom.

"Behold he stands behind our wall, looking through the windows, looking through the lattices" (Song 2:9). Behold, oh, my soul, your loving Jesus, burning with the same love with which he loved you when dying for you on the cross, is now concealed in the Blessed Sacrament under the sacred species; and doing what? "Looking through the lattices." As an ardent lover, desirous to see his love corresponded with, from the host, as from within closed lattices, from where he sees without being seen, he is looking at you, who are this morning about to feed upon his divine flesh. He observes your thoughts, what it is that you love, what you desire, what you seek for, and what offerings you are about to make him.

Awake, then, my soul, and prepare to receive Jesus; and, in the first place, by faith, say to him:

So, then, my beloved Redeemer, in a few moments you are coming to me? Oh, hidden God, unknown to the greater part of men, I believe, I confess, I adore you in the Blessed Sacrament as my Lord and Savior! And in acknowledgment of this truth I would willingly lay down my life. You come to enrich me with your graces and to unite yourself all to me. How great, then, should be my confidence in this your so loving visit!

Act of Confidence. My soul, expand your heart. Jesus can do you every good, and, indeed, loves you. Hope for great things from this your Lord, who, urged by love, comes all love to you. Yes, my dear Jesus, my hope, I trust in your goodness, that, in giving yourself to me this morning, you will enkindle in my poor heart the beautiful flame of your pure love, and a real desire to please you; so that, from this day forward, I may never will anything but what you will.

Act of Love. Ah, my God, my God, true and only love of my soul, and what more could you have done to be loved by me? To die for me was not enough for you, my Lord; you were pleased to institute this great sacrament in order to give yourself all to me, and thus bind and unite yourself heart to heart with so loathsome and ungrateful a creature as I am. And what is more, you yourself invite me to receive you, and desire so much that I should do so. Oh, boundless love! Incomprehensible love! Infinite love! A God would give himself all to me!

My soul, do you believe this? And what do you do? What do you say? Oh God, oh God, oh infinite amiability, only worthy object of all loves, I love you with my whole heart, I love you above all things, I love you more than myself, more than my life! Could I but see you loved by all! Could I but cause you to be loved by all hearts as much as you deserve! I love you, most lovable God, and I unite my miserable heart in loving you to the hearts of the Seraphim, to the heart of the most blessed Virgin

Mary, to the heart of Jesus, your most loving and beloved Son. So that, infinite good, I love you with the love with which the saints, with which Mary, with which Jesus loves you. And I love you only because you are worthy of it, and to give you pleasure. Depart, all earthly affections which are not for God, depart from my heart. Mother of fair love, most holy Virgin Mary, help me to love that God whom you do so ardently desire to see loved!

Act of Humility. Then, my soul, you are even now about to feed on the most sacred flesh of Jesus! And are you worthy? My God, who am I, and who are you? I indeed know and confess who you are who gives yourself to me; but do you know what I am who am about to receive you?

And is it possible, my Jesus, that you who are infinite purity desires to come and reside in this soul of mine, which has been so many times the dwelling of your enemy, and soiled with so many sins? I know, my Lord, your great majesty and my misery; I am ashamed to appear before you. Reverence would induce me to keep at a distance from you; but if I depart from you, my life, whither shall I go? To whom shall I have recourse? What will become of me? No, never will I depart from you; no, I will draw ever nearer and nearer to you. You are satisfied that I should receive you as food; you even invite me to this. I come then, my amiable Savior, I come to receive you this morning, all humbled and confused at the sight of my defects; but full of confidence in your tender mercy, and in the love which you bear me.

Act of Contrition. I am indeed grieved, oh God of my soul, for not having loved you in time past. Still worse, so far from loving you, and to gratify my own inclinations, I have greatly offended and outraged your infinite goodness. I have turned my back against you, I have despised your grace and friendship. Oh, my God, I was deliberately set in will to lose you. Lord, I am sorry, and grieve for it with my whole heart. I detest the sins which I have committed, be they great or small, as the greatest of all my misfortunes, because I have thereby offended you, infinite goodness. I trust that you have already forgiven me. But if you have not yet pardoned me, oh, do so before I receive you. Wash with your blood this soul of mine, in which you are so soon about to dwell.

Act of Desire. And now, my soul, the blessed hour is arrived in which Jesus will come and take up his dwelling in your poor heart. Behold the king of heaven, behold your Redeemer and God, who is even now coming. Prepare yourself to receive him with love, invite him with the ardor of your desire. Come, my Jesus, come to my soul, which desires you. Before you give yourself to me, I desire to give you, and I now do give you my miserable heart. Accept it, and come quickly to take possession of it.

Come, my God, hurry. Delay no longer. My only and infinite good, my treasure, my life, my paradise, my love, my all, my wish is to receive you with the love with which the most holy and loving souls have received you, with which the most blessed Virgin Mary received you. With their communions I unite this one of mine.

Most holy Virgin and my mother Mary, look, I am already approaching to receive your Son. Would that I had the heart and love with which you communicated! Give me this morning your Jesus, as you gave him to the shepherds and to the kings. I intend to receive him from your most pure hands. Tell him that I am your servant and your client; for he will thus look upon me with a more loving eye, and now that he is coming, will press me more closely to himself.

Petitions to the Most Holy Sacrament

Oh, my Jesus, now that you, who are the true life, hast come to me, make me die to the world, to live only for you, my Redeemer. By the flames of your love destroy in me all that is displeasing to you, and give me a true desire to gratify and please you in all things.

Give me that true humility which shall make me love contempt and self-abjection, and take from me all ambition to put myself forward. Give me the spirit of mortification, that I may deny myself all those things that do not tend to your love, and may lovingly embrace whatever is displeasing to the senses and to self-love.

Give me a perfect resignation to your will, that I may accept in peace pains, infirmities, loss of friends or property, desolations, persecutions, and all that comes to me from your hand. I offer you all of myself, that you may dispose of me according to your pleasure. And give me grace always to repeat this entire offering of myself, especially at the time of my death. May I, then, so sacrifice my life to you, with all my affection, in union with the sacrifice that you did make of your life for me to the eternal Father. My Jesus, enlighten me, and make me know your goodness, and the obligation I am under to love you above all, for the love you have borne me in dying for me, and in leaving yourself in the most holy Sacrament.

I pray you to give your light to all infidels who know you not, to all heretics who are out of the Church, and to all sinners who live deprived of your grace. My Jesus, make yourself known, make yourself loved. I recommend to you all the souls in purgatory, and especially ________ ________.

Alleviate the pains they suffer, and shorten the time of their banishment from your sight. Do this through your merits, and those of your most holy mother and all the saints.

My God, enkindle the flame of your love within me, so that I may seek nothing but your pleasure, that nothing may please me but pleasing you; I drive from my heart everything which is not agreeable to you. May I always be able to say with real affection: Oh God, my God, I wish for you alone and nothing more. My Jesus, give me a great love for your most sacred Passion, that your sufferings and death may be always before my eyes to excite me to love you always, and to make me desire to give you some grateful compensation for your so great love. Give me also a great love for the most holy sacrament of the altar, in which you have made known the exceeding tenderness you have for us. I also beg of you to give me a tender devotion to your most holy mother: give me grace always to love and serve her, always to have recourse to her intercession, and to induce others to honor her and confide in her patronage; and grant to me and to all men always to have a great confidence, first in the merits of your Passion, and then in the intercession of Mary.

I pray you to grant me a happy death. Grant that I may then receive you with great love in the most holy Viaticum, that in your embrace, burning with a holy fire, and a great desire of seeing you, I may quit this life to throw myself at your feet the first time it shall be my lot to see you.

Above all, I pray you, Jesus, to give me the grace of prayer, that I may recommend myself always to you and your most holy mother, especially in time of temptation. And I pray you, by your merits, to grant me holy perseverance and your holy love.

Bless me, Jesus, and bless me altogether, my soul, my body, my senses, and my faculties. Bless especially my tongue, that it may only speak for your glory. Bless my eyes, that they may not look at anything that might tempt me to displease you. Bless my taste, that it may not offend you by intemperance; and bless all the members of my body, that they may all serve you and not offend you. Bless my memory, that it may always remember your love and the favors you have accorded me. Bless my understanding, that it may know your goodness and the obligation I have of loving you; and that it may see all that I must avoid, and all that I must do, to conform myself to your holy will. Above all, bless my will, that it may love no other but you, the infinite good, that it may seek for nothing but to please you and may take delight in nothing but what conduces to your glory.

Prayer Before Communion and Thanksgiving Afterward

Cardinal Bona asks why it happens that so many souls, after so many Communions, make so little advance in the way of God. And he answers: "The fault is not in the food, but in the disposition of him who eats it," that is to say, in the lack of due preparation on the part of the communicant. Fire soon burns dry wood, but not that which is green because it is not fit to burn. The saints derived great profit from their Communions, because they were so very careful in their preparation. There are two principal things which we should try to obtain in order to prepare ourselves for Holy Communion. The first is detachment from creatures, by driving from our hearts everything that is not of God and for God. Although the soul may be in a state of grace, yet if the heart is occupied by earthly affections, the more there is of earth in the soul, so much less room will there be for divine love. The second thing that is necessary in order to reap great fruit from Communion is the desire to receive Jesus Christ with the view of loving him more. Gerson says that at this banquet no one is satiated but he who feels great hunger. Hence Saint Francis de Sales writes that the principal intention of a soul in receiving Communion should be to advance in the love of God. "He," says the saint, "should be received for love, who out of pure love alone gives himself to us."

It is also necessary to make a thanksgiving after Communion. There is no prayer more dear to God than that which is made after Communion. We must occupy this time in acts of love and prayers. The devout acts of love which we then make have greater merit in the sight of God than those which we make at other times because they are then animated by the presence of Jesus Christ, who is united to our souls. And as to prayers, Saint Teresa says that Jesus, after Communion, remains in the soul as on a throne of grace, and says to it: "What will you that I should do for you?" Soul, I am come from heaven on purpose to bestow graces upon you. Ask me what you will and as much as you will, and you shall be heard. Oh, what treasures of grace do they lose who pray but a short time to God after Holy Communion!

Novena of the Holy Spirit: Meditations for Each Day of the Novena

The Novena of the Holy Spirit is the chief of all novenas because it was the first that was ever celebrated, and that by the Apostles and Mary in the upper room, and was distinguished by so many remarkable wonders and gifts, principally by the gift of the same Holy Spirit, a gift merited for us by the Passion of Jesus Christ himself. Jesus himself made this known to us when he said to his disciples that if he did not die, he could not send us the Holy Spirit: "If I go not, the Paraclete will not come to you; but if I go, I will send him to you" (Jn 16:7). We know well by faith that the Holy Spirit is the love that the Father and the eternal Word bear one to the other; and therefore the gift of love, which the Lord infuses into our souls, and which is the greatest of all gifts, is particularly attributed to the Holy Spirit, as Saint Paul says, "the charity of God is poured forth in our hearts by the Holy Ghost, who is given to us" (Rom 5:5). In this novena, therefore, we must consider, above all, the great value of divine love, in order that we may desire to obtain it, and endeavor by devout exercises, and especially by prayer, to be made partakers of it, since God has promised it to him who asks for it with humility: "your Father from heaven [will] give the good Spirit to them that ask him!" (Lk 11:13).

Meditation 1:
Love Is a Fire That Inflames the Heart

God had ordered, in the ancient law, that there should be a fire kept continually burning on his altar: "The fire on the altar shall always burn" (Lev 6:12). Saint Gregory says that the altars of God are our hearts, where be desires that the fire of his divine love should always be burning; and therefore the eternal Father, not satisfied with having given us his Son Jesus Christ to save us by his death, would also give us the Holy Spirit, that he might dwell in our souls and keep them constantly on fire with love. And Jesus himself declared that he had come into the world on purpose to inflame our hearts with this holy fire, and that he desired nothing more than to see it kindled: "I am come to cast fire on the earth: and what will I, but that it be kindled?" (Lk 12:49). Forgetting, therefore, the injuries and ingratitude he received from men on this earth, when he had ascended into heaven he sent down upon us the Holy Spirit. Oh, most loving Redeemer, you do, then, love us as well in your sufferings and ignominies as in your kingdom of glory! This is why the Holy Spirit chose to appear in the upper room under the form of tongues of fire: "And there appeared to them parted tongues as it were of fire" (Acts 2:3). And therefore the Church teaches us to pray: "May the Holy Spirit, we beseech you, oh Lord, inflame us with that fire which our Lord Jesus Christ came to cast upon the earth, and which he ardently desired should be enkindled." This was the holy fire which has inflamed the saints to do such great things for God, to love their enemies, to desire contempt, to deprive themselves of all earthly goods, and to embrace with delight even torments and death. Love cannot remain idle and never says, "This is enough." The soul that loves God, the more she does for her beloved the more she desires to do, in order to please him and to attract to herself his affections. This holy fire is enkindled by mental prayer. If, therefore, we desire to burn with love for God, let us love prayer; that is the blessed furnace in which this divine ardor is enkindled.

Meditation 2: Love Is a Light That Enlightens the Soul

One of the greatest evils which the sin of Adam has produced in us is that darkening of our reason by means of the passions which cloud our mind. Oh, how miserable is that soul which allows itself to be ruled by any passion! Passion is, as it were, a vapor, a veil which prevents our seeing the truth. How can he fly from evil who does not know what is evil? Besides, this darkness increases in proportion as our sins increase. But the Holy Spirit, who is called "most blessed light," is he who not only inflames our hearts to love him through his divine splendor but also dispels our darkness and shows us the vanity of earthly things, the value of eternal goods, the importance of salvation, the worth of grace, the goodness of God, the infinite love which he deserves and the immense love which he bears us. "The sensual person perceives not these things that are of the Spirit of God" (1 Cor 2:14). A person who is absorbed in the pleasures of the world knows little of these truths and therefore, unfortunate that he is, loves what he ought to hate and hates what he ought to love. Saint Mary Magdalene of Pazzi exclaimed: "Oh, love not known! Oh, love not loved!" And Saint Teresa said that God is not loved because he is not known. Therefore the saints were always seeking light from God: "Send forth your light; illuminate my darkness; open you my eyes." Yes, because without light we cannot avoid precipices nor find God.

Meditation 3: Love Is a Fountain That Satisfies

Love is also called "a living fountain, fire, and charity." Our blessed Redeemer said to the Samaritan woman: "He that shall drink of the water that I will give him, shall not thirst for ever" (Jn 4:13). Love is the water which satisfies our thirst; he who loves God really with his whole heart neither seeks nor desires anything else, because in God he finds every good. Therefore, satisfied with God, he often joyfully exclaims, "My God and my all!" My God, you are my whole good. But the Almighty complains that many souls go about seeking for fleeting and miserable pleasures from creatures and leave him, who is the infinite good and fountain of all joy: "They have forsaken me, the fountain of living water, and have dug to themselves cisterns, broken cisterns, that can hold no water" (Jer 2:13). Therefore God, who loves us and desires to see us happy, cries out and makes known to all: "If anyone thirst, let them come to me, and drink" (Jn 7:37). He who desires to be happy, let him come to me; and I will give him the Holy Spirit, who will make him blessed both in this life and the next. "He that believes in me" (He goes on to say), "as the scripture saith, out of his belly shall flow rivers of living water" (Jn 7:38). He, therefore, who believes in Jesus Christ and loves him shall be enriched with so much grace that from his heart (the heart, that is the will, is the belly of the soul) shall flow many fountains of holy virtues, which shall not only serve to preserve his own life, but also to give life to others. And this water is the Holy Spirit, the substantial love which Jesus Christ promised to send us from heaven after his ascension: "Now this he said of the Spirit which they should receive, who believed in him: for as yet the Spirit was not given, because Jesus was not yet glorified" (Jn 7:39). The key which opens the channels of this blessed water is holy prayer, which obtains every good for us in virtue of the promise, "Ask, and you shall receive." We are blind, poor, and weak; but prayer obtains for us light, strength, and abundance of grace. Theodoret said: "Prayer, though but one, can do all things." He who prays receives all he wants. God desires to give us his graces; but he will have us pray for them.

Meditation 4: Love Is a Dew That Fertilizes

Thus does Holy Church teach us to pray: "May the infusion of the Holy Spirit cleanse our hearts, and fertilize them by the interior sprinkling of his dew." Love fertilizes the good desires, the holy purposes, and the good works of our souls: these are the flowers and fruits which the grace of the Holy Spirit produces. Love is called dew, because it cools the heart of bad passions and of temptations. Therefore the Holy Spirit is called refreshment and pleasing coolness in the heat. This dew descends into our hearts in time of prayer. A quarter of an hour's prayer is sufficient to appease every passion of hatred or of inordinate love, however ardent it may be: "He brought me into the cellar of wine, he set in order charity in me" (Song 2:4). Holy meditation is the cellar where love is set in order, so that we love our neighbor as ourselves and God above everything. He who loves God loves prayer. He who does not love prayer will find it morally impossible to overcome his passions.

Meditation 5: Love Is a Repose That Refreshes

Love is also called "in labor rest, in mourning comfort." Love is repose that refreshes, because the principal office of love is to unite the will of the lover to that of the beloved one. To a soul that loves God, in every affront it receives, in every sorrow it endures, in every loss which happens to it, the knowledge that it is the will of its beloved for it to suffer these trials is enough to comfort it. It finds peace and contentment in all tribulations merely by saying, This is the will of my God. This is that "peace of God, which surpasses all understanding" (Phil 4:7). Saint Mary Magdalene of Pazzi merely by saying "The will of God" was always filled with joy.

In this life everyone must carry his cross. But as Saint Teresa says, the cross is heavy for him who drags it, not for him who embraces it. Thus our Lord knows well how to strike and how to heal: "He wounds, and cures," as Job said (5:18). The Holy Spirit, by his sweet unction, renders even ignominies and torments sweet and pleasant: "Yea, Father; for so has it seemed good in your sight" (Mt 11:26). Thus ought we to say in all adversities that happen to us: "So be it done, Lord, because so hath it pleased you." And when the fear of any temporal evil that may befall us alarms us, let us always say: "Do what you will, my God; whatever you do, I accept it all." It is a very good thing to offer oneself thus constantly during the day to God, as Saint Teresa did.

Meditation 6: Love Is a Virtue That Strengthens

"Love is strong as death" (Song 8:6). As there is no created strength which can resist death, so there is no difficulty for a loving soul which love cannot overcome. When there is a question of pleasing its beloved, love conquers all, losses, contempt, and sorrow. "Nothing is so hard, but that the fire of love can conquer it." This is the most certain mark with which to know if a soul really loves God, if it is as faithful in love when things are adverse as when they are prosperous. Saint Francis de Sales said that "God is quite as amiable when he chastises as when he consoles us, because he does all for love." Indeed, when he strikes us most in this life, then it is that he loves us most. Saint John Chrysostom esteemed Saint Paul in chains more fortunate than Saint Paul caught up into the third heaven. Hence the holy martyrs in the midst of their torments rejoiced and thanked the Lord, as for the greatest favor that could fall to their lot, that of having to suffer for his love. And other saints, where there were no tyrants to afflict them, became their own executioners by the penances which they inflicted upon themselves in order to please God. Saint Augustine says that "For that which men love, either no labor is felt, or the labor itself is loved."

Meditation 7: Love Causes God to Dwell in Our Souls

The Holy Spirit is called "Sweet Guest of the soul." This was the great promise made by Jesus Christ to those who love him, when he said: "If you love me, keep my commandments. And I will ask the Father, and he shall give you another Paraclete, that he may abide with you forever. The Spirit of truth...shall abide with you, and shall be in you" (Jn 14:15–17). For the Holy Spirit never forsakes a soul if He is not driven away from it; he does not forsake, unless he be first forsaken.

God, then, dwells in a soul that loves him. But he declares that he is not satisfied if we do not love him with our whole heart. Saint Augustine tells us that the Roman Senate would not admit Jesus Christ into the number of their gods because they said that he was a proud god, who would have none other beloved but himself. And so it is. He will have no rivals in the heart that loves him; and when he sees that he is not the only object loved, he is jealous (so to speak). Saint James writes of those creatures who divide up with him the heart which he desires to have all to himself: "Do you think that the scripture saith in vain: To envy doth the spirit covet which dwells in you?" (Jas 4:5). In short, as Saint Jerome says, Jesus is jealous, "*Zelotypus est Jesus.*" Therefore the heavenly spouse praises that soul which, like the turtledove, lives in solitude and hidden from the world (Song 1:9). Because he does not choose that the world should take a part of that love which he desires to have all to himself, therefore he also praises his spouse by calling her "a garden enclosed" (Song 4:12), a garden closed against all earthly love. Do we doubt that Jesus deserves our whole love? "He gave himself wholly to you," says Saint John Chrysostom, "he left nothing for himself." He has given you all his blood and his life; there remains nothing more for him to give you.

Meditation 8: Love Is a Bond That Binds

As the Holy Spirit, who is uncreated love, is the indissoluble bond which binds the Father to the eternal Word, so he also unites the soul with God. "Charity is a virtue," says Saint Augustine, "uniting us with God." Hence, full of joy, Saint Laurence Justinian exclaims: Love, your bond has such strength that it is able to bind even God and unite him to our souls. The bonds of the world are bonds of death; but the bonds of God are bonds of life and salvation (Eccl 6:31), because the bonds of God by means of love unite us to God, who is our true and only life.

Before the coming of Jesus Christ, men fled from God and being attached to the earth refused to unite themselves to their Creator. But a loving God has drawn them to himself by the bonds of love, as he promised through the prophet Hosea: "I will draw them with the cords of Adam, with the bands of love" (11:4). These bands are the benefits, the lights, the calls to his love, the promises of paradise which he makes to us, the gift which he has bestowed upon us of Jesus Christ in the sacrifice of the cross and in the sacrament of the altar, and finally, the gift of his Holy Spirit. Therefore the prophet exclaims, "Loose the bonds from off your neck, O captive daughter of Sion" (Isa 52:2). Oh my soul, you who are created for heaven, loose yourself from the bonds of earth, and unite yourself to God by the bonds of holy love: "Have charity, which is the bond of perfection" (Col 3:14). Love is a bond which unites with herself all other virtues and makes the soul perfect. "Love, and do what you will," said Saint Augustine. Love God, and do what you wish, because he who loves God tries to avoid causing any displeasure to his beloved and seeks in all things to please him.

Meditation 9: Love Is a Treasure of Every Good

Love is that treasure of which the Gospel says that we must leave all to obtain it, because love makes us partakers of the friendship of God, "an infinite treasure to men! which they that use, become the friends of God" (Wis 7:14). Says Saint Augustine, why, then, do you go about seeking for good things? Seek that one good alone in which all other good things are contained. But we cannot find God, who is this sovereign good, if we do not forsake the things of the earth. Saint Teresa writes, "Detach your heart from creatures, and you will find God." He who finds God finds all that he can desire: "Delight in the Lord, and he will give you the requests of your heart" (Ps 36:4). The human heart is constantly seeking after good things that may make it happy; but if it seeks them from creatures, however much it may acquire, it will never be satisfied; if it seeks God alone, God will satisfy all its desires. Who are the happiest people in this world, if not the saints? And why? Because they desire and seek only God.

A tyrant offered gold and gems to Saint Clement, in order to persuade him to renounce Jesus Christ. The saint exclaimed with a sigh, "Is God to be put into competition with a little dirt? Blessed is he who knows this treasure of divine love, and strives to obtain it. He who obtains it will of his own accord divest himself of everything else, that he may have nothing else but God." "When the house is on fire," says Saint Francis de Sales, "all the goods are thrown out of the windows." And Father Paul Segneri the Younger, a great servant of God, used to say that love is a thief which robs us of all earthly affections, so that we can say, "And what else do I desire but you alone, my Lord?"

Novena Resolution

The more we love God, the more holy we become. Saint Francis Borgia says it is prayer that introduces divine love into the human heart and mortification that withdraws the heart from the world and renders it capable of receiving this holy fire. The more there is of the world in the heart, the less room there is for holy love: "Wisdom is [not to be] found in the land of them that live in delights" (Job 28:12–13). Hence the saints have always sought to mortify as much as possible their self-love and their senses. The saints are few, but we must live with the few if we will be saved with the few. Saint Bernard says, "That cannot be perfect which is not singular." He who would lead a perfect life must lead a singular one. But above all, in order to become saints, it is necessary to have the desire to be saints; we must have the desire and the resolution. Some are always desiring, but they never begin to put their hands to the work. "Of these irresolute souls," says Saint

Teresa, "the devil has no fear." On the other hand, the saint said, "God is a friend of generous souls." The devil tries to make it appear to us as pride to think of doing great things for God. It would indeed be pride in us if we thought of doing them all by ourselves, trusting in our own strength; but it is not pride to resolve to become saints trusting in God and saying, "I can do all things in him who strengthens me." We must therefore be of good courage, make strong resolutions, and begin. Prayer can do everything. What we cannot do by our own strength, we can do easily with the help of God, who has promised to give us whatever we ask of him: "You shall ask whatever you will, and it shall be done unto you" (Jn 15:7).

The Glories of Mary

The Great Confidence We Should Have in Mary

The Church justly honors the great Virgin Mary and would have her honored by all men with the glorious title of queen, because she has been elevated to the dignity of mother of the King of Kings. If the Son is King, says Saint Athanasius, his mother must necessarily be considered and entitled queen. From the moment that Mary consented, adds Saint Bernardine of Siena, to become the mother of the eternal Word, she merited the title of queen of the world and of all creatures. If the flesh of Mary, says Saint Arnold, was the flesh of Jesus, how can the mother be separated from the Son in his kingdom? Hence it follows that the regal glory must not only be considered as common to the mother and the Son, but even the same.

Mary, then, is queen, but let all learn for their consolation that she is a mild and merciful queen, desiring the good of us poor sinners. Therefore the Church bids us salute her in prayer and name her the queen of mercy. The very name of queen signifies, as Albertus Magnus remarks, compassion and provision for the poor, differing in this from the title of empress, which signifies severity and rigor. The greatness of kings and queens consists in comforting the wretched, as Seneca says, so that whereas tyrants in reigning have only their own advantage in view, kings should have for their object the good of their subjects. Therefore at the consecration of kings their heads are anointed with oil, which is the symbol of mercy, to denote that in reigning they should above all things cherish thoughts of kindness and good will toward their subjects.

Kings should, then, principally occupy themselves with works of mercy, but not to the neglect of the exercise of justice toward the guilty when it is required. Not so Mary who, although queen, is not queen of justice, intent on the punishment of the guilty, but queen of mercy, solely intent on compassion and pardon for sinners. Accordingly, the Church requires us explicitly to call her queen of mercy. The High Chancellor of Paris, John Gerson, meditating on the wonder of David—"These two things have I heard, that power belongs to God, and mercy to you, O Lord" (Ps 61:12–13)—says that the Lord has divided the kingdom of God consisting of justice and mercy. He has reserved the kingdom of justice for himself and he has granted the kingdom of mercy to Mary, ordaining that all the mercies dispensed to men should pass through Mary's hands and should be bestowed according to her good pleasure. Saint Thomas confirms this in his preface to the Canonical Epistles, saying that the holy Virgin, when she conceived the divine Word in her womb and brought him forth, obtained half of the kingdom of God by becoming queen of mercy, Jesus Christ remaining king of justice.

The eternal Father constituted Jesus Christ king of justice, and therefore made him the universal judge of the world. Hence the prophet sang: "Give to the king your judgment, O God: and to the king's son your justice" (Ps 71:2). Here a learned interpreter takes up the subject and says: "Oh Lord, you have given to your Son your justice, because you have given to the mother of the king your mercy." And Saint Bonaventure happily varies the passage above quoted by saying: "Give to the king your judgment, oh God, and to his mother your mercy." Ernest, Archbishop of Prague, also says that the eternal Father has given to the Son the office of judging and punishing and to the mother the office of compassionating and relieving the wretched. Therefore the prophet David predicted, if I may thus express it, that God himself would consecrate Mary queen of mercy, anointing her with the oil of gladness in order that all of us miserable children of Adam might rejoice in the thought of having in heaven that great queen so full of mercy and pity for us.

And how well Albertus Magnus applies here the history of Queen Esther, who was indeed a type of our Queen Mary. We read in the fourth chapter of the Book of Esther that in the reign of King Assuerus there went forth throughout his kingdom a decree commanding the death of all the Jews. Then Mardochai, who was one of the condemned, committed their cause to Esther, that she might intercede with the king to obtain revocation of the sentence. At first Esther refused to take on herself this office, fearing that it would excite the anger of the king more. But Mardochai rebuked her and bade her remember that she must not think of saving herself alone, as the Lord had placed her on the throne to obtain salvation for all the Jews: "Think not that you may save your life only, because you are in the king's house, more than all the Jews" (Esth 4:13). Thus said Mardochai to Queen Esther, and thus might we poor sinners say to our Queen Mary, if ever she were reluctant to intercede with God for our deliverance from the just punishment of our sins. Think not that you may save your life only because you are in the king's house more than all men. Think not, oh Lady, that God has exalted you to be queen of the world, only to secure your own welfare; but also that you, being so greatly elevated, may more compassionately relieve us miserable sinners.

Assuerus, when he saw Esther before him, affectionately inquired of her what she had come to ask him. Then the queen answered, "If I have found favor in your sight, O king,…give me my people for which I request" (Esth 7:3). Assuerus heard her and immediately ordered the sentence to be revoked. Now if Assuerus granted to Esther, because he loved her, the salvation of the Jews, will not God graciously listen to Mary, in his boundless love for her, when she prays to him for those poor sinners who recommend themselves to her, and when she says to him: If I have found favor in your sight, oh King, my King and my God, if I have ever found favor with you, give me my people for whom I beg. If you love me, she says to him, give me, my Lord, these sinners on whose behalf I entreat you. Is it possible that God will not graciously hear her? Is there anyone who does not know the power of Mary's prayers with God? "The law of clemency is on her tongue" (Prov 31:26). Every prayer of hers is as a law established by our Lord, that mercy shall be exercised toward those for whom she intercedes. Saint Bernard asks why the Church names Mary queen of mercy. And he answers, because we believe that she opens the depths of the mercy of God, to whom she will, when she will, and as she will, so that not even the vilest sinner is lost if Mary protects him.

But it may perhaps be feared that Mary disdains interposing in behalf of some sinners, because she finds them so laden with sins. Perhaps the majesty and sanctity of this great queen should alarm us? No, says Saint Gregory, in proportion to her greatness and holiness are her clemency and mercy toward sinners who desire to amend, and who have recourse to her. Kings and queens inspire terror by the display of their majesty, and their subjects are afraid to enter their presence. But what fear, says Saint Bernard, can the wretched have of going to this queen of mercy, since she never shows herself terrible or austere to those who seek her, but all sweetness and kindness? Mary not only gives, but she herself presents to us milk and wool: the milk of mercy to inspire us with confidence, and wool to shield us from the thunderbolts of divine justice.

Mary Is the Mother of Our Souls

Not by chance nor in vain do the servants of Mary call her mother. They cannot invoke her by any other name and are never weary of calling her mother: mother indeed, for she is truly our mother, not according to the flesh but the spiritual mother of our souls and our salvation. Sin, when it deprived our souls of divine grace, also deprived them of life. Hence, when they were dead in misery and sin, Jesus our Redeemer came with an excess of mercy and love to restore to us by his death upon the cross that lost life, as he has himself declared: "I am come that they may have life, and may have it more abundantly" (Jn 10:10). More abundantly because, as the theologians teach us, Jesus Christ by his redemption brought us blessings greater than the injury Adam inflicted upon us by his sin; he reconciled us to God and thus became the father of our souls, under the new law of grace, as the prophet Isaiah predicted, "the Father of the world to come, the Prince of Peace" (Isa 9:6). But if Jesus is the father of our souls Mary is the mother, for in giving us Jesus she gave us true life, and offering upon Calvary the life of her Son for our salvation she then brought us forth to the life of divine grace.

At two different times, Mary became our spiritual mother. The first time was when she was found worthy of conceiving in her virginal womb the Son of God, as Albertus Magnus says. Saint Bernardine of Siena teaches us that when the most holy Virgin, on the annunciation of the angel, gave her consent to become mother of the eternal Word, which consent he awaited before making himself her Son, she by this act demanded of God our salvation. She was so earnestly engaged in obtaining it that from that time she has borne us, as it were, in her womb, as a most loving mother.

Saint Luke says, speaking of the birth of our Savior, that Mary "brought forth her firstborn son" (Lk 2:7). Therefore, says a certain writer, if the evangelist affirms that Mary brought forth her firstborn, is it to be supposed that she afterward had other children? But the same author adds that if it is of faith that Mary had no other children according to the flesh except Jesus, then she must have other spiritual children and these we are. And this explains what is said of Mary in the holy Canticles: "Your belly is like a heap of wheat, set about with lilies" (7:2). Saint Ambrose explains this: "Although in the pure womb of Mary there was only one grain of wheat, which was Jesus Christ, yet it is called a heap of grain, because in that one grain were contained all the elect of whom Mary was to be the mother." Hence, wrote William the Abbot, Mary in bringing forth Jesus, who is our Savior and our life, brought forth all of us to life and salvation.

The second time in which Mary brought us forth to grace was when on Calvary she offered to the eternal Father with so much sorrow of heart the life of her beloved Son for our salvation. Wherefore, Saint Augustine asserts, having then cooperated with Christ in the birth of the faithful to the life of grace, she became also by this cooperation the spiritual mother of all who are members of our head, Jesus Christ. This is also the meaning of what is said of the blessed Virgin in the sacred Canticles: "They have made me the keeper in the vineyards: my vineyard I have not kept" (1:5). Mary, to save our souls, was willing to sacrifice the life of her Son, as William the Abbot remarks. And who was the true soul of Mary but her Jesus, who was her life and all her love? Wherefore Saint Simeon announced to her that her soul would one day be pierced by a sword of sorrows; which was the very spear that pierced the side of Jesus, who was the soul of Mary. And then she in her sorrow brought us forth to eternal life, so that we may all call ourselves children of Mary's sorrows. She, our most loving mother, was always and wholly united to the divine will. That is why, Saint Bonaventure remarks, when she saw the love of the eternal Father for men, who would have his Son die for our salvation, and the love of the Son in wishing to die for us, she too, with her whole will, offered her Son and consented that he should die so that we might be saved, in order to conform herself to that exceeding love of the Father and Son for the human race.

Be joyful, then, all you children of Mary. Remember that she adopts as her children all those who wish her for their mother. Joyful: for what fear have you of being lost when this mother defends and protects you? Thus, says Saint Bonaventure, everyone who loves this good mother, should take courage and repeat: What do you fear, oh my soul? The cause of your eternal salvation will not be lost, as the final sentence depends upon Jesus who is your brother, and upon Mary who is your mother. And Saint Anselm, full of joy at this thought, exclaims in order to encourage us: "Oh, blessed confidence! Oh, secure refuge! The Mother of God is my mother too. With what certainty may we hope, since our salvation depends upon the sentence of a good brother and a kind mother!" Hear, then, our mother who calls us and says to us: "Whosoever is a little one, let him come to me" (Prov 9:4). Little children have always on their lips the word "mother," and in all the dangers to which they are exposed and in all their fears they cry, "Mother! Mother!" Most sweet Mary, most loving mother, this is exactly what you desire, that we become little children and always call upon you in our dangers and always have recourse to you, for you wish to aid and save us, as you have saved all your children who have had recourse to you.

Mary Obtains for Us the Pardon of Our Sins

In order to understand correctly the reason why the Church calls Mary our life, we must consider that as the soul gives life to the body so divine grace gives life to the soul. For a soul without grace, although nominally alive, in truth is dead. As Mary, then, by her intercession obtains for sinners the gift of grace, she restores them to life. The Church applies to her the following words of Proverbs: "they that in the morning early watch for me, shall find me" (8:17). They shall find me, or, according to the Septuagint, "they shall find grace." Hence, to have recourse to Mary is to find the grace of God, for, as immediately follows: "He that shall find me, shall find life, and shall have salvation from the Lord" (Prov 8:35). Listen, as Saint Bonaventure exclaims here upon these words, listen, all you who desire the kingdom of God. Honor the Virgin Mary, and you shall have life and eternal salvation.

Saint Bernard exhorts us, if we have been so unfortunate as to lose divine grace, to strive to recover it, but to strive through Mary, for if we have lost it she has found it. She is therefore called by this saint "the finder of grace." This the angel Gabriel expressed for our consolation when he said to the Virgin, "Fear not, Mary, for you have found grace." But if Mary had never been without grace, how could the angel say to her that she had found it? A thing is said to be found when it has been lost. The Virgin was always with God and with grace. She was even full of grace, as the archangel himself announced when he saluted her, "Hail! full of grace, the Lord is with you." If, then, Mary did not find grace for herself, for whom did she find it? Cardinal Hugo answers, commenting on this passage, that she found it for sinners who had lost it. Let sinners, then, who have lost grace, flee to Mary. With her they will certainly find it. And let them say: Oh Lady, what is lost must be restored to him who has lost it. This grace which you have found is not yours, you have never lost it. It is ours, for we have lost it, and to us you should restore it. In connection with this, Richard of Saint Laurence remarks, If then we desire to find the grace of God, let us go to Mary, who has found it, and always find it. Since she ever has been and ever will be dear to God, if we have recourse to her we shall certainly find it. She says, in the holy Canticles, that God has placed her in the world to be our defense and therefore she is ordained to be the mediatrix of peace between the sinner and God: "I am become in his presence as one finding peace" (Song 8:10). By which words Saint Bernard gives encouragement to the sinner, and says: "Go to this mother of mercy, and show her the wounds which your sins have inflicted on your soul. Then she will certainly beg her Son that he may pardon you by the milk with which she nourished him, and the Son who loves her so much will certainly hear her." So, too, the Church teaches us to pray the Lord to grant us Mary's powerful intercession so that we may rise from our sins, in the following prayer: "Grant us, oh merciful God, strength against all our weakness, that we who celebrate the memory of the holy Mother of God may by the help of her intercession arise again from our iniquities."

Mary Renders Death Sweet to Her Servants

"He that is a friend loves at all times: and a brother is proved in distress" (Prov 17:17). True friends and relatives are not known in times of prosperity but in the season of adversity and misery. Worldly friends do not desert their friend when he is prosperous but if any misfortune overtakes him, particularly in the hour of death, they immediately abandon him. Not so does Mary desert her devoted servants. In their distresses, and especially at the trying hour of death when our sufferings are the greatest that can be experienced on earth, our good Lady and mother cannot abandon her faithful servants. As she is our life in the time of our exile, so is she also our sweetness in the hour of death, obtaining for us that it may be sweet and blessed. For since that great day in which it was Mary's lot and grief to be present at the death of her Son Jesus, who was the head of the elect, she obtained the grace of aiding all the elect at death. Hence holy Church requires us to pray the Blessed Virgin to aid us especially in the hour of our death: "Pray for us sinners, now and at the hour of our death."

Mary Is the Hope of All

Modern heretics cannot bear the fact that we salute Mary in this way, by calling her our hope. Hail, our hope, *spes nostra salve.* They say that God alone is our hope, and that he who places hope in a creature is accursed of God (Jer 17:5). Mary, they exclaim, is a creature, and as a creature how can she be our hope? Thus say the heretics, but notwithstanding this the Church requires all the clergy and all religious daily to lift their voices and in the name of all the faithful to invoke Mary by the sweet name of our hope, the hope of all: "Hail, our hope!"

In two ways, says the angelic Saint Thomas, we can place our hope in a person, as the principal cause and as the intermediate cause. Those who hope for some favor from a king hope for it from the king as sovereign or hope for it from one of his ministers or a favorite as intercessor. If the favor is granted, it comes in the first place from the king, but if it comes through the medium of his favorite he who has asked the favor justly calls the intercessor his hope. The king of heaven, because he is infinite goodness, greatly desires to enrich us with his graces. But because confidence is necessary on our part, in order to increase our confidence he has given us his own mother for our mother and advocate, and has given her all power to aid us. He therefore wishes us to place in her all our hopes of salvation and every blessing. Those who place all their hope in creatures, without dependence upon God, as sinners do, who to obtain the friendship and favor of others are willing to displease God, are certainly cursed by God as Isaiah says. But those who hope in Mary as Mother of God, powerful to obtain for them graces and life eternal, are blessed and please the heart of God, who wishes to see that noble creature honored who more than all men and angels loved and honored him in this world.

Hence we justly call the Virgin our hope, hoping, as Cardinal Bellarmine says, to obtain by her intercession what we could not obtain by our prayers alone. We pray to her, says Saint Anselm, so that the dignity of the intercessor may supply our own deficiencies. Therefore, the saint adds, to supplicate the Virgin with such hope is not to distrust the mercy of God but only to fear our own unworthiness.

Mary Is a Merciful Advocate

There is no doubt, says Saint Bernard, that Jesus is the only mediator of justice between men and God, who in virtue of his merits can, and according to his promises will, obtain for us pardon and divine grace. But because men recognize and fear in Jesus Christ the divine majesty which dwells in him as God, it was necessary that another advocate should be assigned to us to whom we could have recourse with less fear and more confidence. This is Mary, than whom we can find no advocate more powerful with the divine majesty and more compassionate toward us. We would greatly wrong the mercy of Mary, continues the saint, if we should fear to cast ourselves at the feet of this most sweet advocate, who is in nothing severe or terrible but in all things is kind, lovely, and compassionate. Read and consider as much as you will all the history found in the Gospels, and if you find any act of austerity in Mary, then fear to approach her. But you will never find any. Go then joyfully to her, for she will save you by her intercession.

Exceedingly beautiful is the exclamation which William of Paris puts in the mouth of a sinner who has recourse to Mary: "Oh mother of my God, I come to you full of confidence, even in the miserable state to which I find myself reduced by my sins. If you reject me I will plead with you, for in a certain sense you are bound to help me, since all the Church of the faithful calls you and proclaims you mother of mercy. You, oh Mary, are so dear to God that he always graciously listens to you. Your great mercy has never failed. Your sweet condescension has never despised any sinner, however enormous his sins, who has had recourse to you. Could the whole Church falsely and in vain name you her advocate and the refuge of sinners? No, never let it be said that my sins prevent you, my mother, from exercising the great office of mercy which you hold, by which you are at the same time the advocate and mediator of peace between God and his people, and next to your Son the only hope and secure refuge of sinners. Whatever of grace and glory is yours, even the dignity of being Mother of God itself, if I may so speak, you owe to sinners, since for their sake the divine Word has made you his mother. Far from this divine mother, who brought forth into the world the fountain of mercy, be the thought that she should refuse her compassion to any sinner who recommends himself to her. Since, then, Mary, your office is that of peacemaker between God and man, may your great mercy, which far exceeds all my sins, move you to aid me."

Console yourselves, then, you who are faint of heart. I will say with Saint Thomas of Villanova: Take heart, miserable sinners. This great Virgin, who is the mother of your judge and God, is the advocate of the human race. Powerful and able to obtain whatever she wishes from God; most wise, for she knows every method of appeasing him; universal, for she welcomes all and refuses to defend none.

How Great Is the Mercy of Mary

Saint Bernard, speaking of the great mercy of Mary for us poor sinners, says that she is the very land promised by God, flowing with milk and honey. Saint Leo says that to the Virgin such compassion has been given that she not only deserves to be called merciful, but should be called mercy itself. And Saint Bonaventure—considering that Mary was made the Mother of God for the sake of us sinners and that to her was committed the charge of dispensing mercies, and considering, moreover, the great care she has for all those in misery, which renders her so rich in compassion that she seems to desire nothing else than to relieve the needy—says that when he looked on Mary it seemed to him he no longer beheld divine justice but only divine mercy, with which Mary is filled.

In a word, Mary's mercy is so great that, as Guerric the Abbot says, her love can never for a moment cease to bring forth for us the fruits of mercy. And what but mercy, exclaims Saint Bernard, can flow from a fountain of mercy? For this reason Mary was called the olive tree, like a fair olive tree in the plains (Eccl 24:19), for as the olive tree produces nothing but oil, the symbol of mercy, thus from the hands of Mary nothing but graces and mercies proceed. If, then, we have recourse to this mother and ask of her the oil of her mercy, we cannot fear that she will refuse us as the wise virgins refused the foolish, answering, "[No,] lest perhaps there be not enough for us and for you." No, for she is indeed rich in that oil of mercy. She is called by the Church not only prudent but most prudent, and by this we may understand, as Hugh of Saint Victor says, that Mary is so full of grace and mercy that there is enough for all without exhausting her.

But why, I would ask, is it said that this fair olive tree is in the midst of the plains, and not rather in a garden surrounded by walls and hedges? In order that all may easily see her, Cardinal Hugo answers, and thus may easily have recourse to her to obtain relief for their necessities. And what more secure refuge can we find, says the devout Thomas à Kempis, than Mary's compassionate heart? There the poor find shelter, the sick medicine, the afflicted consolation, the doubtful counsel, the abandoned help.

Wretched should we be if we did not have this mother of mercy, mindful and solicitous to help us in our miseries. "Where there is no wife," say the Holy Spirit, "he mourns that is in want" (Eccl 36:27). This wife, remarks Saint John Damascene, is certainly Mary, without whom the sick suffer and mourn.

Rebecca was the type of Mary, who, when Abraham's servant asked her for a little water, answered that she would give him water enough not only for himself but for his camels also (Gen 24:19). Hence the devout Saint Bernard, addressing the Blessed Virgin, says: Oh Lady, not to the servant of Abraham only but also to his camels give from your overflowing pitcher. By which he means to say: Oh Lady, you are more merciful and liberal than Rebecca, therefore you do not rest contented with dispensing the favors of your unbounded compassion only to the servants of Abraham, by whom are meant the faithful servants of God, but you bestow them also on the camels, who represent sinners. And as Rebecca gave more than she was asked, so Mary gives more than we pray for. The liberality of Mary, says Richard of Saint Laurence, resembles the liberality of her Son, who always gives more than is asked and is therefore named by Saint Paul "rich unto all that call upon him" (Rom 10:12).

When the Samaritans refused to receive Jesus Christ and his doctrine, Saint James and Saint John said to their Master: "Lord, will you that we command fire to come down from heaven, and consume them?" (Lk 9:54). But the Savior answered: "You know not of what spirit you are" (Lk 9:55), as if he had said, I am of so mild and merciful a Spirit that I have come from heaven to save; not to punish sinners, and would you wish to see them lost? What fire? What punishment? Be silent, do not speak to me again of punishment; that is not my Spirit. But we cannot doubt that Mary, whose spirit is in everything so like that of her Son, is wholly inclined to exercise mercy. This is why Mary was seen by Saint John clothed with the sun: "And a great sign appeared in heaven: A woman clothed with the sun" (Rev 12:1). On which passage Saint Bernard remarks, addressing the Virgin: "You have clothed the sun, and are yourself clothed with it. Oh Lady, you have clothed the sun, the divine Word, with human flesh, but he has clothed you with his power and his mercy."

So compassionate, then, and kind is this queen, says Saint Bernard, that when a sinner recommends himself to her mercy, she does not begin to examine his merits, and to judge whether he is worthy or not of being heard, but she graciously hears all and helps them. Hence Saint Idelbert remarks that Mary is called "fair as the moon" (Song 6:9) because as the moon illuminates and benefits the smallest bodies upon the earth, so Mary enlightens and helps the most unworthy sinners. And although the moon receives all light from the sun, she moves more quickly than the sun; for, as a certain author remarks, what the sun does in a year, the moon does in a month. Hence, says Saint Anselm, our relief is sometimes more immediate when the name of Mary is invoked than when we invoke the name of Jesus. Wherefore Hugh of Saint Victor tells us that if because of our sins we fear to draw near to God, because he is an infinite majesty that we have offended, we should not hesitate to have recourse to Mary, because in her we shall find nothing to alarm us. She is indeed holy, immaculate, queen of the world, and Mother of God; but she is of our flesh, and a child of Adam, like ourselves.

In a word, says Saint Bernard, whatever pertains to Mary is full of grace and mercy. For she, as mother of mercy, has become all things to all, and by her great charity has made herself a debtor to the just and to sinners, and opens to all the bowels of her compassion, that all may share it. As the devil, according to Saint Peter, "goes about seeking whom he may devour" (1 Pet 5:8), so, on the contrary, says Bernardine de Bustis, Mary goes about seeking to whom she can give life and salvation.

Let us conclude, then, with the beautiful and sweet exclamation of Saint Bernard upon the words: Oh clement, oh merciful, oh sweet Virgin Mary. "Oh Mary, you are clement to the unhappy, merciful to those who pray to you, sweet to those who love you; and clement to the penitent, merciful to the advancing, sweet to the perfect. You show yourself clement by rescuing us from punishment, merciful by bestowing on us graces, sweet by giving yourself to those who seek you."

Prayer to the Most Holy Mary

Oh most holy, immaculate Virgin and my mother Mary, to you who are the mother of my Lord, the queen of the world, the advocate, the hope, the refuge of sinners, I, the most miserable of all, have recourse today. I adore you, great queen, and thank you for all the favors you have hitherto granted me, especially for having delivered me from hell which I have so often deserved. I love you, most amiable Lady, and through the love I bear you promise that I will always serve you and do all that I can that you may also be loved by others. I place in you all my hopes of salvation. Accept me for your servant and receive me under your mantle, oh mother of mercy. And since you are so powerful with God, deliver me from all temptations, or obtain for me the strength to conquer them always until death. From you I ask a true love for Jesus Christ; from you do I hope to die a good death. Oh my mother, by the love you bear to God, I pray you to help me always, but most of all at the last moment of my life. Do not leave me until you see me actually safe in heaven, blessing you and singing your mercies through all eternity. Amen. Thus I hope. Thus may it be.

On the Immaculate Conception of Mary

How befitting it was to all three of the divine persons that Mary should be preserved from original sin.

In the first place, it was fitting that the eternal Father should create Mary free from the original stain, because she was his daughter and his firstborn daughter, as she herself attests—"I came out of the mouth of the most High, the firstborn before all creatures" (Eccl 24:5)—in a passage that is applied to Mary by the sacred interpreters, by the holy Fathers, and by the Church itself on the solemn festival of her Conception. Whether she is the firstborn on account of her predestination together with her Son in the divine decrees before all creatures, as the school of the Scotists will have it, or the firstborn of grace as predestined to be the mother of the Redeemer after the provision of sin, according to the school of the Thomists, all agree in calling her the firstborn of God. If this is the case, it was not right that Mary should be the slave of Lucifer, but only that she should always be possessed by her Creator, as she herself asserts: "The Lord possessed me in the beginning of his ways" (Prov 8:22). Hence Mary was rightly called by Dionysius, Archbishop of Alexandria, one and only daughter of life, differing in this from others who, being born in sin, are daughters of death.

Moreover, it was right that the eternal Father should create her in his grace, since he destined her for the restorer of the lost world and mediatrix of peace between human beings and God. Now certainly he who treats of peace should not be an enemy of the offended person, still less an accomplice of his crime. Saint Gregory says that to appease the judge his enemy certainly must not be chosen as an advocate, for instead of appeasing him he would enrage him more. Therefore, as Mary was to be the mediatrix of peace between God and man, there was every reason why she should not appear as a sinner and enemy of God, but as his friend and pure from sin.

Besides, it was fitting that God should preserve her from original sin, since he destined her to bruise the head of the infernal serpent, who by seducing our first parents brought death upon all men, as our Lord predicted: "I will put enmities between you and the woman, and your seed and her seed: she shall crush your head" (Gen 3:15). Now, if Mary was to crush Lucifer, surely it was not fitting that she should first be conquered by Lucifer and made his slave, but rather that she should be free from every stain and from all subjection to the enemy. Otherwise, as he had in his pride already corrupted the whole human race, he would also have corrupted the pure soul of this Virgin. May the divine goodness be ever praised for preventing her with so much grace that she remained free from every stain of sin and could overthrow and confound Lucifer's pride.

But it was especially fitting that the eternal Father should preserve his daughter from the sin of Adam, because he destined her to be the mother of his only-begotten Son. She was preordained in the mind of God, before every creature, to bring forth God himself made man. If for no other reason, then, at least for the honor of his Son, who was God, the Father would create her pure from every stain. The angelic Doctor Saint Thomas says that all things ordained by God must be holy and pure from every defilement. If David, when he was planning the temple of Jerusalem with a magnificence worthy of the Lord, said: "a house is prepared not for man, but for God" (1 Chr 29:1), how much greater cause have we to believe that the great Creator, having destined Mary to be the mother of his own Son, would adorn her soul with every grace so that it might be a worthy habitation for a God. Thus the eternal Father could say to this beloved daughter: "As the lily among the thorns, so is my love among the daughters" (Song 2:2). Daughter among all my other daughters, you are like a lily among thorns. For they are all stained by sin, but you were ever immaculate and ever my friend.

In the second place, it was befitting the Son that Mary, as his mother, should be preserved from sin. It is not permitted to other children to select a mother according to their good pleasure; but if this were ever granted to anyone who would choose a slave for his mother when he might have a queen, who a peasant when he might have a noble, who an enemy of God when he might have a friend of God? If, then, the Son of God alone could select a mother according to his pleasure, it must be considered as certain that he would choose one befitting a God. God, indeed, created her, by the nobility of her nature as well as by the perfection of grace, such as it was fitting that his mother should be. And here the words of the Apostle may be applied: "For it was fitting that we should have such a high priest, holy, innocent, undefiled, separated from sinners" (Heb 7:26).

God who is wisdom itself well knew how to prepare upon the earth a fit dwelling for him to inhabit: "Wisdom hath built herself a house" (Prov 9:1). "The Most High has sanctified his own tabernacle...God will help it in the morning early" (Ps 45:5,6). The

Lord says David sanctified his habitation in the early morning, that is from the beginning of her life, to render her worthy of himself, for it was not befitting a God who is holy to select a house that was not holy. How can we think that the Son of God would have chosen to inhabit the soul and body of Mary without first sanctifying her and preserving her from every stain? For, as Saint Thomas teaches us, the eternal Word inhabited not only the soul but the body of Mary. The Church also sings: Oh Lord, you did not shrink from the Virgin's womb. Indeed, a God would have shrunk from incarnating himself in the womb of an Agnes, of a Gertrude, of a Teresa, since those virgins, although holy, were for a time stained with original sin. But he did not shrink from becoming man in the womb of Mary, because this chosen Virgin was always pure from every guilt and never possessed by the infernal serpent. Hence, Saint Augustine wrote, the Son of God has built himself no house more worthy than Mary, who was never taken by the enemy nor robbed of her ornaments.

On the other hand, Saint Cyril of Alexandria says, who has ever heard of an architect building a house for his own use and then giving the first possession of it to his greatest enemy?

Certainly our Lord, who, as Saint Methodius declares, gave us the command to honor our parents, would not fail, when he became man like ourselves, to observe it himself, by bestowing on his mother every grace and honor. Hence, Saint Augustine says, we must certainly believe that Jesus Christ preserved Mary's body from corruption after death, for if he had not done so he would not have observed the law, which as it commands respect to the mother also condemns disrespect. How much less mindful would Jesus have been of his mother's honor if he had not preserved her from the sin of Adam.

In a word, to conclude this point, as Hugh of Saint Victor

says, the tree is known by its fruit. If the Lamb was always immaculate, the mother must also have been always immaculate. Hence this same Doctor saluted Mary by calling her the worthy mother of a worthy Son, by which he meant to say that none but Mary was the worthy mother of such a Son, and that none but Jesus was the worthy Son of such a mother. Therefore let us say with Saint Ildephonsus: "Give suck, then, oh Mary, give suck to your Creator; give suck to him who created you, and made you so pure and perfect that you have merited that he should receive human nature from you."

If, then, it was fitting for the Father to preserve Mary as his daughter from sin, and the Son because she was his mother, it was also fitting for the Holy Spirit to preserve her as his spouse. Mary, says Saint Augustine, was the only person who merited to be called the mother and spouse of God. For, as Saint Anselm affirms, the Holy Spirit came fully upon Mary and rested in her, enriching her with grace beyond all creatures, and dwelt in her and made his spouse queen of heaven and earth. As the saint expresses it, he was with her really, as to the effect, since he came to form from her immaculate body the immaculate body of Jesus Christ, as the archangel predicted—"The Holy Ghost shall come upon you, and the power of the Most High shall overshadow you" (Lk 1:35). For this reason, says Saint Thomas, Mary is called the temple of the Lord, the sanctuary of the Holy Spirit, because by the operation of the Holy Spirit she was made mother of the incarnate Word.

Now, if an excellent painter were allowed to choose a bride as beautiful or as deformed as he himself might paint her, how great would be his care to make her as beautiful as possible! Who, then, will say that the Holy Spirit did not deal thus with Mary, and that, having it in his power to make his spouse as beautiful as it became her to be, he did not do so? Yes, thus it was fitting he should do, and thus he did, as the Lord himself attested when praising Mary: "You are all fair, O my love, and there is not a spot in you" (Song 4:7).

The Holy Spirit signified the same thing when he called his spouse "a garden enclosed, a fountain sealed up" (Song 4:12). Mary, says Saint Jerome, was properly this enclosed garden and sealed fountain, for the enemies never entered to harm her, but she was always uninjured, remaining holy in soul and body. And Saint Bernard also said, addressing the Blessed Virgin, "You are an enclosed garden, where the sinner's hand never entered to rob it of its flowers."

We know that this divine spouse loved Mary more than all the other saints and angels united, as Father Suarez, Saint Lawrence Justinian, and others affirm. He loved her from the beginning and exalted her in sanctity above all creatures, as David expresses it: "The foundations thereof are in the holy mountains: The Lord loves the gates of Sion above all the tabernacles of Jacob…and the Highest himself hath founded her" (Ps 86:1,2,5). All these words signify that Mary was holy from her conception. The same thing is signified by what the Holy Spirit himself says in another place: "Many daughters have gathered together riches: you have surpassed them all" (Prov 31:29). If Mary has surpassed all in the riches of grace, she then must have possessed original justice as Adam and the angels had it. "There are…young maidens without number. One is my dove; my perfect one [the Hebrew reads, 'my uncorrupted, my immaculate'], she is the only one of her mother" (Song 6:7–8). All just souls are children of divine grace; but among these, Mary was the dove without the bitter gall of sin, the perfect one without the stain of original sin, the one conceived in grace. The angel, therefore, before Mary was Mother of God, already found her full of grace, and thus saluted her: "Hail, full of grace." Commenting on these words, Sophronius writes that to the other saints grace is given in part but to the Virgin it was given in fullness. So that, as Saint Thomas says, grace not only made the soul but also the flesh of Mary holy, that with it the Virgin might clothe the eternal Word.

On the Annunciation of Mary

Mary could not humble herself more than she did in the Incarnation of the Word. On the other hand, God could not exalt her more than he has exalted her.

"Whosoever shall exalt himself, shall be humbled: and he that shall humble himself shall be exalted" (Mt 23:12). These are the words of our Lord and cannot fail. Therefore, God having determined to make himself man, in order to redeem lost souls and thus manifest to the world his infinite goodness, being about to choose his mother on earth, sought among women the holiest and most humble. Among them all he saw one, the youthful Virgin Mary, who, as she was the most perfect in all virtues, so was she the most simple, and humble as a dove in her own esteem. "There are…young maidens without number. One is my dove, my perfect one" (Song 6:7–8). Let this one, said God, be my chosen mother. Let us, then, see how humble Mary was, and how God exalted her. Mary could not humble herself more than she did in the Incarnation of the Word; this will be the first point. That God could not exalt Mary more than he exalted her will be the second.

First Point. Our Lord in the holy Canticles, speaking precisely of the humility of this most humble Virgin, said: "While the king was at his repose, my spikenard sent forth the odor thereof." Saint Antoninus, commenting on these words, says that the spikenard, inasmuch as it is a small and lowly plant, was a type of the humility of Mary, whose odor ascended to heaven and drew from the bosom of the eternal Father into her virginal womb the divine Word. Thus the Lord, drawn by the odor of this humble Virgin, chose her for his mother when he wished to become man to redeem the world. But for the greater glory and merit of his mother he would not make himself her Son without first obtaining her consent. He would not take flesh in her without her consent. Therefore, when the humble young Virgin was in her poor dwelling, the Archangel Gabriel came, bearing the great message. He enters and salutes her, saying: "Hail, full of grace, the Lord is with you: blessed are you among women" (Lk 1:28). Hail, oh Virgin, full of grace, for you were always rich in grace above all the other saints. The Lord is with you because you are so humble. You are blessed among women, for all others have incurred the curse of original sin; but you, because you are to be the mother of the Blessed One, have been and will always be blessed, and free from every stain.

And what did the humble Mary answer to this salutation so full of praises? She answered nothing, but she was disturbed thinking about such a greeting: "Who having heard, [she] was troubled at his saying, and thought with herself what manner of salutation this should be" (Lk 1:29). And why was she disturbed, through fear of illusion or through modesty at the sight of a man, as some suppose, remembering that the angel appeared to her in human form? No, the text is plain, she was troubled at his words, as Eusebius Emissenus remarks, not by his appearance but by his speech. Such a disturbance was then wholly owing to her humility at hearing those praises, so far beyond her humble estimate of herself. Hence the more she is exalted by the angel, the more she humbles herself and the more she considers her nothingness.

But, I would remark, the blessed Virgin had already well

learned from the holy Scriptures that the time foretold by the prophets for the coming of the Messiah had arrived, that the weeks of Daniel were now completed, that already, according to the prophecy of Jacob, the scepter of Judah had passed into the hands of Herod, a strange king. And she well knew that a virgin was to be the mother of the Messiah, and she heard those praises offered by the angel to herself, which seemed to belong only to the Mother of God. Did it then come into her mind that perhaps she herself might be that chosen Mother of God? No, her profound humility did not permit this thought. These praises had no other effect than to cause her great fear, so that, as Saint Peter Chrysologus remarks, as Christ wished to be consoled by an angel, so must the Virgin be encouraged by an angel. As the Savior willed to be comforted by an angel, so it was necessary that Gabriel, seeing Mary so full of fear at that salutation, should encourage her, saying: "Fear not, Mary, for you have found grace with God" (Lk 1:30). Do not be afraid, Mary, nor be surprised by the great titles by which I have saluted you, for if you are so little and humble in your own eyes, God, who exalts the humble, has made you worthy to find the grace lost by humans; and therefore he has preserved you from the common stain of all Adam's children; therefore, even from the moment of your conception he has adorned you with a greater grace than that of all the saints; and therefore, finally, he now exalts you to be his mother: "Behold you shall conceive a son; and you shall call his name Jesus" (Lk 1:31).

Now why this delay? The angel, Lady, awaits your answer, or rather, as Saint Bernard says, we who are condemned to death await it. "Behold, Mother," continues Saint Bernard, "to you is now offered the price of our salvation, which will be the divine Word in you made man. If you will accept him for a son, we shall immediately be delivered from death. Look, the price of our salvation is offered to you. We are freed immediately if you consent. Your Lord himself, as he is greatly enamored of your beauty, so much the more desires your consent on which he has made the world's salvation depend." Answer quickly, oh Lady, adds Saint Augustine, delay no longer the salvation of the world, which now depends on your consent.

But look, Mary already answers. She says to the angel: "Behold the handmaid of the Lord; be it done to me according to your word" (Lk 1:38). Oh, what more beautiful, more humble, and more prudent answer could all the wisdom of men and of angels united have invented, if they had thought of it for millions of years! Oh powerful answer, which gave joy in heaven and poured upon the earth a vast flood of graces and blessings! Answer that had no sooner come forth from the humble heart of Mary than it drew, from the bosom of the eternal Father, the only-begotten Son, to become man in her most pure womb! For hardly had she uttered those words when immediately the Word was made flesh. *Verbum caro factum est*: the Son of God became also the Son of Mary.

But let us not wander from our point. Let us consider the great humility of the Virgin in this answer. She was indeed well enlightened to understand how great was the dignity of the Mother of God. She had already been assured by the angel that she was this happy mother chosen by the Lord. But with all this, she is not at all raised in her own esteem, stops not at all to enjoy her exaltation, but considering on one side her own nothingness and on the other the infinite majesty of her God who has chosen her for his mother, she knows how unworthy she is of such an honor but would by no means oppose herself to his will. Hence, when her consent is asked, what does she do, what does she say? Wholly annihilated as to self, all inflamed on the other hand with the desire to unite herself more closely to God by entirely abandoning herself to the divine will, she answers, "Behold the handmaid of the Lord." Behold the slave of the Lord, obliged to do whatever her Lord commands. If the Lord chooses me for his mother, who have nothing of my own, if everything that I have is his gift, then who could think he is selecting me for any merit of my own? "Behold the handmaid of the Lord." What merit can a slave have to be made the mother of her Lord? "Behold the handmaid of the Lord." Let the goodness of God alone be praised and not the slave, since it is wholly God's goodness which has led him to place his glance on a creature so lowly as I am and thus to make her so great.

Second Point. In order to comprehend the greatness to which Mary was elevated, it would be necessary to comprehend the sublime majesty and grandeur of God. It is sufficient, then, only to say that God made this Virgin his mother to have it understood that he could not exalt her more than he did exalt her. Rightly did Saint Arnold Carnotensis affirm that, by making himself the Son of the Virgin, God established her in a superior rank to all the saints and angels.

This, remarks Saint Thomas of Villanova, removes the surprise expressed by some that the holy Evangelists, who have so fully recorded the praises of a Baptist and a Magdalene, have been so brief in their descriptions of the privileges of Mary. For, says the saint, it was enough to say of her that from her Jesus was born. What more would you wish the Evangelists to say, the saint continues, about the grandeur of this Virgin? Let it be enough for you that they attest her to be the Mother of God. Having recorded in these few words the greatest and indeed the whole of her merits, it was not necessary for them to describe each separately. And why not? "Because," as Saint Anselm answers, "to say of Mary this alone, that she was the Mother of God, transcends every other glory that can be attributed to her, in thought or word." Peter of Celles adds that by whatever name you may wish to call her, whether queen of heaven, ruler of the angels, or any other title of honor, you will never succeed in honoring her so much as by calling her only "the Mother of God."

The reason for this is evident, because, as the angelic Doctor teaches, the nearer a thing approaches its author the greater the perfection it receives from him. Therefore Mary, as the creature nearest to God, has partaken more than all others of his grace, perfection, and greatness. To this, Father Suarez traces the cause why the dignity of Mother of God is of an order superior to any other created dignity: because it appertains, in a certain manner, to the order of union with a divine Person, a union with which it is necessarily connected.

Saint Bernardine affirms that in order to become Mother of God, it was requisite that the holy Virgin should be exalted to a certain equality with the divine Persons by an infinity of graces. And as children are esteemed morally one with their parents, so that their possessions and honors are shared in common, therefore Saint Peter Damian says that if God dwells in creatures in different ways, he dwelt in Mary in a unique way, making himself one with her. And then he exclaims in these celebrated words: "Here let every creature be silent and tremble, and scarcely dare to behold the immensity of so great a dignity. God dwells in a virgin with whom he has the identity of one nature."

Saint Thomas asserts that Mary, being made Mother of God, by reason of this close union with an infinite good received a certain infinite dignity. The dignity of Mother of God is the highest dignity that could be conferred on a mere creature. The angelic Doctor teaches that the humanity of Jesus Christ, though it might have received a greater habitual grace from God, yet, as to the union with a divine Person, could not receive greater perfection. For as habitual grace (this is his reasoning) is a created gift, we must acknowledge that its essence is finite. The capacity of every creature is limited in measure, which does not prevent the divine power from being able to form another creature of greater capacity. Although the divine power may, therefore, create something greater and better than the habitual grace of Christ, yet it could not destine it to anything greater than the personal union of the only-begotten Son with the Father. Thus the Blessed Virgin, because she is Mother of God, has a certain infinite dignity from the infinite good which is God. In this respect, nothing greater can be created.

Therefore, Saint Bonaventure wrote another celebrated sentence: God could make a greater world, a greater heaven, but could not exalt a creature to greater excellence than by making her his mother.

But better than all others, the divine mother herself described the height to which God had elevated her when she said: "He that is mighty, has done great things to me" (Lk 1:49).

To conclude, then, this divine mother is infinitely inferior to God, but immensely superior to all creatures. If it is impossible to find a son more noble than Jesus, it is also impossible to find a mother more noble than Mary. This should cause the servants of such a queen not only to rejoice in her greatness but also to increase their confidence in her most powerful protection. For, being Mother of God, as Father Suarez says, she has a certain right to his gifts and a right to obtain them for those for whom she prays. Saint Germanus, on the other hand, says that God cannot refuse to hear the prayers of this mother, for he cannot refuse to recognize her for his true and immaculate mother. Thus, says the saint addressing the Virgin: You prevail with God by a maternal authority; thus even for those who grievously sin you obtain the great grace of reconciliation. For you cannot but be graciously heard, as God in all things conforms to your wishes as to those of a true and pure mother. Therefore, oh Mother of God and our mother, in you the power to help us is not lacking. The will, too, is not lacking. For you know, I will say with your servant the Abbot of Celles, that God has not created you for himself alone, but has given you to the angels for their restorer, to men for their deliverer, and to the demons for their conqueror. For by your means we recover divine grace, and by you the enemy is conquered and crushed.

On the Assumption of Mary

How glorious was the triumph of Mary when she ascended to heaven and how exalted was the throne to which she was raised in heaven!

It would seem just that the Church, on this day of the assumption of Mary into heaven, should rather invite us to weep than to rejoice, since our sweet mother has quitted this earth and left us bereft of her sweet presence. As Saint Bernard says, it seems that we should rather weep than exult. But no, holy Church invites us to rejoice: "Let us all rejoice in the Lord, celebrating a festival in honor of the Blessed Virgin Mary." And justly, if we love this our mother, we ought to congratulate ourselves more upon her glory than upon our own particular consolation. What son does not rejoice, although separated from his mother, if he knows that she is going to take possession of a kingdom? Mary today is to be crowned queen of heaven, and shall we not make a joyful feast if we truly love her? Let us all rejoice, let us rejoice: *Gaudeamus omnes, et gaudeamus.*

After Jesus Christ our Savior had completed the work of our redemption by his death, the angels earnestly desired to have him with them in their heavenly country. Hence they were continually supplicating him, repeating the words of David: "Arise, O Lord, into your resting place: you and the ark which you have sanctified" (Ps 131:8). And let us now consider how the Savior came from heaven to meet his mother, and how he said to her, "Arise, make haste, my love, my dove, my beautiful one, and come. For winter is now past…and gone" (Song 2:10–11). Come, my dear mother, my beautiful and pure dove, leave that valley of tears where you have suffered so much for my love; "come from Libanus, my spouse, come from Libanus, come: you shall be crowned" (Song 4:8). Come with soul and body, to enjoy the reward for your holy life. If you have suffered greatly on earth, far greater is the glory I have prepared for you in heaven. Come there to sit near me, come to receive the crown I will give you as queen of the universe.

Now, behold, Mary leaves the earth, and calling to mind the many graces she had there received from her Lord, she looks on it at the same time both affectionately and compassionately, leaving in it so many poor children in the midst of so many miseries and dangers. And now Jesus offers her his hand and the Blessed Mother rises in the air and passes beyond the clouds and spheres. See her now arrived at the gates of heaven. When monarchs make their entrance to take possession of their kingdom, they do not pass through the gates of the city, for either these are taken off entirely or they pass over them. Hence the angels, when Jesus Christ entered paradise, cried: "Lift up your gates, O ye princes, and be ye lifted up, O eternal gates: and the King of Glory shall enter in" (Ps 23:7). Thus, also, now that Mary is going to take possession of the kingdom of the heavens, the angels who accompany her cry to the others who are within: "Lift up your gates, ye princes, and be ye lifted up, eternal gates: and the queen of glory shall enter in."

And now Mary enters into the blessed country. But on her

entrance, the celestial spirits seeing her so beautiful and glorious ask of those who are without, as Origen describes it, and exclaim as one, all rejoicing in heaven, "Who is this that comes up from the desert, flowing with delights, leaning upon her beloved?" (Song 8:5). Who is this creature, so beautiful, that comes from the desert of the earth, a place full of thorns and tribulations? This one comes so pure and so rich in virtue, supported by her beloved Lord, who deigns to accompany her with such great honor. Who is she? The angels who accompany her answer: This is the mother of our King. She is our queen, the blessed one among women, full of grace, the saint of saints, the beloved of God, the immaculate one, the dove, the most beautiful of all creatures. And then all those blessed spirits begin to bless and praise her, singing, with more reason than the Hebrews sang to Judith, "You are the glory of Jerusalem, you are the joy of Israel, you are the honor of our people" (Judg 15:10). Our lady and our queen, you are the glory of paradise, the joy of our heavenly country, you are the honor of us all. Be ever welcome, be ever blessed. Behold us, we are all your servants, ready for your commands.

If the human mind, says Saint Bernard, cannot attain to comprehension of the immense glory which God has prepared in heaven for those who have loved him on earth, as the Apostle declares, then who will ever attain to comprehension of what he has prepared for her who bore him? What glory did he prepare for his beloved mother, he who on earth loved her more than all men; who even from the first moment of her creation loved her more than all men and angels together? Justly, then, does holy Church sing that Mary, having loved God more than all the angels, has been exalted above all the angels. Yes, she has been exalted above the angels, says William the Abbot, so that she sees no one above her but her Son who is the only-begotten Son of God.

The glory of Mary, which was a full glory and a complete glory, remarks a learned author, is different from that which the other saints have in heaven. It is true that in heaven all the blessed enjoy perfect peace and full content. Yet it will always be true that no one of them enjoys that glory which he could have merited if he had loved and served God with greater fidelity. Therefore, although the saints in heaven desire nothing more than what they possess, yet in fact there is something more they could desire. It is also true that the sins which they have committed and the time which they have lost do not bring suffering. But it cannot be denied that the most good done in life, innocence preserved and time well employed, gives the greatest contentment. Mary in heaven desires nothing and has nothing to desire. Who of the saints in paradise, says Saint Augustine, if asked whether or not he has committed sins, can answer no, except Mary? It is certain, as the holy Council of Trent defined, that Mary never committed any sin, not even the slightest. Not only did she never lose divine grace—never bedim it—but she never kept it unemployed. She never did an action that was not meritorious. She never said a word or had a thought or drew a breath that was not directed to the greatest glory of God. In a word, she never relaxed or stopped one moment in her onward course to God. She never lost anything through negligence, for she always corresponded with grace with all her power and loved God as much as she could love him. Oh Lord, she now says to him in heaven, if I have not loved you as much as you deserve, at least I have loved you as much as I could.

Let us rejoice, then, with Mary, in the exalted throne to which God has elevated her in heaven. And let us rejoice also for her own sake, since if our mother has ceased to be present with us, by rising in glory to heaven, she has not ceased to be present with us in her affection. No, being there nearer and more united to God, she better knows our miseries and therefore pities them more and is better able to relieve us. And will you, as Saint Peter Damian asks, oh Blessed Virgin, because you have been so exalted in heaven, be forgetful of us miserable creatures? No, may God preserve us from the thought. A heart so merciful cannot but pity our miseries which are so great. If the pity of Mary for us was so great when she lived upon earth, much greater, says Saint Bonaventure, is it in heaven where she now reigns.

And with this love of our mother Mary, I leave you, my dear reader and brother, saying to you, continue joyfully to honor and love this good lady. Try also to promote the love of her wherever you can, and do not doubt but securely trust that if you persevere in true devotion to Mary, even until death, your salvation will be certain. I finish, not because I have nothing more to say about the glories of this great queen but so that I may not weary you. The little I have written may indeed be enough to charm you with this great treasure of devotion to the Mother of God, with which she will correspond with her powerful patronage. Accept, then, the desire I have had by this my work, to see you safe and holy, to see you become a loving and ardently devoted child of this most lovable queen. And if you know that this book of mine has aided you somewhat, I pray you of your charity, recommend me to Mary and ask of her the grace which I ask for you, namely, that we may both meet in paradise at her feet, together with all her other dear children.

Little Rosary of the Seven Sorrows of Mary

Incline unto mine aid, oh God! Mother, enable my heart to share your sorrow for the death of your Son.

First Sorrow. I pity you, my afflicted mother, because of the first sword of sorrow that pierced you: when in the temple, by the prophecy of Saint Simeon, all the cruel sufferings that men would inflict on your beloved Jesus were represented to you, sufferings which you had already learned from holy Scripture, even to his death before your eyes upon the infamous wood of the cross, exhausted of blood and abandoned by all, and you without power to defend or relieve him. By that bitter memory, then, which for so many years afflicted your heart, I ask you to obtain for me the grace that always, in life and in death, I may keep impressed upon my heart the passion of Jesus and your sufferings.

(Say the Our Father, Hail Mary, Glory be to God, and the beginning prayer: "Incline unto mine aid..." as above. Repeat at the end of each sorrow.)

Second Sorrow. I pity you, my afflicted mother, because of the second sword that pierced you: when you saw your innocent Son so soon after his birth threatened with death by those very men for whom he had come into the world, so that you were obliged to flee with him by night secretly into Egypt. By the many hardships, then, that you, a delicate young virgin, in company with your exiled infant, endured in the long and wearisome journey through rough and desert countries and during your sojourn in Egypt where, being unknown and a stranger, you lived all those years poor and despised, I ask you, my beloved Lady, to obtain for me the grace to suffer with patience, in your company until death, the trials of this miserable life; that I may be able in the next life to be preserved from the eternal sufferings of hell deserved by me. *(Our Father, etc.)*

Third Sorrow. I pity you, my afflicted mother, because of the third sword that pierced your heart: at the loss of your dear son, Jesus, who remained absent from you in Jerusalem for three days. Not seeing your beloved one at your side and not knowing the cause of his absence, I can understand how in these nights you did not rest, and did nothing but sigh for him who was your only good. By the sighs, then, of those three days and nights, for you so long and bitter, I ask you to obtain for me the grace never to lose my God; that I may always live closely united to God and thus united with him depart from this world. *(Our Father, etc.)*

Fourth Sorrow. I pity you, my afflicted mother, because of the fourth sword that pierced your heart: in seeing your Jesus condemned to death, bound with ropes and chains, covered with blood and wounds, crowned with thorns, and falling under the weight of the heavy cross which he bore on his bleeding back when going like an innocent lamb to die for love of us. Your eye then met his eye, and your glances were so many cruel sorrows with which each wounded the loving heart of the other. By this great grief, then, I ask you to obtain for me the grace to live wholly resigned to the will of my God, joyfully bearing my cross with Jesus to the last moment of my life. *(Our Father, etc.)*

Fifth Sorrow. I pity you, my afflicted mother, because of the fifth sword that pierced your heart: when on Mount Calvary you saw your beloved Son Jesus dying slowly before your eyes, amid so many insults and in anguish on that hard bed of the cross, without being able to give him even the least of those comforts which the greatest criminals receive at the hour of death. And I ask you by the anguish which you, oh my most loving mother, suffered together with your dying Son, and by the tenderness you felt when for the last time he spoke to you from the cross, and taking leave of you left all of us to you in the person of Saint John as your children, and you, still constant, saw him bow his head and expire. I ask you to obtain for me the grace, by your crucified love, to live and die crucified to everything in this world, in order to live only for God throughout my whole life, and thus to enter one day into paradise, to enjoy him face to face. *(Our Father, etc.)*

Sixth Sorrow. I pity you, my afflicted mother, because of the sixth sword which pierced your heart: when you saw the kind heart of your Son pierced through and through after his death—a death endured for those ungrateful men who even after his death were not satisfied with the tortures they had inflicted on him. By this cruel sorrow, then, which was wholly yours, I ask you to obtain for me the grace to abide in the heart of Jesus which was wounded and opened for me—in that heart which is the beautiful abode of love, where all the souls who love God repose; that living there, I may never love or think of anything but God. Most holy Virgin, you can do it; from you, I hope for it. *(Our Father, etc.)*

Seventh Sorrow. I pity you, my afflicted mother, because of the seventh sword that pierced your heart: on seeing in your arms your Son who had just died, no longer fair and beautiful as you once received him in the stable of Bethlehem but covered with blood, livid, and lacerated by wounds which exposed his very bones. My Son, you said, my Son, to what has love brought you? And when he was borne to the sepulcher, you wanted to accompany him yourself and help to put him in the tomb with your own hands. And bidding him a last farewell, you left your loving heart buried with your Son. By all the anguish of your pure soul, obtain for me, oh mother of fair love, pardon for the offenses I have committed against my God, whom I love, and of which I repent with my whole heart. Will you defend me in temptation? Help me at the hour of my death; that, being saved by the merits of Jesus and by yours, I may come one day with your aid, after this miserable exile, to sing in paradise the praises of Jesus and of you through all eternity. Amen. *(Our Father, etc.)*

Pray for us, oh most sorrowful Virgin,
That we may be worthy of the promises of Christ.

Let us Pray. Oh God, at whose Passion, according to the prophecy of Simeon, the sword of sorrow pierced through the most sweet soul of the glorious virgin and mother Mary, grant that we who commemorate and reverence her sorrows may experience the blessed effect of your Passion, who lives and reigns world without end. Amen.

On the Love of God, and the Means to Acquire It

1 ◆ Our good Lord, because he loves us much, desires to be loved much by us. Therefore he has not only called us to love him by many invitations repeated again and again in Scripture, and by many blessings both general and individual, but he also obliges us to love him by an express commandment. He threatens those who do not love him with hell, while to those who do love him he promises paradise. His will is that no one shall be lost but that all attain salvation, as Saint Peter and Saint Paul most clearly teach: "Who will have all men to be saved" (1 Tim 2:4): "The Lord…deals patiently for your sake, not willing that any should perish, but that all should return to penance" (2 Pet 3:9). But since God wishes all men to be saved, why has he created hell? He did so, not to see us damned, but in order to be loved by us. If he had not created hell, who in the whole world would love him? If with hell, existing as it really does, the greater part of men choose rather to be damned than to love almighty God, who, I repeat, would love him were there no hell? And therefore the Lord threatens those who will not love him with eternal punishment, so that they who will not love him out of love may at least love him by force, being constrained to do so through fear of falling into hell.

2 ◆ Oh God, how fortunate and honored would that person esteem himself to whom his king should say, "Love me because I love you!" An earthly monarch would take good care not to humble himself to such an extent as to ask one of his subjects for his love; but God, who is infinite goodness, the Lord of all, almighty, all-wise, who merits an infinite love, who has enriched us with spiritual and temporal gifts, does not disdain to ask of us our love. He exhorts and commands us to love him, and he cannot obtain it. What does he ask of each one of us but to be loved? "What does the Lord your God require of you, but that you fear the Lord your God…and love him?" (Deut 10:12). It was for this end that the Son of God came to converse with us even upon earth, as he himself said: "I am come to cast fire on the earth: and what will I, but that it be kindled?" (Lk 12:49). Notice those last words—"and what will I, but that it be kindled?" It is as if a God, who possesses in himself infinite happiness, could not be happy without seeing himself loved by us: "As if," says Saint Thomas, "he could not be happy without you."

3 • We cannot doubt, then, that God loves us, and loves us exceedingly. Because he loves us exceedingly, he wishes us to love him with our whole heart: "You shall love the Lord your God with your whole heart." And then he adds: "And these words…shall be in your heart:…and you shall meditate upon them sitting in your house, and walking on your journey, sleeping and rising. And you shall bind them as a sign on your hand, and they shall be and shall move between your eyes. And you shall write them in the entry, and on the doors of your house" (Deut 6:5–9). We can see in all these words how earnest is the desire which God has to be beloved by each one of us. He wishes that the injunction of loving him with our whole heart should be imprinted in our heart, and that we may never be unmindful of these words, he wishes us to meditate upon them when we are sitting at home, when we are walking abroad, when we lie down to sleep, and when we wake from it again. He wishes us to hold them in our hands bound up with some significant memento in order that, wherever we may be, our eyes may ever rest upon them. Hence it was that the Pharisees, taking the words only in their literal sense, as we are told by Saint Matthew, used to wear them inscribed on broad pieces of parchment on their foreheads (Mt 23:5).

4 ◆ Saint Gregory of Nyssa exclaims, "Blessed is the arrow which carries along with it into the heart the God by whom it is aimed!" What the holy Father means is this: that when God wounds the heart with an arrow of love, it acts like a flash or ray of special illumination, whereby the soul becomes aware of his goodness and of the love which he bears toward her, and also of the desire which he has to possess the love of that soul; while at the same moment he himself comes together with that arrow of his love, he who is the archer being himself also loved. And as an arrow remains fixed in the heart which it has wounded, so in the same way does God, when he wounds a soul with his love, come to remain forever united with that soul which he has wounded. Let us be assured that it is God only who loves us truly. The love of parents, of friends, and of all others who profess to love us (except those who love us solely out of regard for God) is not a true but a self-interested love, and arises from some motive of self-love for the sake of which we are loved. My God, I know full well that it is you alone who loves me, and desires for me every good, not for any selfish interests of thine own but solely out of thine own goodness and out of the pure affection which you bear toward me, while I am so ungrateful as to have caused no one so much displeasure and so many griefs as I have done to you, who hast loved me so much. My Jesus, do not permit me to be ungrateful to you any more. You have loved me truly, and I wish to love you truly in whatever of this life may still be mine. With Saint Catherine of Genoa, I say to you: "My

Love, no more sins, no more sins." I wish to love you only, and nothing else.

5 ◆ Saint Bernard says that a soul which truly loves God cannot will anything but what God wills. "Let us pray God to wound us with his holy love, for a soul thus wounded has neither the faculty nor the power to have a will for anything but that which God wills, and divests itself of every desire arising out of self-love. This self-spoliation, together with giving oneself unreservedly to God, is the arrow by which he declares that he himself is Wounded by the Soul, as he said to the Sacred Spouse in the Canticles: "You have wounded my heart, my Sister, my Spouse" (Song 4:9).

6 ◆ How beautifully Saint Bernard expresses himself on this subject when he says: "Let us learn to dart our hearts at God!" When a soul gives herself up wholly and unreservedly to God, it is as if she darted her own heart like a spear toward the heart of God, who declares himself to be, as it were, captured and taken prisoner by the soul which has made over to him the gift of herself in full. This is the employment of such souls in the prayers which they offer, "they dart their hearts at God"; they give themselves wholly up to God and they are ever renewing that gift in these or similar ejaculations of love: My God and my all: my God, I long for you and for nothing else.

Oh Lord, I give myself wholly to you; and if I do not know how to make the gift as perfect as I ought, do you manage it yourself.

And what would I love, my Jesus, if I do not love you, who has died for me?

Draw me after you: my Savior, drag me out of the mire of my sins, and draw me after you.

Bind me, Lord, and fetter me with the chains of your love, so that I may never leave you more.

I wish to be all yours. Lord, have you understood me? I wish to be wholly, wholly your own: it is for you to make me so.

And what would I have but you, my love, my all?

Since you have called me to your love, enable me to please you as you desire.

And what would I love but you, who art infinite goodness, deserving infinite love?

You have inspired me with the desire of being wholly yours: oh, make the work complete!

And what would I have in this world but you, who art the sovereign good?

I give myself to you without reserve: accept me, and give me the strength to be faithful to you till death!

I wish to love you greatly in this life, that I may love you greatly for all eternity.

Jesus, my true, my only love,
I wish for nothing but you:
Behold me all your own, my God;
Do what you will with me.

Whoever says this little canticle from the heart causes joy in paradise.

7 • Blessed, in short, is that soul which can truly say, "My beloved to me, and I to him" (Song 2:16): My God has given himself wholly to me, and I have given myself wholly to him; I am no longer my own; I belong entirely to my God. Saint Bernard says that whoever can say this from his heart would most readily and willingly embrace all the pains of hell (provided that he could do so without separating himself from God) rather than see himself, even for one single moment, disunited from God: "It would be more tolerable to such a one to suffer hell than to withdraw from him." Oh, what a beautiful treasure is the treasure of divine love! He who possesses it is happy indeed. Let him take every care, and make use of all the means which are necessary to preserve and increase it. He who does not yet possess it ought to employ every means in order to acquire it. Let us now see what are the means most necessary and proper for its acquisition and preservation:

8 • The *first* of these means is the detachment of oneself from worldly affections. In a heart which is full of the world there is no room to be found for the love of God. The more the worldly element predominates, so much the less does the divine love hold sway. Therefore, he who desires to have his heart filled with divine love should study to remove out of it all that is of the world. To become saints, we must follow the example of Saint Paul who, that he might gain the love of Jesus Christ, despised as so much dung all the good things of this world (Phil 3:8). Oh, let us pray the Holy Spirit to enkindle within us his holy love, for then we too shall despise and reckon as mere vanity, smoke, and dirt all this world's riches, pleasures, honors, and distinctions, for the sake of which men involve themselves so miserably in destruction.

9 • Whenever holy love enters into the heart, it no longer regards as of any value all that the world holds in esteem: "If a person should give all the substance of his house for love, he shall despise it as nothing" (Song 8:7). Saint Francis de Sales observes that when a house is in flames the goods are all thrown out through the windows, meaning that when the heart is on fire with divine love a person does not need the preachings and exhortations of a spiritual father, but of his own accord sets himself to work to divest himself of the good things of this world, of its honors, its riches, and of all earthly things, in order that he may love nothing but God. Saint Catherine of Genoa used to say that she did not love God for the sake of his gifts, but that she loved the gifts of God so that she might love him the more.

10 • Gilbert observes: "Oh, how hard it is for the lover to divide his heart between Christ and the world!" Saint Bernard says that the divine love is, on the other hand, insolent, because God will not suffer that, in a heart which loves, there should be others to share with him in its love, wishing as he does to have it all for himself. Does God claim too much, in wishing that a soul should love him, and him alone? "The sovereign loveliness," observes Saint Bonaventure, "ought to be loved exclusively." Such a one as God, whose loveliness and goodness are infinite and worthy of an infinite love, has a just claim to be alone in his possession of the love of a heart created by himself for the express purpose of making him the object of its love. In order that he might be loved exclusively, he has gone so far as to expend himself wholly for that heart, as Saint Bernard says when speaking of himself and of the love which Jesus Christ had borne toward him: "He was utterly spent for my benefit." What each one of us can most truly say when thinking of Jesus Christ is that for each one of us he has sacrificed all his life and all his blood, dying upon a cross, consumed by pain, and that, although his death be past, he has bequeathed to us his body and his blood, his soul and his whole self in the sacrament of the altar, that it may be the meat and drink of our souls and that we may each of us be united to himself.

11 ◆ Happy is the soul, as Saint Gregory observes, which has arrived at a state wherein everything is intolerable which is not the God whom it exclusively loves. We must, then, be on our guard against setting our affections on creatures, lest they steal from us a portion of the love which God wishes to be wholly for himself. Even when such affections are right, as in the case of those we feel toward parents or friends, we should never forget the saying of Saint Philip Neri, that whatever love we entertain for creatures is so much taken away from God.

12 ◆ We should, therefore, try to make ourselves "gardens enclosed," as the sacred spouse in the Canticles was styled by her Lord. The title of "a garden enclosed" applies to that soul which keeps itself closed up against the entrance of all mere earthly affections. Whenever, therefore, any creature seeks to enter in and to lay hold of a portion of our heart, we must utterly refuse it admission. Then we ought to turn to Jesus Christ and say to him: My Jesus, you alone are sufficient for me. I do not wish to love anyone but you: "You are the God of my heart, and the God that is my portion for ever." On this account let us not cease from praying continually to God, that he would bestow upon us the gift of his pure love; since, as Saint Francis de Sales observes, "The pure love of God consumes all that is not God, to transform everything into itself."

13 ◆ Meditation on the Passion of our Lord Jesus Christ is the *second* means for acquiring divine love. It is certain that the fact of Jesus Christ being so little loved in the world arises from the negligence and ingratitude of humankind, and from people not considering, at least occasionally, how much he has suffered for us and the love with which he suffered for us. "To humankind it has appeared foolish," as Saint Gregory observes, "that God should die for us." It seems folly, says the saint, that God should have been willing to die in order to save us miserable servants; but nevertheless it is of faith that he did so. "He has loved us, and delivered himself for us." And he has willed to shed all his blood, in order to wash away our sins therewith (Rev 1:5).

14 • Saint Bonaventure says, "My God, you have loved me so much that through your love for me you seem to have gone so far as even to have hated yourself." Besides, he has further willed that he himself should be our food in Holy Communion. Saint Thomas, speaking of the Blessed Sacrament, says that God has so humbled himself with us that it is as if he were our servant and each of us his God.

15 • Hence it is that the Apostle says, "the charity of Christ presses us" (2 Cor 5:14). Saint Paul says that the love which Jesus Christ has borne us constrains us, in a certain sense forces us to love him. My God, what is there that men will not do out of their love for some creature on which they have set their affections! And how little is their love for one who is God, whose goodness and loveliness are infinite, and who has even gone so far as to die on a cross for each of us! Let us follow the example of the Apostle who said: "But God forbid that I should glory, save in the cross of our Lord Jesus Christ" (Gal 6:14). So spoke the holy Apostle, and what greater glory can I hope for in the world than that of having had a God to sacrifice his blood and life out of his love for me? This is what everyone who has faith must say; if he has faith, how shall it be possible for him to love anything other than God? How can a soul, contemplating Jesus crucified, as he hangs suspended on three nails and dies of sheer anguish through his love for us, not perceive itself drawn and as it were forced to love him with all its powers?

16 • The *third* means of gaining a perfect love of God is the bringing of our own will into uniformity with the divine will in all things. Saint Bernard says that he who loves God perfectly "cannot will anything except that which God wills." There are many who profess themselves to be thoroughly resigned to whatever God wills, but when any adverse circumstance or any troublesome infirmity befalls them they cannot retain their peace of mind. It is not so with souls in a state of true uniformity. They say, "Thus it pleases or has pleased him whom I love," and they are immediately at rest. "To holy love," says Saint Bonaventure, "all things are sweet." These souls know that everything which happens in the world is either ordered or permitted by God. Consequently, in all that comes to pass, they humbly bow down their heads and live contented with what God assigns. Although it is frequently the case that he does not will that those who persecute and injure us should do so, yet he nevertheless wills, and for wise ends, that we should suffer with patience the persecution or the injury by which we are afflicted.

17 • Saint Catherine of Genoa used to say, "If God had placed me in the depths of hell, I would sincerely have said, it is good for us to be here." I would have said, it is enough for me that I am here by the will of him whom I love, who loves me more than all others do and who knows what is best for me. Sweet is the rest of those who rest in the arms of the divine will.

18 • Saint Teresa says the great thing to be acquired by one who practices the habit of prayer is the conformity of his own will with the divine, for in that consists the highest perfection. Therefore we must be ever repeating to God that prayer of David: "Teach me to do your will" (Ps 142:9). The most perfect act of love which a soul can perform toward God is that of Saint Paul, when on his conversion he said, "Lord, what will you have me do?" (Acts 9:6). Lord, tell me what you desire of me, for I am ready to do it. This act is worth more than a thousand fasts and a thousand disciplines. This ought to be the object of all our works, desires, and prayers, the accomplishment of the divine will. We ought to beg our Blessed Mother, our patron saints and guardian angels to obtain for us the grace to fulfill the will of God. And whenever things which are opposed to our self-love befall us, we may then by one act of resignation gain treasures of merit. Let us accustom ourselves on such occasions to repeat those words which Jesus himself has, by his own example, taught us: "The chalice which my Father has given me, shall I not drink it?" (Jn 18:11). Or again: "Yea, Father; for so has it seemed good in your sight" (Mt 11:26). Or again, with holy Job, let us say: as it has pleased the Lord so is it done: blessed be the name of the Lord" (Job 1:21). Juan of Avila used to say that a single "Blessed be God" under adverse circumstances is worth more than a thousand thanksgivings when things go smoothly. And here we may say again, what has already been said, beautiful is the rest of those who rest themselves in the arms of the will of God, for then will the declaration of the Holy Spirit be fulfilled in them: "Whatever shall befall the just person, it shall not make him sad" (Prov 12:21).

19 ◆ The *fourth* means for becoming enamored of God is mental prayer. The eternal truths are not discernible by the natural eye, like the things which are visible in this world. They are to be discerned solely by means of meditation and contemplation. Therefore, unless we pause for a certain length of time, in order to consider the eternal truths and more especially our obligation to love God, because he is so deserving of our love and also because of the great blessings he has conferred upon us and the love which he has borne us, we shall hardly loose ourselves from the love of creatures, to fix our whole love on God. It is in the time of prayer that God gives us to understand the worthlessness of earthly things, and the value of the good things of heaven. Then it is that he inflames with his love those hearts which do not offer resistance to his calls. There are many, however, who complain that they go to prayer and do not find God. The reason is that they carry with them a heart full of earth. Detach the heart from creatures, says Saint Teresa, seek God, and you will find him: "The Lord is good…to the soul that seeks him" (Lam 3:25). Therefore, to find God in prayer, the soul must be stripped of its love for the things of earth; then God will speak to it: "I will …lead her into the wilderness: and I will speak to her heart" (Hos 2:14). But in order to find God, the solitude of the body, as Saint Gregory observes, is not enough; that of the heart is necessary too. The Lord one day said to Saint Teresa: "I would willingly speak to many souls, but the world makes such a noise in their hearts that my voice cannot make itself heard." When a detached soul is engaged in prayer, truly does God speak to it and make it understand the love which he has borne it. Then the soul (as a certain author says), burning with holy love, speaks not. But in that silence, oh, how much does it say! The silence of charity says more to God than could be said by the utmost powers of human eloquence: each sigh that it utters is a manifestation of its whole interior. It then seems as if it could not repeat often enough: "My beloved to me, and I to him."

20 • The *fifth* means of attaining to a high degree of divine love is prayer. We are poor in all things; but if we pray, we are rich in all things, for God has promised to grant the prayer of him who prays. He says: "Ask, and it shall be given you" (Mt 7:7). What greater love can one friend show toward another than to say to him, Ask of me what you will, and I will give it you? This is what the Lord says to each one of us. God is Lord of all things. He promises to give us as much as we ask. If, then, we are poor, the fault is our own, because we do not ask him for the graces of which we stand in need. It is on this account that mental prayer is morally necessary for all: for when prayer is laid aside while we are involved in this world's cares, we pay too little attention to the soul; but when we practice it, we discover the needs of the soul and then ask for the corresponding graces and obtain them.

21 ◆ The whole life of the saints has been one of meditation and prayer. All the graces by means of which they have become saints were received by them in answer to their prayers. If, therefore, we would be saved and become saints, we ought always to stand at the gates of the divine mercy to beg and pray for, as an alms, all that we need. We need humility: let us ask for it and we shall be humble. We need patience under tribulation: let us ask for it and we shall be patient. Divine love is what we desire: let us ask for it and we shall obtain it. "Ask, and it shall be given you," is God's promise which cannot fail. And Jesus Christ, in order to inspire us with greater confidence in our prayers, has promised us that whatever graces we shall ask of the Father in his name, for the sake of either his love or his merits, the Father will give us all of them: "Amen, amen I say to you: If you ask the Father anything in my name, he will give it you" (Jn 16:23). And in another place he says: "If you shall ask me anything in my name, that I will do" (Jn 14:14).

22 ◆ Let a soul be as cold as it can be in divine love, if it has faith, I do not know how it is possible for it not to feel urged to love Jesus Christ, on even the most hasty consideration of what Scripture tells us of the love which he has manifested toward us in his

Passion, and in the most holy sacrament of the altar. As regards his Passion, we read in Isaiah: "Surely he has borne our infirmities and carried our sorrows" (53:4), and in the verse which follows: "he was wounded for our iniquities, he was bruised for our sins." So it is of faith, that Jesus Christ has willed to suffer in his own Person pains and afflictions, to set free from them ourselves to whom they were justly due. And why is it that he has done so, if not for the love he has borne toward us? "Christ also has loved us, and has delivered himself for us" (Eph 5:2), Saint Paul says. And Saint John: "Christ has loved us, and washed us from our sins in his own blood" (Rev 1:5). While with respect to the sacrament of the Eucharist, it was Jesus himself who said to us all, when he instituted it, "Take ye, and eat; this is my body" (1 Cor 11:24). And in another passage: "He that eats my flesh, and drinks my blood, abides in me, and I in him" (Jn 6:57). How can anyone who has faith read this without feeling himself, as it were, forced to love his Redeemer who, after having sacrificed his blood and life out of love for him, has left him his own Body in the sacrament of the altar to be the food of his soul and the means of uniting him wholly to himself in Holy Communion?

23 • We may add one more brief reflection on the Passion of Jesus Christ. He shows himself to us on the cross pierced by three nails, with blood issuing from every pore, and agonizing in the pangs of death. I ask, why is it that Jesus shows himself to us in such a pitiable condition? Is it, perhaps, that we may compassionate him? No, it is not so much to gain our compassion as to become the object of our love that he has reduced himself to so miserable a state. It ought to have been a motive more than sufficient to secure our love, had he given us to know that his love for us is from all eternity: "I have loved you with an everlasting love" (Jer 31:3). But seeing that this was not enough for our lukewarmness, the Lord, in order to move us to love him according to his desires, has willed thus to give us a practical demonstration of the love he bore us, by making us behold him, covered with wounds, dying of anguish through his love for us, that by means of his sufferings we might understand the immensity and tenderness of the love which he cherishes toward us.

The Practice of the Love of Jesus Christ

Jesus Christ Deserves Our Love

The whole sanctity and perfection of a soul consist in loving Jesus Christ, our God, our sovereign good, and our Redeemer. Whoever loves me, says Jesus Christ himself, shall be loved by my eternal Father: My Father loves you, because you have loved me (Jn 16:27). Some, says Saint Francis de Sales, think perfection means an austere life, others prayer, others frequenting the sacraments, others works. But they deceive themselves. Perfection means loving God with our whole heart. The Apostle wrote, "above all things have charity, which is the bond of perfection" (Col 3:14). It is charity which keeps united and preserves all the virtues that render a person perfect. Hence Saint Augustine said: "Love God, and do whatever you please," because a soul that loves God is taught by that same love never to do anything that will displease him and to leave nothing undone that may please him.

But perhaps God does not deserve all our love? He has loved us with an everlasting love (Jer 31:3). Oh, says the Lord, behold I was the first to love you. You were not yet in the world, the world itself was not created, and I already loved you. As long as I am God, I love you; as long as I have loved myself, I have also loved you.

As almighty God knew that human beings are won by kindness, he determined to lavish his gifts upon him and so to take captive the affections of his heart. For this reason he said,

"I will draw them with the cords of Adam, with the bands of love" (Hos 11:4). I will catch men by those very snares by which they are naturally caught, the snares of love. And such exactly are all the favors of God to human beings. After having given them a soul created in his own image, with memory, understanding, and will, and a body with its senses, he created heaven and earth for them, all that exists, all for the love of humans—the firmament, the stars, the planets, the seas, the rivers, the fountains, the hills, the plains, metals, fruits, and a countless variety of animals, and all these creatures so that they might minister to the uses of people and so that humans might love him in gratitude for so many admirable gifts. "Heaven and earth, and all things, tell me to love you," says Saint Augustine. "My Lord," he said, "whatever I behold on the earth, or above the earth, all speak to me, and exhort me to love you, because all assure me that you have made them for the love of me." The Abbot de Rancé, founder of La Trappe, when from his hermitage he stood and surveyed the hills, the fountains, the birds, the flowers, the planets, and the skies, felt himself animated by each one of these creatures to love that God who had created all through love of him.

In the same way, whenever Saint Mary Magdalene of Pazzi held any beautiful flower in her hand, she was moved by the sight of it with love of God, and she would say: "And God, then, has thought from all eternity of creating this flower for love of me!" Thus did that flower become an arrow of love, which sweetly wounded her and united her more and more to her God. On the other hand, Saint Teresa, at the sight of trees, fountains, rivers, lakes, or meadows, declared that all of these fair things upbraided her for her ingratitude in loving so coldly a God who created them that he might be loved by her. And it is said of a pious hermit that when walking through the country it seemed to him that the plants and flowers in his path reproached him for the cold return of love he made to God, so that he went along gently striking them with his staff, saying to them: "Oh be silent. You call me an ungrateful wretch, you tell me God made you for love of me, and yet I do not love him. But now I understand you. Be silent, be silent; do not reproach me any more."

But God was not satisfied with giving us so many beautiful creatures. He has gone to such lengths to gain our love as to give himself to us. The eternal Father did not hesitate to give us even his only-begotten Son: "For God so loved the world, as to give his only begotten Son" (Jn 3:16). When the eternal Father saw that we were all dead and deprived of his grace by sin, what did he do? For the immense love, as the Apostle writes, for the too great love he bore us, he sent his beloved Son to make atonement for us, and so to restore to us that life which sin had robbed us of, who "for his exceeding charity wherewith he loved us, even when we were dead in sins, has quickened us together in Christ" (Eph 2:4–5). And in granting us his Son (not sparing his Son, that he might spare us), he has granted us every good together with him, his grace, his love, and paradise, since assuredly all these gifts are much less than that of his Son.

And so, likewise, the Son through his love for us has given himself wholly to us. In order to redeem us from everlasting death and to recover for us the divine grace and heaven which we had forfeited, he became man and put on flesh like our own. Behold then a God reduced to nothingness. Behold the sovereign of the world humbling himself so low as to assume the form of a servant and to subject himself to all the miseries which the rest of men endure.

But what is more astonishing still is that he could very well have saved us without dying and without suffering at all. But no, he chose a life of sorrow and contempt, and a death of bitterness and ignominy even to expiring on a cross—the gibbet of infamy, the award of vilest criminals. But why, if he could have ransomed us without suffering, why should he choose to die, and to die on a cross? To show us how he loved us. He loved us, and because he loved us, he delivered himself up to sorrows and ignominies and to a death more cruel than ever anyone endured in this world.

Hence that great lover of Jesus Christ, Saint Paul, took occasion to say: "the charity of Christ presses us" (2 Cor 5:14), wishing to show us by these words that it is not so much the sufferings themselves of Jesus Christ as his love in enduring them that obliges us and constrains us to love him. Let us hear what Saint Francis de Sales says on this text: "When we remember that Jesus Christ, true God, has loved us to such an excess as to suffer death, and the death of the cross, for us, our hearts are as it were put in a wine press and they suffer violence until love be extorted from them, a violence which becomes the more delightful the stronger it is."

The love of Jesus Christ toward men created in him a longing desire for the moment of his death, when his love should be fully shown to them. Therefore he said: "I have a baptism wherewith I am to be baptized: and how am I straightened until it be accomplished" (Lk 12:50). I have to be baptized in my own blood; and I feel myself anxious with the hope that the hour of my Passion may soon arrive, for then human beings will know the love which I bear him. Hence Saint John, speaking of that night in which Jesus began his Passion, writes, "Jesus knowing that his hour was come, that he should pass out of this world to the Father: having loved his own who were in the world, he loved them unto the end" (Jn 13:1). The Redeemer called that hour his own hour, because the time of his death was the time desired by him. It was then that he wished to give humankind the final proof of his love by dying for them upon a cross, overwhelmed by sorrows.

But what could have ever induced a God to die like a criminal on a cross between two sinners, with such insult to his divine majesty? "Who did this?" asks Saint Bernard and he answers, "It was love, careless of its dignity." Love, indeed, when it tries to make itself known, does not seek what is becoming to the dignity of the lover, but rather what will serve best to declare itself to the object loved. Saint Francis of Paula therefore had good reason to cry out at the sight of a crucifix, "Oh charity, charity, charity!" And in like manner, when we look upon Jesus on the cross, we should all exclaim, Oh love, love, love!

If faith had not assured us of it, who could ever have believed that a God, almighty, most happy, and the Lord of all, should have condescended to love us to such an extent that he seems to go out of himself for love of us? We have seen wisdom itself, that is the eternal Word, become foolish through the excessive love he bore to us—so said Saint Laurence Justinian. Saint Mary Magdalene of Pazzi said the same. One day, being in ecstasy, she took a wooden crucifix in her hands, and then cried out: "Yes, my Jesus, you are mad with love. I repeat it, and I will say it forever, my Jesus, you are mad with love." But, "No," Says Denis the Areopagite, "no, it is not madness, but the ordinary effect of divine love, which makes him who loves go out of himself in order to give himself up entirely to the object of his love: divine love causes ecstasy."

Oh, if men would only pause and consider, looking at Jesus on the cross, the love that he has borne each one of them. "With what love," says Saint Francis de Sales, "would not our souls become enkindled at the sight of those flames in the Redeemer's breast. And oh, what happiness to be able to be consumed by that same fire with which our God burns for us. What joy, to be united to God by the chains of love!" Saint Bonaventure called the wounds of Jesus Christ wounds which pierce the most hardened hearts and which inflame the most icy souls. How many darts of love come forth from those wounds to wound the hardest hearts! What flames issue from the burning heart of Jesus Christ to inflame the coldest souls! And chains, how many, from that wounded side, to bind the most stubborn wills!

Who can deny that of all devotions devotion to the Passion of Christ is the most useful, the most tender, the most agreeable to God, one that gives the greatest consolation to sinners and at the same time most powerfully enkindles loving souls? From what do we receive so many blessings, if not from the Passion of Jesus Christ? Why do we have hope of pardon, courage against temptations, confidence that we shall go to heaven? From where come so many lights to know the truth, so many loving calls, so many spurrings to change our life, so many desires to give ourselves up to God, except from the Passion of Jesus Christ? The Apostle therefore had only too great reason to declare him who did not love Jesus Christ to be excommunicated: "If anyone love not our Lord Jesus Christ, let them be anathema" (1 Cor 16:22).

Saint Bonaventure says there is no devotion more fitted for sanctifying a soul than meditation on the Passion of Jesus Christ. Therefore he advises us to meditate every day upon the Passion if we would advance in the love of God. And before him Saint Augustine said that one tear shed in memory of the Passion is worth more than to fast weekly on bread. That is why the saints were always occupied in considering the sorrows of Jesus Christ. Saint Francis of Assisi was found by a gentleman one day when he was shedding tears and crying out with a loud voice. Being asked the cause, the saint replied, "I am weeping over the sorrows and ignominies of my Lord, and what causes me the greatest sorrow is that men, for whom he suffered so much, live in forgetfulness of him." And on saying this, he wept even more, so that this gentleman too began to weep. When the saint heard the bleating of a lamb, or saw anything which reminded him of the Passion of Jesus, he immediately shed tears. On another occasion when he was sick, someone told him to read some pious book. "My book," he replied, "is Jesus crucified." Hence he did nothing but exhort his brethren always to think of the Passion of Jesus Christ. Tiepoli writes: "He who does not become inflamed with the love of God by looking at Jesus dead on the cross will never love at all."

How We Are Obliged to Love Jesus Christ

Jesus Christ as God has a claim on all our love; but by the love which he has shown us, he wished to put us under the necessity of loving him, at least out of gratitude for all he has done and suffered for us. He has loved us greatly, that we might love him greatly. "Why does God love us, but that he may be loved?" wrote Saint Bernard. And Moses had said the same before him: "And now, Israel, what doth the Lord your God require of you, but that you fear the Lord your God…and love him?" (Deut 10:12). Therefore the first command which God gave us was this: "You shall love the Lord your God with your whole heart" (Deut 6:5).

In the great mystery of our redemption, we must consider how Jesus employed all his thoughts and zeal to discover every means of making himself loved by us. Had he merely wished to die for our salvation, it would have been enough to have been slain by Herod with the other children. But no, he chose before dying to lead for thirty-three years a life of hardship and suffering, and during that time, with a view to winning our love, to appear in several different guises: first of all as a poor child born in a stable, then as a little boy helping in a workshop, and finally as a criminal executed on a cross. But before dying on the cross, we see him in many states, one and all calculated to excite our compassion and to make him loved: in agony in the garden, bathed from head to foot in a sweat of blood; afterward, in the court of Pilate, torn with scourges; then treated as a mock king, with a reed in his hand, a ragged garment on his shoulders and a crown of thorns on his head; then dragged publicly through the streets to death, with the cross on his shoulders; and at length, on the hill of Calvary, suspended on the cross by three iron nails. Tell me, does he merit our love or not, this God who was willing to endure all these torments and to use so many means to captivate our love?

To acquire, then, a true love of Jesus Christ should be our only care. The masters of the spiritual life describe the marks of true love. Love, they say, is fearful, and its fear is none other than that of displeasing God. It is generous, because, trusting in God, it is never daunted, even at the greatest enterprises for his glory. It is strong, because it subdues all its evil appetites, even in the midst of the most violent temptations and the darkest desolations. It is obedient, because it immediately flies to execute the divine will. It is pure, because it loves God alone and for the sole reason that he deserves to be loved. It is ardent, because it would inflame all men and willingly see them consumed with divine love. It is inebriating, for it causes the soul to live as it were out of herself, as if she no longer saw, nor felt, nor had any more senses left for earthly things, bent wholly on loving God. It is unitive, by producing a close union between the will of the creature and the will of the Creator. It is longing, for it fills the soul with desires to leave this world, to fly and unite herself perfectly with God in her true and happy country where she may love him with all her strength.

But no one teaches us the real characteristics and practice of charity as well as the great preacher of charity, Saint Paul. In his first epistle to the Corinthians, he says in the first place that without charity we are nothing and nothing profits us: "if I should have all faith, so that I could move mountains, and have not charity, I am nothing. And if I should distribute all my goods to feed the poor, and if I should deliver my body to be burned, and have not charity, it profit me nothing" (1 Cor 13:2–3). Then Saint Paul gives us the marks of true charity, and at the same time teaches us the practice of those virtues which are the daughters of charity. He goes on to say: "Charity is patient, is kind; charity envies not, deals not perversely; is not puffed up; is not ambitious, seeks not her own; is not provoked to anger, thinks no evil; rejoices not in iniquity, but rejoices with the truth; bears all things, believes all things, hopes all things, endures all things" (1 Cor 13:4–7). Let us, therefore, in the present book proceed to consider these holy practices, to see if the love which we owe Jesus Christ truly reigns within us and also so that we may understand what virtues we should chiefly practice in order to persevere and advance in this holy love.

Charity Is Patient

The soul that loves Jesus Christ loves to suffer. This earth is the place for meriting, and therefore it is a place for suffering. Our true country, where God has prepared for us repose in everlasting joy, is heaven. We have but a short time to stay in this world, but in this short time we have many labors to undergo: "Man born of a woman, living for a short time, is filled with many miseries" (Job 14:1). We must suffer, all must suffer; be they just or be they sinners, each one must carry his cross. He who carries it with patience is saved; he who carries it with impatience is lost. Saint Augustine says that the same miseries send some to heaven and some to hell: "One and the same blow lifts the good to glory and reduces the bad to ashes." The same saint observes that by the test of suffering the chaff in the Church of God is distinguished from the wheat: he who humbles himself under tribulations, and is resigned to the will of God, is wheat for paradise; he that grows haughty and is enraged, and so forsakes God, is chaff for hell.

He that loves God in suffering earns a double reward in heaven. Saint Vincent de Paul said that it was a great misfortune to be free from suffering in this life. And he added that a congregation or an individual that does not suffer and is applauded by all the world is not far from a fall. It was on this account that Saint Francis of Assisi, on the day he had suffered nothing for God, became afraid lest God had forgotten him. Saint John Chrysostom says that when God endows anyone with the grace of suffering he gives them a greater grace than that of raising the dead to life, because in performing miracles people remain God's debtor, whereas in suffering God makes himself the debtor of us humans. And he adds that whoever endures something for God, even if he had no other gift than the strength to suffer for the God whom he loves, this would procure an immense reward. Therefore he affirmed that Saint Paul received a greater grace in being bound in chains for Jesus Christ than in being caught up to the third heaven in ecstasy.

"And patience has a perfect work" (Jas 1:4). The meaning of this is that nothing is more pleasing to God than to see a soul bearing with patience all the crosses sent by him. The effect of love is to liken the lover to the person loved. Saint Francis de

Sales said, "All the wounds of Christ are so many mouths, which preach to us that we must suffer for him. The science of the saints is to suffer constantly for Jesus; and in this way we shall soon become saints." A person who loves Jesus Christ is anxious to be treated like Jesus Christ—poor, persecuted, and despised. Saint John beheld all the saints "clothed with white robes, and palms in their hands" (Rev 7:9). The palm is the symbol of martyrs, and yet all the saints did not suffer martyrdom; why, then, do all the saints bear palms in their hands? Saint Gregory replies that all the saints have been martyrs either of the sword or of patience, so that "we can be martyrs without the sword, if we keep patience."

Saint Teresa used to say that whenever anyone does something for God, the Almighty repays him with some trial. And therefore the saints, on receiving tribulations, thanked God for them. Saint Louis of France, referring to his captivity in Turkey, said: "I rejoice, and thank God more for the patience which he accorded me in the time of my imprisonment than if he had made me master of the universe." And when Saint Elizabeth, princess of Thuringia, after her husband's death was banished with her son from the kingdom and found herself homeless and abandoned by all, she went to a convent of the Franciscans and there had the *Te Deum* sung in thanksgiving to God for the signal favor of being allowed to suffer for his love.

Saint Joseph Calasanctius used to say: "All suffering is slight to gain heaven." The Apostle had already said the same: "the sufferings of this time are not worthy to be compared with the glory to come, that shall be revealed in us" (Rom 8:18). It would be a great gain for us to endure all the torments of all the martyrs during our whole lives in order to enjoy one single moment of the bliss of heaven. With what readiness, then, should we embrace our crosses when we realize that the sufferings of this transitory life will gain for us everlasting happiness!

The person who strives with the greatest patience shall have the greatest reward. Wonderful indeed! When the temporal goods of this world are in question, the worldly try to get as much as they can. But when it is a question of the goods of eternal life, they say, "It is enough if we get a little corner in heaven." Such is not the language of the saints. They are satisfied with anything whatever in this life, and even more, they strip themselves of all earthly goods. But concerning eternal goods, they strive to obtain them in as large a measure as possible. Which of the two acts with more wisdom and prudence?

But even with regard to the present life, it is certain that he who suffers with the most patience enjoys the greatest peace. It was a saying of Saint Philip Neri that in this world there is no purgatory; it is either all heaven or all hell. He who patiently supports tribulations enjoys a heaven; he who does not do so suffers a hell.

Let us be convinced that in this valley of tears true peace of heart cannot be found, except by him who endures and lovingly embraces sufferings to please almighty God. This is the result of that corruption in which all are placed by the infection of sin. The condition of the saints on earth is to suffer and to love; the condition of the saints in heaven is to enjoy and to love.

A soul that loves God has no other end in view but to be wholly united with him. But let us learn from Saint Catherine of Genoa what it is necessary to do to arrive at this perfect union: "To attain union with God, adversities are indispensable, because by them God aims at destroying all our corrupt tendencies within and without. And therefore all injuries, contempts, infirmities, abandonment by relations and friends, confusions, temptations, and other mortifications, all are in the highest degree necessary for us, in order that we may carry on the fight until by repeated victories we come to extinguish within us all vicious movements so that they are no longer felt. And we shall never arrive at divine union until adversities, instead of seeming bitter to us, become all sweet for God's sake."

It follows, then, that a soul which sincerely wants to belong to God must be resolved, as Saint John of the Cross writes, not to seek enjoyments in this life but to suffer in all things. She must embrace all voluntary mortifications with eagerness, and with still greater eagerness those which are involuntary, since they are the more welcome to almighty God: "The patient person is better than the valiant." God is pleased with a person who practices mortifications by fasting and disciplines, because of the courage displayed in such mortifications. But he is much more pleased with those who have the courage to bear patiently and gladly such crosses as come from his own divine hand. Saint Francis de Sales said, "Such mortifications as come to us from the hand of God, or from men by his permission, are always more precious than those which are the offspring of our own will. For it is a general rule that wherever there is less of our own choice, God is better pleased and we ourselves derive greater profit." Saint Teresa taught the same thing: "We gain more in one day by the oppositions which come to us from God or our neighbor than by ten years of mortifications self-inflicted."

Charity Is Kind

He that loves Jesus Christ loves meekness. The spirit of meekness is peculiar to God: "my spirit is sweet above honey" (Eccl 24:27). This is why a soul that loves God also loves those whom God loves, her neighbors, so that she eagerly seeks every occasion to help all, to console all, and to make all happy as much as she can.

This meekness should be particularly observed toward the poor, who because of their poverty are often treated haughtily by men. It should also be especially practiced toward the sick who are suffering under infirmities and who, for the most part, meet with small help from others. Meekness is more especially to be observed in our behavior toward enemies: "Overcome evil by good" (Rom 12:21). Hatred must be overcome by love and persecution by meekness. Thus the saints acted, and thus they won over the affections of their most bitter enemies.

"There is nothing," says Saint Francis de Sales, "that gives so much edification to our neighbor as meekness of behavior." Saint Francis was therefore generally seen smiling, and with a countenance beaming with charity which gave a tone to all his words and actions. This gave occasion to Saint Vincent de Paul to declare that he never knew a kinder man in his life. He said further that it seemed to him that in this his lordship of Sales was a true likeness of Jesus Christ. Even in refusing what he could not in conscience comply with, he did so with such sweetness that all, even those unsuccessful in their requests, went away satisfied and well-disposed toward him. He was gentle toward all, toward superiors, toward equals and toward inferiors, at home and abroad, in contrast with some people who, as he used to say, "seemed angels abroad, but were devils at home." Moreover, the saint never complained of the neglect or laxity of servants; at most he would give them an admonition, but always in the gentlest terms. This is a thing most praiseworthy in superiors. The superior should use all kindness toward those under him. When telling them what they have to do, he should request rather than command. Saint Vincent de Paul said: "A superior will never find a better means of being readily obeyed than meekness." And to the same effect was the saying of Saint Jane

Frances of Chantal: "I have tried various methods of governing, but I have not found any better than that of meekness and forbearance."

More than this, the superior should be kind even in the correction of faults. It is one thing to correct with firmness and another with harshness. It is necessary at times to correct with firmness, when a fault is serious, and especially if it is repeated after the subject has already once been admonished. But let us always be on our guard against harsh and angry correction; he who corrects with anger does more harm than good. This is that bitter zeal reproved by Saint James. Some make a boast of keeping their family in order by severity, and they say it is the only successful method of treatment; but not Saint James: "if you have bitter zeal…glory not" (Jas 3:14). If on some rare occasion it is necessary to speak a cross word in order to bring an offender to a proper sense of his fault, in the end we ought invariably to leave him with a gentle countenance and a word of kindness. Wounds must be healed after the fashion of the good Samaritan in the Gospel, with wine and oil: "But as oil," said Saint Francis de Sales, "always swims on the surface of all other liquids, so must meekness prevail over all our actions." And when it happens that the person under correction is agitated, then the scolding must be deferred until his anger has subsided, or else we should only increase his indignation. The Canon Regular Saint John said: "When the house is on fire, one must not cast wood into the flames."

Kindness should be observed toward all on all occasions and at all times. Saint Bernard remarks that certain persons are gentle as long as things fall out to their taste, but scarcely do they experience some opposition or contradiction than they are instantly on fire, like Mount Vesuvius itself. These may be called burning coals, but hidden under the embers. Whoever would become a saint must during this life resemble the lily among thorns, which however much it may be pricked by them never ceases to be a lily and is always equally sweet and serene. The soul that loves God maintains an imperturbable peace of heart; she shows this in her very countenance, being always mistress of herself, alike in prosperity and adversity.

Whenever it happens that we have to reply to someone who insults us, let us be careful to answer with meekness: "A wild answer breaks wrath" (Prov 15:1). A mild reply is enough to quench every spark of anger. And in case we feel irritated, it is best to stay silent, because then it seems only just to give vent to all that rises to our lips; but when our passion has subsided, we shall see that all our words were full of faults.

And when it happens that we ourselves commit some fault, we must also practice meekness in our own regard. To be exasperated at ourselves after a fault is not humility but a subtle pride, as if we were anything else but the weak and miserable things that we are. Saint Teresa said: "The humility that disturbs does not come from God but from the devil. To be angry at ourselves after the commission of a fault is a fault worse than the one committed, and will be the occasion of many other faults. It will make us quit our devotions, prayers, and communions, or if we do practice them they will be done very badly." Saint Aloysius Gonzaga said that we cannot see in troubled waters and that the devil fishes in them. A soul that is troubled knows little of God and of what she ought to do. Whenever, therefore, we fall into any fault, we should turn to God with humility and confidence and, craving his forgiveness, say to him with Saint Catherine of Genoa: "Oh Lord, this is the product of my own garden. I love you with my whole heart, and I repent of the displeasure I have given you. I will never do the same again. Grant me your help."

Charity Envies Not

The soul that loves Jesus Christ does not envy the great ones of this world, but only those who are greater lovers of Jesus Christ. Saint Gregory explains this next characteristic of charity in saying that as charity despises all earthly greatness, this cannot possibly provoke her envy. "She does not envy, since she desires nothing in this world, she cannot envy earthly prosperity." Hence we must distinguish two kinds of envy, one evil and the other holy. The evil kind is that which envies and repines at the worldly goods possessed by others on this earth. But holy envy, far from wishing to be like them, rather compassionates the great ones of the world who live amid honors and earthly pleasures. She seeks and desires God alone and has no other aim than that of loving him as much as she can, and therefore she has a pious envy of those who love him more than she does, for she would if possible surpass the very seraphim in loving him.

This is the sole end which pious souls have in view on earth, an end which so charms and ravishes the heart of God with love that it causes him to say: "You have wounded my heart, my Sister, my Spouse, you have wounded my heart with one of your eyes" (Song 4:9). By "one of your eyes" is meant that one goal which the espoused soul sees in all her devotions and thoughts, namely, to please almighty God. Men of the world look on things with many eyes, that is, they have several inordinate views in their actions, as, for instance, to please others, to become honored, to obtain riches, and if nothing else at least to please themselves. But the saints have but a single eye, with which they keep in sight in all that they do the sole pleasure of God. With David they say: "What have I in heaven? and besides you what do I desire upon earth?" (Ps 72:25). "Let the rich," said Saint Paulinus, "enjoy their riches, let the kings enjoy their kingdoms, you, Christ, are my treasure and my kingdom!"

And here we must remark that we must not only perform good works but must perform them well. In order that our works may be good and perfect they must be done with the sole aim of pleasing God. This was the admirable praise bestowed on Jesus Christ: "He has done all things well" (Mk 7:37). Many actions may in themselves be praiseworthy, but from being performed for some other purpose than for the glory of God, they are often of little or no value in his sight. Saint Mary Magdalene of Pazzi said, "God rewards our actions by the weight of pure intention," as much as to say that the Lord accepts and rewards our actions according to the purity of our intention in performing them. But, God, how difficult it is to find an action done solely for you! I remember a holy old man, a religious, who had labored greatly in God's service and died in the reputation of sanctity. Now one day, as he cast a glance back at his past life, he said to me in a tone of sadness and fear, "Woe is me! When I consider all the actions of my past life, I do not find one done entirely for God." Oh, this accursed self-love, that makes us lose all or the greater part of the fruit of our good actions! How many in their most holy employments, such as priests preaching, hearing confessions, giving missions, labor and exert themselves greatly and yet gain little or nothing because they do not regard God alone, but worldly honor, or self-interest, or the vanity of making an appearance, or at least their own inclination.

The following are the signs which indicate whether we work solely for God in any spiritual undertaking: (1) If we are not disturbed at the failure of our plans, because when we see that something is not God's will, neither is it any longer our will. (2) If we rejoice at the good done by others as heartily as if we ourselves had done it. (3) If we have no preference for one task more than another, but willingly accept that which obedience to superiors directs us. (4) If after our actions we do not seek the thanks or approval of others, nor are in any way affected if we are found fault with or scolded, being satisfied with having pleased God. And if when the world applauds us we are not puffed up but meet the vainglory which might make itself felt with the reply of Juan of Avila: "Get away, you come too late, for all has been already given to God."

Those who have nothing else in view in their undertakings than the divine will enjoy that holy liberty of spirit which belongs to the children of God. This enables them to embrace everything that pleases Jesus Christ, however revolting it may be to their own self-love or human respect. The love of Jesus Christ establishes his lovers in a state of total indifference, so that all is the same to them, whether sweet or bitter; they desire nothing for their own pleasure, but all for the pleasure of God. With the same feelings of peace, they address themselves to small and great works, to the pleasant and the unpleasant. It is enough for them if they please God.

Many, on the other hand, are willing to serve God but it must be in such an employment, in such a place, with such companions, or under such circumstances, or else they either quit the work or do it with ill will. Such persons do not have freedom of spirit but are slaves of self-love and on that account gain very little merit by what they do. They lead a troubled life because the yoke of Jesus Christ becomes a burden to them. The true lovers of Jesus Christ care only about doing what pleases him, and for the reason that it pleases him, when he wills and where he wills and how he wills and whether he wishes to employ them in a state of life honored by the world or in a life of obscurity and insignificance. This is what is meant by loving Jesus Christ with a pure love. In this we ought to exercise ourselves, battling against the craving of our self-love which would urge us to seek important and honorable functions and such as suit our inclinations.

We must, moreover, be detached from all exercises, even spiritual ones, when the Lord wishes us to be occupied in other works of his good pleasure. One day Father Alvarez, finding himself surrounded with business, was anxious to get rid of it in order to go and pray, because it seemed to him that during that time he was not with God. But our Lord then said to him: "Though I do not keep you with me, let it suffice you that I make use of you." This is a profitable lesson for those who are sometimes disturbed at being obliged by obedience or by charity to leave their accustomed devotions. Let them be assured that such disturbances do not come from God, but either from the devil or from self-love. "Give pleasure to God, and die." This is the grand maxim of the saints.

Charity Deals Not Perversely

He that loves Jesus Christ avoids lukewarmness and seeks perfection, the means of which are: (1) Desire, (2) Resolution, (3) Mental Prayer, (4) Communion, (5) Prayer. Saint Gregory, in his explanation of the words "deals not perversely," says that charity, giving herself up more and more to the love of God, ignores whatever is not right and holy. The Apostle had already written to the same effect when he called charity a bond that unites the most perfect virtues together in the soul: "Have charity, which is the bond of perfection" (Col 3:14). Since charity delights in perfection, she abhors that lukewarmness with which some persons serve God to the great risk of losing charity, divine grace in their soul, and their all.

At the same time it must be observed that there are two kinds of tepidity or lukewarmness, one unavoidable, the other avoidable. From that which is unavoidable saints themselves are not exempt. This comprises all the feelings which we experience without full consent but merely as a result of our natural frailty. Such are, for example, distractions at prayers, interior disquiet, useless words, vain curiosity, the wish to make a good appearance, special tastes in eating and drinking, movements of concupiscence not instantly repressed, and the like. We ought to avoid these defects as much as we possibly can, but owing to the weakness of our nature, caused by the infection of sin, it is impossible to avoid them altogether. We ought, indeed, to detest them after committing them, because they are displeasing to God, we ought to beware of making them a subject of alarm. Saint Francis de Sales wrote: "Thoughts which create disquiet are not from God, who is the prince of peace; they come from the devil, or from self-love, or from the good opinion we have of ourselves." Such thoughts, therefore, as disturb us must be rejected immediately. It was said also by the same saint, with regard to undeliberate faults, that as they were involuntarily committed so are they canceled involuntarily. An act of sorrow or an act of love is sufficient to cancel them.

The type of tepidity that does hinder perfection is that which is avoidable, when a person commits *deliberate* venial faults. All faults committed willingly with open eyes can effectually be avoided by the help of divine grace. This is why Saint Teresa said, "May God deliver you from deliberate sin, however small it may be." We should, therefore, tremble at all deliberate faults, since they cause God to keep from bestowing on us his clearer lights and stronger helps and they deprive us of spiritual sweetnesses. The result is to make the soul perform spiritual exercises with great weariness and pain, and so in the course of time begin to leave off prayer, communions, visits to the Blessed Sacrament, and novenas. Finally unhappy souls will probably stop everything, as has frequently been the case.

This is the meaning of that threat which our Lord makes to the tepid: "you are neither cold nor hot. I would you were cold, or hot. But because you are lukewarm...I will begin to vomit you out of my mouth" (Rev 3:15–16). He says, "I would you were cold!" What? Is it better to be cold, that is to be deprived of grace, than to be tepid? Yes, in a certain sense it is better to be cold, because a person who is cold may more easily change his life, being stung by the reproaches of conscience, whereas a tepid person contracts the habit of slumbering on in his faults, without bestowing a thought or taking any trouble to correct himself and thus making his case desperate. Saint Gregory says, "Tepidity which has cooled down from fervor is a hopeless state."

All the evil arises from the little love souls have for Jesus Christ. Those who are puffed up with self-esteem, those who frequently take to heart events that work out contrary to their wishes, who practice great indulgence toward themselves on account of their health, who keep their hearts open to external objects and their minds always distracted, with an eagerness to listen to and to know so many things that have nothing to do with the service of God but merely serve to gratify private curiosity, those who are ready to resent every little inattention from others and consequently are often troubled and grow remiss in prayer and recollection—one moment they are all devotion and joy, the next all impatience and melancholy, as things happen according to or against their humor—all such persons do not love Jesus Christ, or love him very little. They cast discredit on true devotion.

But suppose anyone should find himself sunk in this unhappy state of tepidity, what should he do? Certainly, it is a hard thing for a soul grown lukewarm to resume her former fervor. But our Lord has said: "What is impossible for mortals is possible with God" (Lk 18:27). Whoever prays and uses the right means is sure to accomplish his desire. The means to cast off tepidity and to walk in the path of perfection are five in number: (1) the desire of perfection, (2) the resolution to attain it, (3) mental prayer, (4) frequenting Holy Communion, (5) prayer.

Charity Is Not Puffed Up

He that loves Jesus Christ is not vain about his own worth, but humbles himself and is glad to be humbled by others. A proud person is like a balloon filled with air which seems great but whose greatness in reality is nothing more than a little air which, as soon as the balloon is opened, is quickly dispersed. He who loves God is humble, because he knows that whatever he possesses is the gift of God and that on his own he has only emptiness and sin, so that this knowledge of divine favors bestowed on him humbles him all the more as he is conscious of being so unworthy and yet so favored by God.

Two things are chiefly required for the stability of a house: the foundation and the roof. The foundation in us must be humility, acknowledging ourselves as good for nothing and capable of nothing. The roof is divine assistance, in which alone we ought to put all our trust.

It was the saying of Saint Teresa, "Think not that you have advanced far in perfection, until you consider yourself the worst of all and want to be placed below all." On this maxim the saint acted, and so have all the saints. Saint Francis of Assisi, Saint Mary Magdalene of Pazzi, and the rest considered themselves the greatest sinners in the world and were surprised that the earth sheltered them and did not rather open under their feet to swallow them up alive.

We, too, must act in this way if we would save our souls and keep ourselves in the grace of God until death, resting all our confidence in God alone. The proud person relies on his own strength and falls on that account, but the humble person, by placing all his trust in God alone, stands firm and does not fall, however violent the temptations may be, for his watchword is, "I can do all things in him who strengthens me" (Phil 4:13). The devil at one time tempts us to presumption, at another time diffidence. Whenever he suggests to us that we are in no danger of falling, then we should tremble the more for if God were for an instant to withdraw his grace from us, we would be lost. When again he tempts us to diffidence, then let us turn to God and address him with great confidence: "In you, O Lord, have I hoped, let me never be confounded" (Ps 30:2). We ought to exercise ourselves continually, even to the last moments of our life, in these acts of diffidence in ourselves and of confidence in God.

How is it possible for a soul who sees how her God was buffeted and spit on and how he suffered in his Passion? For this purpose our Redeemer wishes us to keep his image exposed on our altars, not representing him in glory but nailed to the cross, that we might have his ignominies constantly before our eyes, a sight which made the saints rejoice at being vilified in this world. Such was the prayer which Saint John of the Cross addressed to Jesus Christ, when he appeared to him with the cross upon his shoulders: "Lord, let me suffer and be despised for you!"

If a person pretending to spirituality practices prayer, frequents Communion, fasts, and mortifies himself, and yet cannot put up with an affront or a biting word, of what is this a sign? It is a sign that he is a hollow cane, without humility and without virtue. And what indeed can a soul do that loves Jesus Christ, if she is unable to endure a slight for the love of Jesus Christ, who has endured so much for her? Thomas à Kempis, in his *Imitation of Christ*, writes as follows: "Since you have such an abhorrence of being humbled, it is a sign that you are not dead to the world, have no humility, and that you do not keep God before your eyes. He that has not God before his eyes is disturbed at every syllable of censure that he hears."

What scandal does that person occasion who communicates often and then is ready to resent every little word of contempt! And on the contrary, what edification does a soul give that answers contempt with words of mildness, spoken to conciliate the offender, or makes no reply at all, nor complains of it to others, but continues with placid looks, without showing the least sign of indignation!

The great occasion for practicing humility is when we receive correction for some fault from others. Some people resemble the hedgehog: they seem all calmness and meekness as long as they remain untouched, but no sooner does a superior or a friend touch them by an observation on something which they have done imperfectly, than they become all prickles and answer warmly that so and so is not true, or that they were right in doing so, or that such a correction is quite uncalled for. In a word, to rebuke them is to become their enemy; they behave like persons who rave at the surgeon for paining them in the care of their wounds. "When the virtuous and humble person is corrected for a fault," says Saint John Chrysostom, "he grieves for having committed it. The proud person, on the other hand, on receiving correction, grieves also; but he grieves that his fault is detected, and on this account he is troubled, gives answers, and is angry at the person who corrects him."

This is the golden rule given by Saint Philip Neri, with regard to receiving correction: "Whoever would really become a saint must never excuse himself, even though what is laid to his charge is not true." There is only one case to be excepted from this rule, and that is when self-defense may appear necessary to prevent scandal. Oh, what merit with God has that soul which is wrongfully accused and yet keeps silence. Saint Teresa said: "There are occasions when a soul makes more progress and acquires a greater degree of perfection by refraining from excusing herself than by listening to ten sermons; because by not excusing herself she begins to obtain freedom of spirit and to be heedless whether the world speaks well or ill of her."

Charity Is Not Ambitious

He that loves Jesus Christ desires nothing but Jesus Christ. He that loves God does not desire to be loved by his fellows. The single desire of his heart is to enjoy the favor of almighty God. Saint Hilary writes that all honor paid by the world is the business of the devil. And so it is, for the enemy traffics in hell when he infects the soul with the desire for esteem. By thus laying aside humility, the soul runs great risks of plunging into every vice. Saint James writes: "God resists the proud, and gives grace to the humble" (Jas 4:6). He says God resists the proud, signifying that he does not even listen to their prayers. And certainly among the acts of pride we may reckon the desire to be honored by the world and one's self-exaltation at receiving honors from it.

Many persons make profession of a spiritual life but are

worshipers of self. They have the semblance of certain virtues but they are ambitious to be praised in all their undertakings. If nobody else praises them, they praise themselves. In short, they strive to appear better than others. If their honor is touched they lose their peace, leave off Holy Communion, omit all their devotions, and find no rest until they imagine they have got back their former standing. The true lovers of God do not behave this way. They not only carefully shun every word of self-esteem and all self-complacency, but further are sorry to hear themselves commended by others. Their gladness is to see themselves held in small repute by the rest of men.

What security is found in the hidden life for such as wish cordially to love Jesus Christ! Jesus Christ himself set us the example by living hidden for thirty years. And with the same view of escaping men's esteem, saints hid themselves in deserts and in caves. It was said by Saint Vincent de Paul that a love of appearing in public and of being spoken about in terms of praise and of hearing our conduct commended, is an evil which makes us unmindful of God, contaminates our best actions, and proves the most fatal drawback to the spiritual life.

In order, then, to be pleasing to God, we must avoid all ambition to appear and to make a display. And we must avoid with still greater caution the ambition to govern others. Sooner than see ambition set foot in the convent, Saint Teresa declared she would prefer to have the whole convent burned, and all the nuns with it. The ambition of a soul that loves God should be to surpass all others in humility, according to the counsel of Saint Paul: "in humility, let each esteem others better than themselves" (Phil 2:3).

Charity Seeks Not Her Own

He that loves Jesus Christ seeks to detach himself from every creature. Whoever desires to love Jesus Christ with his whole heart must banish from his heart all that is not God but is merely self-love. This is what God requires of us all when he says, "You shall love the Lord your God with your whole heart" (Mt 22:37). Two things are needed to love God with our whole heart: (1) To clear it of earth; and (2) To fill it with holy love. Saint Philip Neri said that "as much love as we bestow on the creature is so much taken from the Creator." In the first place, how must the earth be purged away from the heart? Truly, by mortification and detachment from creatures. Some souls complain that they seek God and do not find him. Let them listen to what Saint Teresa says: "Wean your heart from creatures and seek God, and you will find him."

The mistake is that some indeed wish to become saints, but after their own fashion. They would love Jesus Christ, but in their own way, without forsaking those diversions, that vanity of dress, those delicacies in food. They love God, but if they do not succeed in obtaining such and such an office, they live discontented. If they happen to be touched in a point of esteem, they are all on fire. If they do not recover from an illness, they lose all patience. They love God, but they refuse to let go of attachment to the riches and the honors of the world, to the vanity of being reckoned of good family or of great learning. Such people as these practice prayer and frequent Holy Communion, but inasmuch as they take with them hearts full of earth they derive little profit.

When once the love of God takes full possession of a soul, she of her own accord strives to divest herself of everything that could prove a hindrance to belonging wholly to God. Saint Francis de Sales remarked that when a house catches fire, all the furniture is thrown out of the window, meaning that when a person gives himself entirely to God he needs no persuasion to get rid of every earthly affection. Father Segneri the Younger called divine love a robber which happily despoils us of all, that we may come into possession of God alone. A certain man of respectable position in life, having renounced everything in order to become poor for the love of Jesus Christ, was asked by a friend how he fell into such poverty. He took from his pocket a small volume of the Gospels, and said: "Behold, this is what has stripped me of all." The Holy Spirit says: "If a person should give all the substance of his house for love, he shall despise it as nothing" (Song 8:7). And when a soul fixes her whole love on God she despises wealth, pleasures, dignities, territories, kingdoms; all her longing is after God alone.

Anyone who would belong wholly to God must be free of all human respect. How many souls does this accursed respect keep aloof from God? For instance, if they hear mention made of some one or other of their failings, what do they not do to justify themselves and to convince the world that it is a calumny? If they perform some good work, how industrious they are to publicize it everywhere! They would have it known to the whole world, in order to be universally applauded. The saints behave in a very different way. They would rather publish their defects to the whole world, in order to pass in the eyes of all for the miserable creatures which they really are in their own eyes. In practicing any act of virtue they prefer to have God alone know of it, for their only care is to be acceptable to him. It is on this account that so many of them are enchanted with solitude, mindful as they are of the words of Jesus Christ: "But when you give alms, let not your left hand know what your right hand doth" (Mt 6:3). And again: "But you, when you shall pray, enter into your chamber, and having shut the door, pray to your Father in secret" (Mt 6:6).

But of all things, detachment from self-will is most needed. Only once succeed in subduing yourself and you will easily triumph in every other combat. "Conquer yourself," was the maxim which Saint Francis Xavier taught to all. Jesus Christ said: "If any person will come after me, let him deny himself" (Mt 16:24). Here in a few words is all we need to practice to become saints: to deny ourselves and not to follow our own will—"Go not after your lusts, but turn away from your own will" (Sir 18:30). And this is the greatest grace, said Saint Francis of Assisi, that we can receive from God, the power to conquer ourselves by denying self-will. Saint Bernard writes that if all would resist self-will, none would ever be damned: "Let self-will cease, and there will be no hell."

The same saint writes that it is the baneful effect of self-will to contaminate even our good works. For instance, if a penitent is obstinately bent on mortification or on fasting or on taking the discipline against the will of his director, this act of penance, done at the instigation of self-will, becomes very defective. Unhappy the person who lives the slave of self-will! He shall yearn for many things and shall not possess them, while on the other hand he will be forced to undergo many things distasteful and bitter to his inclinations. "From whence are wars and contentions among you? Are they not hence, from your concupiscences, which war in your members? You covet, and have not" (Jas 4:1–2).

The first war springs from the appetite for sensual delights. Let us take away the occasion, let us mortify the eyes, let us recommend ourselves to God, and the war will be over. The second war arises from the covetousness of riches. Let us cultivate a love of poverty, and this war will cease. The third war has its source in ambitiously seeking after honors. Let us love humility and the hidden life, and this war too will be no more. The fourth war, and the most ruinous of all, comes from self-will. Let us practice resignation in all things which happen by the will of God, and the war will cease.

We must therefore love God in the way that pleases God, not the way that pleases us. God will have the soul divested of all in order to be united to himself and to be replenished with his divine love. Saint Teresa writes as follows: "The prayer of union appears to me to be nothing more than to die utterly, as it were, to all things in this world, for the enjoyment of God alone."

Charity Is Not Provoked to Anger

He that loves Jesus Christ is never angry with his neighbor. Humility and meekness were the favorite virtues of Jesus Christ, so that he bade his disciples: "Learn of me, because I am meek and humble of heart" (Mt 11:29). Our Redeemer was called the Lamb—"Behold the Lamb of God"—because of his having to be offered in sacrifice on the cross for our sins and also because of the meekness exhibited by him during his entire life, but more especially at the time of his Passion. When in the house of Caiaphas he received a blow from that servant who at the same time upbraided him presumptuously—"Answer you the high priest so?" (Jn 18:22)—Jesus only answered, "If I have spoken evil, give testimony of the evil; but if well, why do you strike me?" (Jn 18:23). He observed the same meekness until death. While on the cross, made the object of universal scorn, he only sought the eternal Father to forgive them: "Father, forgive them, for they know not what they do" (Lk 23:34).

"Blessed are the dead, who die in the Lord" (Rev 14:13). We must, indeed, die in the Lord to be blessed. And to enjoy in the present life that blessedness as can be had before entering heaven, happiness which, though certainly much below that of heaven yet far surpasses all the pleasures of sense in this world—the Apostle wrote to his disciples, "the peace of God, which surpasses all understanding, keep in your hearts" (Phil 4:7). To gain this peace, even in the midst of affronts and calumnies, we must be dead in the Lord.

A dead person, however much he may be ill-treated and trampled on by others, does not resent it. In the same way, he who is meek, like a dead body which no longer sees or feels, should endure all outrages committed against him. Whoever loves Jesus Christ from his heart easily attains this, because he accepts with equal composure prosperous and adverse occurrences, consolations and afflictions, injuries and courtesies. And, in truth, of what use are all the riches and all the honors of the world to one who lives in disturbance and whose heart is not at peace?

In short, in order to remain constantly united with Jesus Christ, we must do everything with tranquillity and not be troubled at any contradiction we may encounter. "The Lord is not in the earthquake" (1 Kings 19:11).

Let us listen to the beautiful lessons given on this subject by that master of meekness, Saint Francis de Sales: "Never put yourself in a passion, nor open the door to anger on any pretext whatever, because when once it has gained an entrance it is no longer in our power to banish it or moderate it.

"The remedies against it are: (1) To check it immediately, by diverting the mind to some other object, and not to speak a word; (2) To imitate the Apostles when they beheld the tempest at sea, and to have recourse to God, to whom it belongs to restore peace to the soul; and (3) If you feel that, owing to your weakness, anger has already got footing in your breast, do yourself violence to regain your composure, and then try to make acts of humility and of sweetness toward the person against whom you are irritated. But all this must be done sweetly and calmly, for it is of the utmost importance not to irritate the wounds."

The saint said that he himself was obliged to work hard during his life to overcome two passions, namely, anger and love: to subdue the passion of anger, he avowed, had cost him twenty-two years' hard struggle. As to the passion of love, he had succeeded in changing its object, by leaving creatures and turning all his affections to God. And in this manner the saint acquired so great an interior peace that it was visible even in his exterior, for he was invariably seen with a serene countenance and a smile on his features.

We must prepare ourselves in our mental prayer to bear the crosses that may befall us. This was the practice of the saints and they were therefore always ready to receive injuries, blows, and chastisements with patience and meekness. When we meet with an insult from our neighbor, unless we have frequently trained ourselves beforehand, we shall find it extremely difficult to know what course to take in order not to yield to the force of anger. At that moment, our passion will make it seem reasonable for us to retort boldly to the audacity of the person who affronts us. But Saint John Chrysostom says it is not the right way to quench the fire which is raging in the mind of our neighbor by the fire of an indignant reply. To do so will only enflame it more: "One fire is not extinguished by another." Someone may say, but why should I use courtesy and gentleness toward an impertinent fellow who insults me without cause? Saint Francis de Sales replies: "We must practice meekness, not only with reason, but against reason."

When the mind is troubled, the best expedient will be to keep silence. Saint Bernard writes: "The eye troubled by anger does not see straight." When the eye is dimmed with passion, it no longer distinguishes between what is and what is not unjust. Anger is like a veil drawn over the eyes, so that we can no longer choose between right and wrong. Therefore we must, like Saint Francis de Sales, make a compact with our tongue never to speak while our hearts are disturbed.

But there are moments when it seems absolutely necessary to check insolence with severe words. David said: "Be angry, and sin not" (Ps 4:5). Occasions do exist, therefore, when we may be lawfully angry, provided it is without sin. But here is just the point. Speculatively speaking, it seems expedient at times to speak and reply to some people in severe terms, in order to make an impression on them, but in practice it is very difficult to do this without some fault on our part, so that the sure way is always to admonish, or to reply, with gentleness, and to guard scrupulously against all resentment. Saint Francis de Sales said: "I have never been angry without afterward repenting of it." When for some reason or other we still feel warm, the safest way, as I said before, is to keep silence and to reserve the answer until a more convenient moment when the heart is cooled down.

Meekness is also especially necessary when we have to correct others. Corrections made with bitter zeal often do more harm than good, especially when he who must be corrected is himself excited. In such cases the correction should be put off; we must wait until he is cool. And we ourselves ought no less to refrain from correcting while we are under the influence of ill-temper. For then our admonition will always be accompanied by harshness, and the person in fault, when he sees that he is corrected in such a way, will take no heed of the admonition, considering it the mere effect of passion. This is true as far as the good of our neighbor is concerned. As for our personal advantage, let us show how dearly we love Jesus Christ by patiently and gladly supporting every sort of ill-treatment, injury, and contempt.

Charity Thinks No Evil

He that loves Jesus Christ wants only what Jesus Christ wants. Charity and truth always go together, so that charity, conscious that God is the only true good, detests iniquity, which is directly opposed to the divine will, and takes no satisfaction in anything except what pleases almighty God. Blessed Henry Suso said: "That person stands well with God who strives to conform himself to the truth, and for the rest is utterly indifferent to the opinion or treatment of humankind."

Our conformity to the divine will must be complete, without any reserve, and constant without withdrawal. In this consists the height of perfection, and to this all our works, all our desires, and all our prayers ought to tend. If we really desire to be saints we must aspire after true union with God, which is to unite our will entirely to his will. Saint Teresa said, "Those persons are deceived who fancy that union with God consists in ecstasies, raptures, and sensible enjoyments of him. It consists in nothing else than in submitting our will to the will of God. This submission is perfect when our will is detached from everything and so completely united with that of God that all its movements depend solely on the will of God. This is the real and essential union which I have always sought after, and continually beg of the Lord." Many of us say: Lord, I give you my will, I desire nothing but what you desire. But, on some trying occasion, we are at a loss as to how to yield calmly to the divine will. And so we complain that we are the victims of misfortune, the butt of every mishap. And so we drag on in an unhappy life.

If we were conformed to the divine will in every trouble, we should undoubtedly become saints and be the happiest of humankind. This, then, should form the chief object of our attention, to keep our wills in unbroken union with the will of God in every event, be it pleasant or unpleasant. Some people resemble weather vanes, which turn about with every wind that blows; if the wind is favorable to their desires they are all gladness and graciousness, but if a contrary wind blows and things fall out against their desires they are all sadness and impatience. This is why they do not become saints and why their life is unhappy, because in the present life adversity will always befall us in a greater measure than prosperity.

Many manufacture a sort of sanctity according to their own inclinations: Some people, inclined to melancholy, make sanctity consist of living in seclusion. Others, with an active temperament, make it consist of preaching and making up quarrels. Some, possessing an austere nature, make it penitential in inflictions and lacerations. Others, who are naturally generous, make it consist of distributing alms. And all the sanctity of such people consists of such practices. External acts are the fruit of the love of Jesus Christ; but true charity consists of a complete conformity to the will of God, and as a consequence of preferring what is most pleasing to God, solely because he deserves it.

Others wish to serve God, but it must be in this employment, in that place, with these companions, and in those circumstances, or else they either neglect their duty or at least do it with bad grace. Such people are not free in spirit, but are slaves of self-love who on that account reap little merit even from good works they perform. Moreover, they live in perpetual disquiet, since their attachment to self-will makes the yoke of Jesus Christ heavy to them. True lovers of Jesus Christ love when it pleases Jesus Christ, where it pleases him, and how it pleases him, whether he chooses to employ them in honorable functions or in mean and lowly occupations, in a life of notoriety in the world or in one hidden and despised. This is the real drift of what is meant by the pure love of Jesus Christ. So we must work to overcome the cravings of our self-love, which seeks to be employed only in those works that are glorious or are according to our own inclinations.

We must receive with resignation not merely the crosses which come directly from God—ill-health, scanty talents, accidental reverses of fortune—but such as come indirectly from God and directly from our fellows—persecutions, thefts, injuries. All, in reality, come from God. David was one day insulted by one of his vassals called Semei, who not only upbraided him with words of abuse but even threw stones at him. One of the courtiers would have immediately avenged the insult by cutting off the head of the offender, hut David replied: "Let him alone and let him curse: for the Lord has bid him curse David" (2 Kings 16:10). In other words, God made use of him to chastise me for my sins, and therefore allowed him to abuse me.

"Never consider yourselves," said Saint Francis de Sales, "to have arrived at the purity which you ought to have as long as your will is not cheerfully obedient, even in things that are the most repulsive, to the will of God." "Because," as Saint Teresa remarks, "giving up our will to God draws him to unite himself with our loneliness." But this can never be obtained except by means of mental prayer and of continual petitions addressed to the divine Majesty.

Charity Bears All Things

He that loves Jesus Christ bears all things for Jesus Christ, and especially illnesses, poverty, and contempt. Someone who is sick will say: It is not so much the infirmity itself that afflicts me as the fact that it prevents me from going to church to perform my devotions, to communicate, and to hear Holy Mass; I cannot celebrate Mass; I cannot pray, for my head is aching with pain and light almost to fainting. But tell me now, if you please, why do you wish to go to church? Why would you like to communicate and to say or hear Mass? Is it to please God? But now it is not God's pleasure that you say the Office, that you communicate or hear Mass, but that you remain patiently on your bed and bear the pains of your infirmity. But you are displeased with my speaking in this way? Then you are not seeking to do what is pleasing to God, but what is pleasing to yourself. Juan of Avila wrote as follows to a priest who thus complained to him: "My friend, do not busy yourself with what you would do if you were well, but be content to remain ill as long as God thinks fit. If you seek the will of God, what does it matter to you whether you are well or ill?"

You say you are unable even to pray, because your head is weak. Let it be so. You cannot meditate, but why not make acts of resignation to the will of God? If you would only make these acts, you could not make a better prayer, welcoming with love all the torments that assail you. That is what Saint Vincent de Paul did. When attacked by a serious illness, he used to keep himself tranquilly in the presence of God, without forcing his mind to dwell on any particular subject. His sole exercise was to elicit some short acts from time to time, as of love, of confidence, of thanksgiving, and even more frequently of resignation, especially at the point of crisis in his sufferings. Saint Francis de Sales made this remark: "Considered in themselves, tribulations are terrifying; but considered in the will of God, they are lovely and delightful." You cannot pray? What is more exquisite prayer than to look on your crucified Lord and to offer him your pains, uniting the little that you endure with the overwhelming torments that afflicted Jesus on the cross?

Above all, in time of sickness we should be ready to accept death, and that death which God pleases. We must die; our life must finish in our last. And we do not know which will be our last illness. Therefore in every illness we must be prepared to accept that death which God has appointed for us. A sick person says: "Yes; but I have committed many sins and have done no penance. I should like to live not for the sake of living but to make some satisfaction to God before my death." But tell me, my brother, how do you know that if you live longer you will do penance and not rather do worse than before? At present you can cherish the hope that God has pardoned you. What penance can be more satisfactory than to accept death with resignation, if God so wills it?

The bereavement of relations and friends by death belongs also, in some measure, to holy poverty. In this we must especially practice patience. Some people, at the loss of a parent or friend, can find no rest. They shut themselves up in their room to weep and, giving free vent to their sorrow, become insupportable to all around them. I would ask these persons for whose gratification they thus lament and shed tears? For that of God? Certainly not, for God's will is that they should be resigned to his dispensations. For that of the departed soul? By no means. If the soul is lost, she detests both you and your tears. If she is saved and already in heaven, she would have you thank God on her behalf. If still in purgatory, she craves the help of your prayers and wishes you to bow with resignation to the divine will and to become a saint, so that she may one day enjoy your society in heaven. Of what use, then, is all this weeping?

Let us now draw this chapter to a conclusion. That we may be able to practice patience to advantage in all our difficulties, we must be fully persuaded that every trial comes from the hands of God, either directly, or indirectly through men. We must therefore give God thanks whenever we are beset with sorrows, and accept with gladness of heart every event, prosperous or adverse, that proceeds from him, knowing that all happens by his disposition for our welfare: "to them that love God all things work together unto good" (Rom 8:28).

Charity Believes All Things

He that loves Jesus Christ believes all his words. Whoever loves a person believes all that proceeds from the lips of that person. Consequently, the more a soul loves Jesus Christ the more lively and unshaken is her faith. Faith is the foundation of charity; but faith afterward receives her perfection from charity. His faith is most perfect whose love of God is most perfect. Charity produces not merely the faith of the understanding, but the faith of the will also.

There are those who believe only with the understanding but not with the will, as is the case with sinners who are perfectly convinced of the truths of the Faith but who do not choose to live according to the divine commandments—such people have a very weak faith. For if they had a more lively belief that the grace of God is a priceless treasure and that sin, because it robs us of this grace, is the worst of evils, they would assuredly change their lives. If, then, they prefer the miserable creatures of this earth to God, it is either because they do not believe or because their belief is very weak. On the contrary, there are those who believe not only with the understanding but also with the will, so that they not only believe but will to believe in God as the revealer of truth, and because of the love they have for God they rejoice in so believing—such people have a perfect faith and constantly seek to make their lives conformable to the truths that they believe.

The true lover of Jesus Christ keeps the eternal truths constantly in view, and orders all his actions according to them. How thoroughly does he who loves Christ understand the saying of the Wise One, "Vanity of vanities, all is vanity," realizing that all earthly greatness is mere smoke, dirt, and delusion, that the soul's only welfare and happiness lie in loving her Creator and in doing his blessed will.

Charity Hopes All Things

He that loves Jesus Christ hopes for all things from him. Saint Thomas defines Christian hope as a "sure expectation of eternal happiness." Its certainty arises from the infallible promise of God to give eternal life to his faithful servants. Now charity, by taking away sin, at the same time takes away all the obstacles to our obtaining the happiness of the blessed. The greater our charity, the greater also and the firmer therefore is our hope. Hope, on the other hand, can in no way interfere with the purity of love because, according to the observation of Saint Denis, the Areopagite, love tends naturally to union with the object loved. Saint Augustine asserts in stronger terms, love itself is like a chain of gold that links together the hearts of the lover and the loved. And as this union can never be effected at a distance, the person that loves always longs for the presence of the object of his love. The sacred spouse languished in the absence of her beloved, and entreated her companions to acquaint him with her sorrow, that he might come and console her with his presence: "I adjure you, oh daughters of Jerusalem, if you find my beloved, that you tell him that I languish with love" (Song 5:8). A soul that loves Jesus Christ exceedingly can only, as long as she remains on earth, desire and hope, to go without delay and be united to her beloved Lord in heaven.

Thus we see that the desire to go and see God in heaven, not so much for the delight we shall experience in loving God as for the pleasure we shall afford God by loving him, is pure and perfect love. Neither is the joy of the blessed in heaven any hindrance to the purity of their love. Such joy is inseparable from their love, but they take far more satisfaction in their love of God than in the joy that it gives them. Someone will perhaps say that the desire of a reward is rather a love of concupiscence than a love of friendship. We must therefore make a distinction between temporal rewards promised by men and the eternal rewards of paradise promised by God to those who love him. The rewards given by men are distinct from and independent of their own persons, since they do not bestow themselves but only their goods when they reward others. In contrast, the principal reward which God gives to the blessed is the gift of himself: "I am your…reward exceeding great" (Gen 15:1). Thus to desire heaven is the same as to desire God, who is our last end.

I wish here to propose a doubt which may arise in the mind of one who loves God. If it should ever be revealed to such a person that he would be eternally lost, would he be obliged to bow to it with resignation in order to practice conformity with the will of God? Saint Thomas says no, and further that he would sin by consenting to it, because he would be consenting to live in a state which involves sin and which is contrary to the last end for which God created him; for God did not create souls to hate him in hell but to love him in heaven, so that he does not wish the death even of the sinner but rather that all should be converted and saved. The holy Doctor says that God wishes no one to be damned except through sin. Therefore a person, by consenting to his damnation, would not be acting in conformity with the will of God but with the will of sin. But suppose that God, foreseeing the sin of a person, should have decreed his damnation, and this decree should be revealed to him, would he be bound to coincide in it? In the same passage the saint says, No, by no means, because such a revelation must not be taken as an irrevocable decree but as one made merely by way of communication, as a threat of what would follow if he persists in sin.

But let everyone banish such thoughts only calculated to cool his confidence and love. Let us love Jesus Christ as much as possible here below. Let us always be sighing to go from here and to behold him in heaven, that we may there love him perfectly. Let us make it the grand object of all our hopes, to go there to love him with all our strength.

See, then, the scope of all our desires and aspirations, of all our thoughts and ardent hopes, to go and enjoy God in heaven, in order to love him with all our strength and to rejoice in the enjoyment of God. The blessed certainly rejoice in their own felicity in that kingdom of delights, but the chief source of their happiness and that which absorbs all the rest is to know that their beloved Lord possesses an infinite happiness, for they love God incomparably more than themselves. Each one of the blessed has such a love for him that he would willingly forfeit all happiness and undergo the most cruel torments rather than that God should lose (if it were possible for him to lose) one, even the least, particle of his happiness. Hence the sight of God's infinite happiness and the knowledge that it can never suffer diminution for all eternity constitutes his paradise. This is the meaning of what our Lord says to every soul on whom he bestows the possession of eternal glory: "enter you into the joy of your Lord" (Mt 25:21). It is not the joy that enters into the blessed soul, but the soul that enters into the joy of the blessed. Thus the good of God will be the good of the blessed, the riches of God will be their riches, and the happiness of God will be their happiness.

Charity Endures All Things

He that loves Jesus Christ with a strong love does not cease to love him in the midst of all sorts of temptations and desolations

Temptations: Temptations are the most grievous trials that can happen to a soul that loves Jesus Christ. She accepts with resignations every other evil, as calculated only to bind her in closer union with God, but temptations to commit sin drive her toward separation from Jesus Christ. We must know, however, that although no temptation to evil can ever come from God, but only from the devil or our own corrupt inclinations, "for God is not a tempter of evils, and he tempts no one" (Jas 1:13), nevertheless God does at times permit his most cherished souls to be the most grievously tempted. In the first place, he does so in order that from temptations the soul may better learn her own weakness and the need she has of the divine assistance not to fall. While a soul is favored with heavenly consolations she feels as if she were able to vanquish every assault of the enemy and to achieve every undertaking for the glory of God. But when she is strongly tempted, almost reeling on the edge of the precipice and just ready to fall, then she becomes better acquainted with her own misery and with her inability to resist if God does not come to her rescue.

Says the Apostle: "God is faithful, who will not suffer you to be tempted above that which you are able: but will make also with temptation issue, that you may be able to bear it" (1 Cor 10:13). Thus a person, far from losing anything by temptations, derives great profit from them. On this account God frequently allows the souls dearest to him to undergo the severest temptations, that they may turn them into a source of greater merit on earth and of greater glory in heaven. Stagnant water soon grows putrid; a soul left at ease, without any struggle or temptation, stands in great danger of perishing from self-conceit at her own merit. She perhaps has little fear and takes little pains to recommend herself to God and to secure her salvation. When, on the contrary, she is agitated by temptations and sees herself in danger of rushing headlong into sin, then she has recourse to God; she goes to the divine mother; she renews her resolution to die rather than to sin; she humbles herself and casts herself into the arms of the divine mercy. In this manner, as experience shows us, the soul acquires fresh strength and closer union with God.

This must not, however, lead us to seek after temptations. On the contrary, we must pray to God to deliver us from temptations, and especially from those by which God foresees we should be overcome. This is precisely the object of that petition of the Our Father, "Lead us not into temptation." When, by God's permission, we are beset with temptations, we must, without either being alarmed or discouraged by those foul thoughts, rely wholly on Jesus Christ and beseech him to help us. Saint Augustine says: "Throw yourself on him, and fear not; he will not withdraw to let you fall."

Let us come now to the means which we have to employ in order to vanquish temptation. Spiritual masters prescribe a variety of means; but the most necessary and the safest is to have immediate recourse to God with all humility and confidence, saying: "Incline unto my aid, oh God; oh Lord, make haste to help me!" This short prayer will enable us to overcome the assaults of all the devils of hell: for God is infinitely more powerful than all of them. Almighty God knows well that of ourselves we are unable to resist the temptations of the infernal powers, and on this account the most learned Cardinal Gotti remarks "that whenever we are assailed and in danger of being overcome, God is obliged to give us strength enough to resist as often as we call upon him for it."

Almighty God will frequently have decreed success not to the first prayer but to the second, third, or fourth. In short, we must be thoroughly persuaded that all our welfare depends on prayer: our change of life depends on prayer; our victory over temptations depends on prayer; our obtaining divine love depends on prayer.

There may be some who will accuse me of tediousness in so often recommending the importance and necessity of having continual recourse to God by prayer. But I seem to myself to have said not too much but far too little. I know that without divine help we do not have strength to repel the assaults of the devils and that therefore the Apostle exhorts us to put on the armor of God. And what is this armor with which Saint Paul warns us to clothe ourselves in order to conquer our enemies? It consists of this: "By all prayer and supplication, praying at all times in the spirit, and in the same watching with all instance" (Eph 6:18). This armor is constant and fervent prayer to God, that he may help us to gain the victory. I know, moreover, that in every page of Scripture, both in the Old and New Testament, we are repeatedly admonished to pray: "Call upon me in the day of trouble: I will deliver you" (Ps 49:15); "Cry to me and I will hear you" (Jer 33:3); "We ought always to pray, and not to faint" (Lk 18:1); "Ask, and it shall be given you" (Mt 7:7); "Watch and pray" (Mk 13:33); "Pray without ceasing" (1 Thess 5:17). So that I think, far from having spoken too much on prayer, I have not said enough.

Desolations: Saint Francis de Sales says: "It is a mistake to estimate devotion by the consolations which we feel. True devotion in the way of God consists of having a determined will to execute all that is pleasing to God." God often makes use of aridities in order to draw his most cherished souls closer to him. Attachment to our own inordinate inclinations is the greatest obstacle to true union with God and, therefore, when God intends to draw a soul to his perfect love, he tries to detach her from all affection for created goods. Thus he may deprive her of temporal goods, of worldly pleasures, of property, honors, friends, relations, or bodily health. By means of losses, troubles, neglects, bereavements, and infirmities, he wipes out by degrees all earthly attachments so that the affections may be set on him alone.

When God in his mercy deigns to console us with his loving visitations and to let us feel the presence of his grace, it is not good to reject the consolations, as some false mystics advised. Let us thankfully receive them but beware of settling down on them and seeking delight in those feelings of spiritual tenderness. Saint John of the Cross calls this a "spiritual gluttony" which is faulty and displeasing to God. Let us try in such moments to banish from our mind the sensible enjoyment of these sweetnesses and be especially on guard against supposing that these favors are a token of our standing better with God than others, for such a thought of vanity would oblige God to withdraw from us and to leave us in our miseries. We must certainly at such times return most fervent thanks to God, because such spiritual consolations are signal gifts of the divine bounty to our souls, far greater than all the riches and honors of this world. Let us not, however, pride ourselves on these sensible sweetnesses but rather humble ourselves by remembering the sins of our past life. For the rest, we must consider this loving treatment as the pure result of the goodness of God, perhaps sent as the forerunner of some great tribulation soon to befall us, so that we may be strengthened to endure all with patience and resignation.

When a soul is morally certain of being in the grace of God, although she may be deprived of worldly pleasures as well as of those which come from God, she nevertheless rests satisfied with her state, conscious as she is of loving God and of being loved by him. But God, who wishes to see her purified and divested of all sensible satisfaction, in order to unite her entirely to himself by means of pure love, what does he do? He puts her in the crucible of desolation, more painful to bear than the most severe trials. She is left in a state of uncertainty. Is she in God's grace or not? In the dense darkness that shrouds her, there seems no prospect of her ever finding God any more. God, moreover, will sometimes permit her to be assailed by violent sensual temptations, accompanied by irregular movements of the body, or perhaps by thoughts of unbelief, of despair, and even of hatred of God, when she imagines herself cast off by him and that he no longer hears her prayers. Her fears of having lost God are thus very much increased, and from her fancied infidelity in struggling against the temptations, she thinks herself deservedly abandoned by God. The saddest of all calamities seems to have befallen her, to be able no longer to love God and to be hated by him.

When a soul that loves God finds herself in this state, she must not lose courage. Neither must he who directs her become alarmed. These sensual movements, these temptations against faith, these feelings of distrust, and these attacks which urge her to hate God are fears, tortures of the soul, efforts of the enemy, but they are not voluntary and therefore they are not sins. The sincere lover of Jesus Christ resists valiantly on such occasions and withholds all consent to such suggestions but, because of the darkness which envelops her, the soul does not know how to make distinctions, she is thrown into confusion, and the privation of the awareness of divine grace makes her fearful and sad. But even in the state of desolation, if asked whether she would willingly commit one single deliberate venial sin, such a soul will reply that she is ready to suffer not one but a thousand deaths rather than be guilty of such displeasure to almighty God.

It is necessary, therefore, to make this distinction: it is one thing to perform an act of virtue, such as to repel a temptation, to trust in God and to will what he wills, and another thing entirely to have the consciousness of making these good acts. Consciousness of doing good contributes to our pleasure, but profit comes from the first point, that is from actually doing good. With the actuality God is satisfied and may deprive the soul of the awareness of doing good, in order thus to remove from her all self-satisfaction, which adds nothing to the merit of the action, for our Lord seeks more our real advantage than our own satisfaction.

Saint John of the Cross wrote the following words of comfort to a desolate soul: "You were never in a better state than at present, for you were never so deeply humbled and so cut off from all attachment to this world, and at the same time you were never so thoroughly impressed with the conviction of your own wickedness. Neither were you ever so divested and purified of all self-seeking as now." Let us then not believe that when we feel a greater tenderness of devotion we are more beloved of God, for perfection does not consist in that but in mortifying our own will in union with the will of God.

Therefore, when in this state of desolation the soul must not heed the devil's suggestion that God has abandoned her nor must she leave off prayer. This is the object at which the devil is aiming, in order afterward to drag her down some precipice. Saint Teresa writes: "The Lord proves his true lovers by dryness and temptations. What though the dryness should be of lifelong duration? Let the soul never relax in prayer; the time will arrive when all will be abundantly repaid." In such a state of suffering, a person should humble himself by reflecting that his offenses against God are undeserving of any milder treatment. He should humble himself and be fully resigned to the divine will, saying: Lord, behold me at your feet; if it be your will that I should remain thus desolate and afflicted for my whole life, only grant me your grace and do with me whatever you will.

It may be useless and perhaps a source of still greater disquiet to wish to assure yourself that you are in the grace of God and that what you are experiencing is only a trial and not abandonment on God's part. At such times it is God's will that you should not have this assurance. And he so wills this for your greater advantage, in order that you may humble yourself more and increase your prayers and acts of confidence in his mercy. You desire to see, and God wills that you should not see. For the rest, Saint Francis de Sales says: "The resolution not to consent to any sin, however small, is a sure sign that we are in God's grace." But a soul in profound desolation cannot clearly discern this resolution. Nevertheless, in such a state she must not aim at feeling what she wills; it is enough to will with the point of the will.

In this manner she entirely abandons herself into the arms of the divine goodness. Oh, how such acts of confidence and resignation ravish the heart of God, when made in the midst of the darkness of desolation!

Let these souls, then, so dear to God and resolutely determined to belong entirely to him, take comfort even though they see themselves deprived of every comfort. Their desolation is a sign of their being very acceptable to God, a sign that he has prepared a place for them in his heavenly kingdom which overflows with consolations as full as they are lasting. And let them hold for certain that the more they are afflicted in the present life so much the more shall they be consoled in eternity: "According to the multitude of my sorrows in my heart, your comforts have given joy to my soul" (Ps 93:19).

For the encouragement of souls in desolation, I will here mention what is related in the life of Saint Jane de Chantal, who for forty years was tormented by the most fearful interior trials, by temptations, by fears of being the enemy of God, and even of being quite forsaken by him. Her afflictions were so excruciating and unremitting that she declared her sole ray of comfort came from the thought of death. Moreover, she said, "I am so furiously assaulted that I do not know where to hide my poor soul. I seem at times on the point of losing all patience and of giving up all as utterly lost. The tyrant of temptation is so relentless that any hour of the day I would gladly barter it with the loss of my life, and sometimes I can neither eat nor sleep." During the last eight or nine years of her life, her temptations became still more violent. The saint endured assaults against every virtue except chastity, and had likewise to contend with doubts, darkness, and disgusts. Sometimes God would withdraw all lights from her and seem indignant with her and just on the point of expelling her from him, so that terror drove her to look in some other direction for relief—but failing to find any, she was obliged to return to look on God and to abandon herself to his mercy. The divine assistance did not indeed forsake her, but it seemed to her to have done so, since instead of finding satisfaction in anything she found only weariness and anguish in prayer, in reading spiritual books, in Communion, and in all other exercises of piety.

Her sole resource in this state of dereliction was to look upon God and to let him do his will. The saint said: "In all my abandonments my mere life is a cross to me, and my incapability of action adds considerably to its heaviness." She compared herself to a sick person overwhelmed with sufferings, unable to turn from one side to the other, speechless so as not to be able to express his ills, and blind so as not to discern whether the attendants were administering to him medicine or poison.

Nevertheless, the saint maintained continual serenity of countenance and affability in conversation and kept her gaze fixedly bent toward God, in the bosom of whose blessed will she constantly reposed. Therefore Saint Francis de Sales, her director, who knew well what an object of special love her beautiful soul was to God, wrote thus of her: "Her heart resembled a deaf musician who, though he may sing most exquisitely, can derive no pleasure from it himself." To her he wrote as follows: "You must try to serve your Savior solely through love of his blessed will, utterly deprived of consolations and overwhelmed by a deluge of fears and sadness."

It is thus that saints are formed. The saints are precisely those choice stones, of whom the Church sings, which are reduced to shapeliness and beauty by the strokes of the chisel, that is by temptations, fears, darkness, and other torments, internal and external, until at length they are made worthy to be enthroned in the blessed kingdom of paradise.

The Virtues of One Who Loves Jesus Christ

Here is an abstract of the virtues treated in this work, and which should be practiced by him who loves Jesus Christ:

1 ◆ We must patiently endure the tribulations of this life—ill health, sorrows, poverty, losses, bereavement of kindred, affronts, persecutions, and all that is disagreeable. Let us look on the trials of this world as signs of God's love for us and of his desire to save us in the world to come. And let us, moreover, be fully persuaded that the involuntary mortifications which God himself sends us are far more pleasing to him than those which are the fruit of our own choice.

2 ◆ In sickness let us endeavor to resign ourselves entirely to the will of God; no devout exercise is more acceptable to him than this. If at such times we are unable to meditate, let us fix our eyes on our crucified Lord and offer him our sufferings in union with all that he endured for us upon the cross. And when we are told that we are about to die, let us accept the tidings with tranquillity and in the spirit of sacrifice; that is, with the desire to die in order to give pleasure to Jesus Christ: it was this desire that gave all the merit to the death of the martyrs. We should say: Oh, Lord, behold me here with no other will but thine own blessed will: I am willing to suffer as much as you please; I wish to die whenever you will it.

3 • We must likewise practice conformity with the will of God in bearing poverty and the various inconveniences which accompany it: cold, hunger, fatigue, contempt, and scorn.

4 • Nor should we be less resigned to losses, whether of property or of relatives and friends, on whom our ease and happiness depended. Let us acquire the good habit of saying in every adversity: God has so willed it, so I will it too. And at the death of our relations, instead of wasting time in fruitless tears let us employ it in praying for their souls, and offer to Jesus Christ, in their behalf, the pain of our bereavement.

5 • Let us, moreover, force ourselves to endure scorn and insult with patience and tranquillity. Let us answer words of outrage and injury with words of gentleness. But as long as we feel ourselves disturbed, the best plan is to keep silence until the mind grows tranquil. And meanwhile let us not be fretfully speaking to others of the affront we have received, but in silence offer it to Jesus Christ who endured so much for us.

6 • Behave kindly to all, to superiors and inferiors, to the highborn and peasant, to relations and strangers; but more especially to the poor and infirm, and above all to those who regard us with an evil eye.

7 • Gentleness in correcting faults is more effective than any other means or reasons that may be employed. Be therefore on your guard against correcting in a fit of passion, for then harshness is sure to be mingled with it either in word or action. Beware likewise of correcting a person in fault while he is excited, for in such cases the result is exasperation instead of improvement.

8 • Do not envy the great ones of this world their riches, honors, dignities, or applause given them by men, but envy rather those who most love Jesus Christ, who undoubtedly enjoy greater happiness than the first monarchs of the earth. Return thanks to the Lord for enlightening you to discover the vanity of all worldly things, for the sake of which so many perish unhappily.

9 • In all our actions and thoughts let us seek only the pleasure of almighty God, not our private satisfaction; and let us therefore lay aside all disquietude when our efforts are met with failure. And when we succeed, let us be no less cautious against seeking the thanks and approbation of men. Should they murmur against us, let us pay no attention to it. Our consolation will be to have tried to please God and not men.

The chief means of perfection are:

10 • In the first place, to avoid all deliberate sin, however small. Should we, however, unfortunately happen to commit a fault, let us refrain from becoming angry and impatient with ourselves. We must on such occasions quietly repent, and while we make an act of love to Jesus Christ and beg his help, promise him not to repeat the fault.

11 • In the second place, to have an earnest desire to acquire the perfection of the saints and to suffer all things to please Jesus Christ. And if we do not have this desire, to beseech Jesus Christ through his bounty to grant it to us, since as long as we do not feel a sincere desire to become saints we shall never make one step forward in the way of perfection.

12 • In the third place, to have a firm resolution to arrive at perfection. Whoever lacks this resolution works but languidly and does not succeed in overcoming his repugnances, whereas a resolute soul, by the divine aid which never fails her, rises above every obstacle.

13 • In the fourth place, to make daily two, or at least one, hour's mental prayer; and except in case of urgent necessity never to relinquish it for the sake of any weariness, dryness, or trouble we may experience.

14 • In the fifth place, to frequent Holy Communion in obedience to the advice of a spiritual director. It is good for everyone to have his own director, so that all may be regulated in obedience to him. With regard to external mortifications, such as fasting, mortifications when practiced without obedience to our spiritual director will either destroy health or produce vanity.

15 • In the sixth place, to pray continually, by having recourse to Jesus Christ in all our needs, by invoking likewise the intercession of our guardian angel, of our patron saints, and most particularly of the Blessed Mother, through whose hands almighty God bestows all graces upon us. It has already been shown that our welfare depends entirely on prayer. We must not pass a day without begging God to grant us the gift of perseverance in his grace; whoever asks for this perseverance obtains it, but he who does not ask for it does not obtain it. We must pray, too, that Jesus Christ may grant us his holy love and perfect conformity with his divine will. Neither should we forget to pray for every grace through the merits of Jesus Christ. We must first make these prayers when we rise in the morning, and afterward repeat them in our meditation, at Communion, at the visit to the Blessed Sacrament, and again in the evening at the examination of conscience. We must particularly cry to God for help in time of temptation. He who prays conquers; he who does not pray is conquered.

16 • With regard to humility, not to pride ourselves on riches, honors, high birth, talents, or any other natural advantage, and still less on any spiritual gift, remembering that all are gifts from God. To consider ourselves the worst of all, and consequently to delight in being despised by others, and not to act as some do, who declare themselves the worst of men and at the same time wish to be treated as the best. Moreover, to receive corrections humbly and without attempting to excuse ourselves, and this even though blamed wrongfully—except when to defend ourselves would be necessary in order to prevent others from being scandalized.

17 • To banish all desire to appear in public and to be honored by the world. The maxim of Saint Francis should never be out of our sight: "We are just what we are before God." It would be still worse for a religious to covet posts of honor and superiority in his community. The true honor of a religious is to be the most humble of all; and he is the humblest of all who most joyfully embraces humiliations.

18 • To detach our hearts from all creatures. One who continues bound by fondness to worldly things can never rise to a perfect union with God.

19 • To detach ourselves especially from an undue affection for our relatives. In deciding on a state of life, we must be quite unbiased by the advice of parents, who generally keep their own interests in view rather than our real welfare. Cast away all considerations of human respect and of the empty esteem of men, and above all be detached from self-will. We must leave all, in order to gain all. "*Totum pro toto*, All for all," writes Thomas à Kempis.

20 • Not to give way to anger, whatever happens; but if by chance the sparks of passion are suddenly lighted in our breasts, let us call on God and refrain from acting or speaking until we are sure that our anger has subsided. We shall find it of great value to arm ourselves in prayer against every chance of irritation that may befall us, in order not then to give way to culpable resentment.

21 • All sanctity consists in loving God, and all love of God consists in doing his blessed will. We must, therefore, bow with resignation to all the dispositions of providence without reserve, and submit cheerfully to the adversity as well as prosperity which God sends, to the state of life in which God places us, to the sort of health which God bestows on us. This should be the great aim of all our prayers, that God will enable us to fulfill his holy will in all things. And in order to be certain of the divine will, a religious must depend on obedience to his superiors and those who are in the world to their confessors, for nothing is more certain than that saying of Saint Philip Neri: "We shall have no account to render to God of what is done through obedience"—which is to be understood, of course, as long as there is no evident sin in a command.

22 • There are two remedies against temptations: resignation and prayer. Although temptations do not come from God, yet he permits them for our good. Therefore beware of yielding to vexation, however annoying the temptations may be. Be resigned to the will of God, who allows them, and take up the weapon of prayer, the most powerful and most certain way to overcome our enemies. Bad thoughts, however abominable, are not sins; it is only the consenting to them which makes sin. During assaults of temptation, it is useful to renew the resolution to suffer death rather than to offend God. It is also a good practice repeatedly to sign ourselves with the Sign of the Cross and with holy water. It is of great help, too, to reveal the temptation to the confessor. But prayer is the most necessary remedy, and continual cries for help to Jesus and Mary.

23 ◆ As to spiritual desolations, there are two acts in which we ought principally to exercise ourselves: first, to humble ourselves, with the sincere admission that we deserve no better treatment; second, to resign ourselves to the will of God and to abandon ourselves into the arms of his divine goodness. When God favors us with consolations, let us be prepared for coming trials, which frequently follow consolations. And if it pleases God to leave us in desolation, let us be humble and fully resigned to his divine will, and we shall thus reap far greater advantage from desolations than from consolations.

A Christian's Way of Life

Part I: The Means of Preserving God's Grace

In order to obtain eternal salvation, it is not enough to wish to be saved, but we must further take the means which have been left us by Jesus Christ. If we commit sins, it will not help us on the day of judgment to excuse ourselves by saying that the temptations were great and we were weak, because God has given us through his grace the means to conquer all the assaults of our enemies. If, then, we will not take advantage of them and are overcome, the fault is our own. All people desire to be saved, but because they do not employ the means of salvation, they sin and are lost.

Flying From Occasions of Sin

The first means of preserving grace is to avoid all occasions of sin. It is impossible for anyone who does not try to fly from the occasions of sin, especially in the matter of sensual pleasures, to avoid falling into sin. Saint Philip Neri said: "In the war of the senses, the conquerors are the cowards who fly." The occasion is like a veil put before our eyes, so that we can see nothing else—neither God, nor hell, nor the resolutions we had made. So it is morally impossible for anyone to put himself voluntarily into the occasion of sin and not to fall, although he may have made a thousand resolutions and a thousand promises to God. Anyone who has had the evil habit of sins of impurity must know that in order to restrain himself it is not enough merely to avoid those occasions which are absolutely proximate, for if he does not also fly from those which are not altogether proximate, he will easily fall again.

A temptation may begin in a spiritual way, and end carnally. The great servant of God, the Jesuit Sertorio Caputo said that the devil may first induce one to love a person's virtue, then the person, and then blind a person and bring him to ruin. We must also fly from evil companions. The devil is tempting us continually and drawing us to evil; a bad companion is all that is needed to make us fall. Therefore, the first thing we have to do to save ourselves is to avoid evil occasions and bad companions. And we must in this matter use violence with ourselves, resolutely overcoming all human respect. We must not place confidence in our own strength but only in divine help, but God wills that we should do our part in using violence with ourselves, when it is necessary to do so in order to gain paradise: "the violent bear it away" (Mt 11:12).

Mental Prayer

The second means is mental prayer. Without it, the soul will find it almost impossible to remain long in the grace of God. The Holy Spirit says: "In all your works remember your last end, and you shall never sin" (Eccl 7:40). He who often meditates on the four last things, namely death, judgment, and the eternity of hell and paradise, will not fall into sin. These truths are not to be seen by the natural eyes, but only with the eyes of the mind. If they are not meditated on, they vanish from the mind; and then the pleasures of the senses present themselves, and those who do not keep before themselves the eternal truths are easily taken up by them. All Christians know and believe that they must die and that we shall all be judged, but because they do not think about it they live far from God.

Without mental prayer, we walk in the dark; and walking in

the dark we do not see the danger we are in, we do not make use of the means we ought, nor pray to God to help us, and so we are lost. Without prayer we have neither light nor strength to advance in the ways of God, because without prayer we do not ask God to give us his grace, and without so praying we shall certainly fall. For this reason Cardinal Bellarmine declared it to be morally impossible for a Christian who did not meditate to persevere in grace. But one who makes his meditation every day can scarcely fall into sin; for if he should fall on some occasion, by continuing his prayer he will return to God.

Resolve, then, to make every day, either in the morning or in the evening—half an hour's meditation. For the rest, it is enough that during that time you should entertain your thoughts by reading some book of meditations, and from time to time excite some good affection or some aspiration. Above all, I beg you never to leave off this prayer, which you should practice at least once a day, although you may be in great aridity and feel great weariness in doing it. If you do not discontinue it, you will certainly be saved.

Together with prayer, it is of great use to do spiritual reading in private, in some book which treats of the life of a saint or of the Christian virtues, for half or at least a quarter of an hour. How many by reading a pious book have changed their way of living and become saints, such as Saint John Colombino, Saint Ignatius Loyola, and so many others. It would also be a most useful thing if you were every year to make a retreat in some religious house. But at any rate do not omit your daily meditation.

Frequenting the Sacraments

The third means is frequenting the sacraments of confession and Communion. By confession the soul keeps itself purified and not only obtains remission of sins but also greater strength to resist temptations. For this purpose you should choose your director, and always confess to him, consulting him on all more important matters, even temporal ones. Obey him in everything, especially if you are distressed by scruples. He who obeys his confessor need not fear he will go astray: "He that hears you, hears me" (Lk 10:16). The voice of the confessor is the voice of God.

Holy Communion is called heavenly bread, because as common bread preserves the life of the body so Communion preserves the life of the soul: "except you eat the flesh of the Son of Man…you shall not have life in you" (Jn 6:54). On the other hand, to those who often eat this bread eternal life is promised: "If anyone eat of this bread, he shall live forever" (Jn 6:52). You should, then, resolve to go to Communion frequently, being determined not to give it up for anything in the world.

Hearing Mass

The fourth means is to hear Mass every day. When we assist at Mass we give more honor to God than all the angels and saints in heaven can give him, because theirs is the honor of creatures, but in the Mass we offer to God Jesus Christ who gives him infinite honor.

Visiting the Blessed Sacrament and the Blessed Virgin

The fifth means is to make a visit every day to the most holy Sacrament in some church, and to the Blessed Mother before some devout image. Jesus Christ dwells on the altars of so many churches in order to dispense graces to all who come to visit him. Thus the souls of those who practice this beautiful devotion receive innumerable benefits from it. The graces you ought especially to ask for, both from Jesus and Mary, are the love of God and holy perseverance till death.

Prayer

The sixth means which I recommend you above all to put in practice is holy prayer. It is certain that without divine assistance we can do nothing good for our souls. God has declared that graces are granted only to those who ask for them: "Ask, and it shall be given you" (Mt 7:7). Therefore, as Saint Teresa says, he who does not seek does not receive. Hence it is a common opinion of the Fathers and of Saint Thomas that without prayer it is impossible to persevere in grace and to save oneself. But he who prays is sure of God's help. We have his word for it, which cannot fail, repeated so often in the gospels: "all things, whatsoever you ask when ye pray, believe that you shall receive, and they shall come unto you" (Mk 11:24). If, then, we wish to be saved we must pray, and pray with humility and confidence and above all with perseverance. This is why mental prayer is so useful, because then we remember to pray. Otherwise we forget it and so are lost. Saint Teresa says that out of her desire to see everyone saved, she would have wished to go to the top of a mountain and then to cry out, so as to be heard by all men, nothing but these words, "Pray! Pray!" The ancient fathers of the desert in their conferences decided that there was no better means of saving ourselves than by continually repeating the prayer of David: "Incline unto my aid, oh God! Lord, make haste to help me!"

Part II: Devout Exercises

Acts on Rising in the Morning

Make the Sign of the Cross and then say: (1) My God, I adore you and love you with all my heart; (2) I thank you for all your benefits, and especially for having preserved me this night; (3) I offer you whatever I may do or suffer this day, in union with the actions and sufferings of Jesus and of Mary, with the intention of gaining all the indulgences I can; (4) I resolve to fly from all sin this day, and especially from (here place your intention; it is good to make a particular resolution about the fault into which we fall most often)—and I beg you to give me perseverance for the love of Jesus Christ. I resolve to conform myself to your holy will, and particularly in those things which are contrary to my inclination, saying always, Lord, your will be done.

Jesus, keep your hand over me this day. Most holy Mary, take me beneath your mantle. And do thou, eternal Father, help me, for the love of Jesus and Mary. My angel guardian and my patron saints, assist me. An Our Father and a Hail Mary and the Creed, with three Hail Marys in honor of Mary's purity.

When you begin any work, say: Lord, I offer you this work.

When you eat: My God, bless this food and me, that I may commit no fault concerning it; and may all be for your glory. After having eaten: I thank you, Lord, for having done good to one who was thine enemy.

When the clock strikes: My Jesus, I love you; never permit me to offend you again, and let me never be separated from you.

In difficult circumstances: Lord, since you have so willed it, I will it also.

In time of temptation often repeat: Jesus and Mary!

When you know or doubt of some fault or sin you have committed, say immediately: My God, I repent of having offended you, infinite goodness; I will do so no more. And if it was a grievous sin, confess it directly.

It would be a good thing for parents and teachers to make the children under them learn these acts by heart, that they may make use of them afterward throughout their whole life.

Method of Making Mental Prayer

Mental prayer consists of three parts: preparation, meditation, and conclusion. The preparation consists of three acts: one of faith in the presence of God; one of humility, with a short act of contrition; and one of prayer to be enlightened. Say as follows, for the first: My God, I believe that you are present with me, and I adore you with all the affection of my soul. For the second, say: Lord, by my sins I deserve to be now in hell; with my whole heart I repent having offended you, infinite goodness. For the third: My God, for the love of Jesus and Mary, give me light in this prayer, that I may profit by it. Then say a Hail Mary to the most Blessed Virgin, that she may obtain light for us; and a Glory Be to the Father, to Saint Joseph, to your guardian angel, and to your patron saint, for the same purpose. These acts should be made with attention, but briefly. And then go on directly to your meditation.

In the meditation you can always make use of some book, at least at the beginning. Stop where you find yourself most touched. Saint Francis de Sales says that in this we should do as the bees, which stop on a flower as long as they find any honey on it and then pass on to another. The fruits to be gained by meditation are three in number: to make affections, to pray, and to make resolutions; and in these consists the profit to be derived from mental prayer.

After you have meditated on some eternal truth and God has spoken to your heart, you must also speak to God. Do this, in the first place, by forming affections, acts of faith, thanksgiving, humility, or hope, but above all by acts of love and contrition. Saint Thomas says that every act of love merits for us the grace of God and heaven: "Every act of love merits eternal life." Each act of contrition obtains the same thing. Acts of love are such as these: My God, I love you above all things. I love you with all my heart. I desire to do your will in all things. I rejoice that you are infinitely happy. For an act of contrition it is enough to say: I repent having offended you, infinite goodness.

In the second place, you must pray. Ask God to enlighten you, to give you humility or other virtues, to grant you a good death and eternal salvation, but above all, ask for his love and for holy perseverance. When the soul is suffering great aridity, it is sufficient to repeat: My God, help me. Lord, have mercy on me. My Jesus, have mercy. If you do nothing but this, your prayer will succeed exceedingly well.

In the third place, before finishing your prayer, you must form a particular resolution, as for instance to avoid some occasion of sin, to bear with an annoyance from some person, or to correct some fault.

Finally, in conclusion, three acts are to be made: in the first, we must thank God for the inspirations we have received; in the second, we must make a determination to observe the resolutions we have made; in the third, we must ask God, for love of Jesus and Mary, to help us keep our purpose. The prayer concludes by the recommendation of the souls in purgatory, the prelates of the Church, sinners, and all our relations and friends, for which we may say an Our Father and a Hail Mary. Saint Francis de Sales exhort us to choose some thought which may have struck us especially in our prayer, that we may remember it during the rest of the day.

Acts to Be Made Before and After Confession and Communion

Before confessing, the penitent should beg for light from God to enable him to know what sins he has committed and to obtain the grace of true sorrow and purpose of amendment. He should also particularly recommend himself to Our Lady of Sorrows, that she may obtain contrition for him. Then he may make the following acts:

Act Before Confession:
God of infinite majesty, behold at your feet a traitor who has offended you over and over again, but who now humbly seeks forgiveness. Lord, do not reject me; "A contrite and humbled heart, O God, you will not despise" (Ps 50:19). I thank you that you have waited for me until now and have not let me die in sin, casting me into hell as I deserved. Since you have waited for me, my God, I hope that by the merits of Jesus Christ you will pardon me in this confession for all the offenses I have committed against you. I repent and am sorry for them, because by them I have merited hell and lost heaven. But above all, it is not so much on account of hell, which I have deserved, but because I have offended you, infinite goodness, that I am sorry from the bottom of my heart. I love you, sovereign good, and because I love you, I repent of all the insults I have offered you. I have turned my back on you; I have not respected you; I have despised your grace and your friendship. Lord, I have lost you by my own free will. Forgive me all my sins for the love of Jesus Christ, now that I repent with all my heart; I hate, detest, and abominate them above every ill. And I repent not only of mortal sins but also of venial sins, because these are also displeasing to you. I resolve for the future, by your grace, never more willingly

to offend you. Yes, my God, I would rather die than ever sin again.

If a person confesses a sin into which he has often relapsed, it is a good thing to resolve particularly not to fall into it again but promising to avoid the occasion of it and to take the means pointed out by the confessor, or such as he may himself judge to be most effective for correcting himself of it.

Act After Confession:

My dear Jesus, how much I owe you! By the merits of your blood I hope that I have this day been pardoned. I thank you above all things. I hope to reach heaven, where I shall praise your mercies forever. My God, if I have hitherto lost you so often, I now desire to lose you no more. From this day forward I will change my life in earnest. You merit all my love. I will love you truly. I will no longer see myself separated from you. I have promised you this already; now I repeat my promise of being ready to die rather than offend you again. I promise also to avoid all occasions of sin and to take such means as shall prevent my falling again. My Jesus, you know my weakness, give me grace to be faithful to you until death and to have recourse to you when I am tempted. Most holy Mary, help me. You are the mother of perseverance; I place my hope in you.

Preparation For Communion:

There is no means more effective in freeing us from our sins and in enabling us to advance in the love of God than Holy Communion. Why is it, then, that some souls find themselves always in the same lukewarm state, committing the same faults, notwithstanding the many Communions they make? This happens through lack of a proper disposition and preparation. Two things are required for preparation. The first is to disengage our hearts from all affections which are an impediment to divine love. The second is to have a great desire to love God. And this, says Saint Francis de Sales, should be our chief intention when we communicate, namely, to increase in divine love. Out of love alone, says the saint, should our God be received, who out of love alone gives himself to us. For this end let us make the following acts.

Acts Before Communion:

My beloved Jesus, true Son of God, who died for me on the cross in a sea of sorrows and ignominy, I firmly believe that you are present in the Blessed Sacrament; and for this faith I am ready to give my life.

My dear Redeemer, I hope by your goodness and through the merits of your blood that when you do come to me this morning you will inflame me with your holy love and wilt give me all those graces which I need to keep me obedient and faithful to you until death.

My God, true and only lover of my soul, what more could you do to oblige me to love you? You were not satisfied, my love, with dying for me, but you would also institute the Blessed Sacrament, making yourself my food and giving yourself all to me, thus uniting yourself most closely to such a miserable and ungrateful creature. You yourself invite me to receive you and greatly desire that I should receive you.

Depart from my soul, all earthly affections; to you alone, Jesus, my treasure, my all, will I give all my love. This morning you give yourself all to me, and I give myself all to you. Permit me to love you, for I desire none but you, and nothing but what is pleasing to you. I love you, my Savior, and I unite my poor love to the love of all the angels and saints and of your mother Mary and the love of your eternal Father. Oh, that I could see you loved by all! Oh, that I could make you loved by all men, and loved as much as you deserve!

Domine, non sum dignus. Lord, I am not worthy to remain in your presence; I ought to be in hell forever, far away, and abandoned by you. But out of your goodness you call me to receive you. Behold, I come, I come humbled and in confusion for the great displeasure I have given you, but trusting entirely to your mercy and to the love you have for me. I am exceedingly sorry, my loving Redeemer, for having so often offended you in the past. You did even give your life for me, and I have so often despised your grace and your love and have exchanged you for nothing. I repent, and am sorry with all my heart for every offense I have offered you, whether grievous or light, because it was an offense against you, who art infinite goodness. I hope you have already pardoned me, but if you have not yet forgiven me, pardon me, my Jesus, before I receive you. Receive me quickly into your grace, since it is your will soon to come and dwell within me.

Come, then, Jesus, come into my soul which sighs after you. My only and infinite good, my life, my love, my all, I desire to receive you this morning with the same love with which those souls who love you most have received you, and with the same fervor with which your most holy mother received you; to her Communions I wish to unite this one of mine.

Acts After Communion:

The time after Communion is a precious time for gaining treasures of grace, because the acts and prayers made while the soul is thus united to Jesus Christ have more merit and are of more value than when they are made at any other time. Saint Teresa says that our Lord then dwells in the soul, enthroned as on a seat of mercy, and speaks to it in these words: My child, ask me what you will; for this purpose I have come to you, to do you good. What great favors those receive who converse with Jesus Christ after Communion! Let the communicant, then, make the following acts, and try during the rest of the day to go on making acts of love and prayer in order to keep himself united to Jesus Christ whom he has received in the morning.

Behold, my Jesus, you are now within me and have made yourself all mine. Welcome, my beloved Redeemer. I cast myself at your feet; I embrace you, I press you to my heart. Oh Mary, my patron saints, my guardian angel, do all of you thank him for me! My divine King, since you visit me with so much love, I give you my will, my liberty, and my whole self. You have given yourself wholly to me, I will give myself wholly to you; I will no longer belong to myself; from this day forward I will be altogether yours. I desire that my soul, my body, my faculties, my senses, should all be thine, that they may be employed in serving and pleasing you. To you I consecrate all my thoughts, my desires, my affections, and my life. I have offended you enough, Jesus; I desire to spend the remainder of my life in loving you who hast loved me so much.

Accept, oh God of my soul, the sacrifice which I, a miserable sinner, make to you. I desire only to love and please you. Work in me and dispose of me and of all things belonging to me as you please. May your love destroy in me all those affections which displease you, that I may be all thine and may live only to please you!

I ask you not for goods of this world, for pleasures, for honors. Give me, I pray you, by the merits of your Passion, a constant sorrow for my sins. Make me know the vanity of worldly goods and how much you deserve to be loved. Separate me from all attachment to the world and bind me entirely to your love, so that from now on my will may neither seek nor desire anything but what you will. Give me patience and resignation in infirmities, in poverty, and in all those things which are contrary to my self-love. Make me gentle toward those who despise me. Give me a holy death. Give me your holy love. And above all, I pray you to give me perseverance in your grace until death. Never permit me to separate myself from you again. And I also ask of you the grace always to have recourse to you and to invoke your aid in all my temptations.

Most holy Mary, my mother and my hope, obtain for me these graces I so desire, as also a great love for you, my queen. May I always recommend myself to you in all my necessities.

Method of Hearing Mass

The same action is performed in the Mass as was accomplished on Calvary, except that there the blood of Jesus Christ was shed physically while on the altar it is shed mystically. In the Mass the merits of the Passion of Jesus are applied to each one in particular. To hear Mass, therefore, with great fruit, we must pay attention to the ends for which it was instituted, namely: (1) To honor God; (2) To thank him for his benefits; (3) To satisfy for our sins; (4) To obtain graces.

For this reason you may use the following prayer during Mass: Eternal Father, in this sacrifice I offer you your Son Jesus, with all the merits of his Passion: (1) In honor of your majesty; (2) In thanksgiving for all the favors you have shown me and for all those which I hope to receive for all eternity; (3) In satisfaction for my sins and for those of all the living and dead; (4) To obtain eternal salvation and all the graces which are necessary for me to gain it.

At the elevation of the Host: My God, for the love of this your Son, pardon me and give me holy perseverance. At the elevation of the Chalice: By the blood of Jesus, give me your love and a holy death. At the Communion of the priest make a spiritual Communion, saying: My Jesus, I love you and I embrace you, and I will never again separate myself from you.

Prayer Upon Visiting the Blessed Sacrament and the Blessed Virgin

My Lord Jesus Christ who remains night and day in this sacrament, full of love, awaiting, calling, and receiving all who come to visit you, I believe that you are present in the sacrament of the altar. I adore you from the depths of my own nothingness. I thank you for the many graces you have given me, and especially for having given me yourself in this sacrament, for having given me Mary your mother as my advocate, and for having called me to visit you in this church. I salute your loving heart, first, in thanksgiving for this great gift; second, to atone for all the insults you have received in this sacrament; third, I intend in this visit to adore you in all those places where, veiled in the Blessed Sacrament, you are least reverenced and most abandoned. My Jesus, I love you with my whole heart. I am sorry that I have so often offended your infinite goodness. With the help of your grace, I resolve to displease you no more; and unworthy as I am I now consecrate myself wholly to you. I renounce and give to you my will, my affections, my desires, and all that is mine. Henceforward do with me and with all that belongs to me whatever you please. I ask for nothing but you and your holy love, final perseverance, and a perfect fulfillment of your will. I recommend to you the souls in purgatory, especially those who were most devoted to this sacrament. I also recommend to you all poor sinners. And lastly, my beloved Savior, I unite all my affections with those of your most loving heart, and thus united I offer them to your eternal Father. In your name I beseech him to accept them.

Prayer Upon Visiting Any Image of the Blessed Virgin

Most holy Immaculate Virgin Mary, my mother, I, the most miserable of sinners, have this day recourse to you, mother of my Lord and refuge of sinners. I thank you for the many favors you have obtained for me, especially for having delivered me from hell which I have so often deserved. I love you, most amiable lady, worthy of all love. And for the love I bear you, I promise to serve you always. I place my salvation in your hands. Accept me for your servant, receive me under your mantle, mother of mercy. You are all-powerful with God. Free me, then, from all temptations, or at least obtain for me strength to conquer them as long as I live. From you I beg a true love of Jesus Christ. By your help I hope for a good death. I beseech you, Mother, by the love you bear to God, that you will always help me, but especially at the last moment of my life. Do not leave me until you see me safe in heaven, blessing you and singing your mercies for all eternity. Amen. This is my hope. So may it be.

Acts to Be Made Before Going to Bed

Before going to rest, make your examination of conscience in the following manner. First thank God for all the favors you have received. Then cast a glance over all your actions and words during the day, repenting all the faults you have committed. Afterward make Christian acts in the following manner:

Act of Faith:

My God, who are infallible truth, because you have revealed it to your Church, I believe all that she proposes to my belief. I believe that you are my God, the creator of all things; that you do reward the just with an eternal paradise and do punish the wicked in hell for all eternity. I believe that you are one in essence, and three in persons, namely, Father, Son, and Holy Ghost. I believe in the Incarnation and death of Jesus Christ. I believe, in short, all that the Church believes. I thank you for having made me a Christian, and I protest that I will live and die in this holy faith.

Act of Hope:

My God, confiding in your promises because you are powerful, faithful, and merciful, I hope through the merits of Jesus Christ to obtain pardon for my sins, final perseverance, and the glory of heaven.

Act of Love and Contrition:

My God, because you are infinite goodness, worthy of infinite love, I love you with all my heart above all things, and for love of you I love my neighbor also. I repent with all my heart, and am sorry above all things for all my sins, because by them I have offended your infinite goodness. I resolve, by the help of your grace, which I beseech you to grant me now and always, rather to die than ever to offend you again.

Prayer for Final Perseverance:

Eternal Father, I humbly adore and thank you for having created me and for having redeemed me by means of Jesus Christ. I thank you for having made me a Christian by giving me the true faith and by adopting me for your child in holy baptism. I thank you for having given me time for repentance after my many sins, and for having (as I hope) pardoned all my offenses against you. I renew my sorrow for them, because I have displeased you. I thank you also for having preserved me from falling again, as often as I should have done if you had not held me up and saved me.

But my enemies do not cease to fight against me, nor will they until death, that they may again have me for their slave. If you do not keep and help me continually by your assistance, I shall be wretched enough to lose your grace anew. I therefore pray you, for the love of Jesus Christ, to grant me holy perseverance till death. Your Son Jesus has promised that you will grant us whatever we ask for in his name. By the merits then of Jesus Christ, I beg you, for myself, and for all those who are in your grace, the grace of never more being separated from your love, but that we may always love you in this life and in the next. Mary, Mother of God, pray to Jesus for me.

Prayer for Confidence in the Merits of Jesus Christ and in the Intercession of Mary:

Eternal Father, I thank you for myself and on behalf of all humankind for the great mercy you have shown us in sending your Son to be made man and to die to obtain our salvation. I thank you for it, and I wish to offer you in thanksgiving all that love which is due for such an inestimable benefit. By his merits our sins are pardoned and your justice is satisfied for the punishment we had merited. By these merits do you receive us miserable sinners into your grace, while we deserve nothing but hatred and chastisement. Finally, you have bound yourself, in consideration of these merits, to grant all gifts and graces to those who ask for them in the name of Jesus Christ.

I thank you also, infinite goodness, that, in order to strengthen our confidence, besides giving us Jesus Christ as our Redeemer, you have also given us your beloved daughter Mary as our advocate, so that with the heart full of mercy which you have given her she may never cease to help by her intercession any sinner who may have recourse to her, and this intercession is so powerful with you that you cannot deny her any grace she asks of you.

Hence it is your will that we should have great confidence in the merits of Jesus and in the intercession of Mary. But this confidence is your gift, and it is a great gift which you grant to those only who ask you for it. This confidence, then, in the blood of Jesus Christ and in the patronage of Mary, I beg of you through the merits of Jesus and Mary. To you also, my dear Redeemer, do I turn; it was to obtain for me this confidence in your merits that you did sacrifice your life on the cross for me, who was worthy only of punishment. Accomplish, then, the end for which you died; enable me to hope for all things through confidence in your passion. And you, Mary, my mother, and my hope after Jesus, obtain for me a firm confidence, first in the merits of Jesus your Son, and then in the intercession of your prayers. My beloved Jesus, my sweet Mary, I trust in you, to you I give my soul. You have loved it so much, have pity on it and save it.

Prayer to Obtain the Grace of Being Constant in Prayer: God of my soul, I hope in your goodness that you have pardoned all my offenses against you and that I am now in a state of grace. I thank you for it with all my heart and hope to thank you for all eternity. I know I have fallen because I have not had recourse to you when I was tempted, to ask for holy perseverance. For the future, I firmly resolve to recommend myself always to you, and especially when I see myself in danger of offending you again. I will always fly to your mercy, invoking the most holy names of Jesus and Mary with full confidence that when I pray you will not fail to give me the strength which I have not of myself to resist my enemies. This I resolve and promise to do. But of what use, my God, will all these resolutions and promises be to have recourse to you in all dangers, if you do not assist me with your grace to put them in practice? Eternal Father, help me, for the love of Jesus Christ, and let me never omit recommending myself to you whenever I am tempted. I know you will always help me when I have recourse to you, but my fear is that I may forget to recommend myself to you and so my negligence will be the cause of my ruin, that is, the loss of your grace, the greatest evil that can happen to me. By the merits of Jesus Christ, give me grace to pray to you. But grant me such an abundant grace that I may always pray, and pray as I ought! My mother Mary, whenever I have had recourse to you, you have obtained for me the help which has kept me from falling! Now I come to beg of you to obtain a still greater grace, that of recommending myself always to your Son and to you in all my times of need. My queen, you obtain all you desire from God by the love you bear for Jesus Christ. Obtain for me now this grace which I beg of you, namely, to pray always and never to cease praying until I die. Amen.

Prayer to Obtain the Graces Necessary for Salvation:
Eternal Father, your Son has promised that you will grant us all the graces for which we ask you in his name. In the name, therefore, and by the merits of Jesus Christ, I ask the following graces for myself and for all humankind.

First, I pray you to give me a lively faith in all that the holy Roman Church teaches me. Enlighten me also that I may know the vanity of the goods of this world and the immensity of the infinite good that you are. Make me also see the deformity of the sins I have committed, that I may humble myself and detest them as I should, and on the other hand show me how worthy you are because of your goodness, that I should love you with all my heart. Make me know also the love you have borne me, that from this day forward I may try to be grateful for so much goodness.

Second, give me a firm confidence of receiving your merciful pardon for my sins, holy perseverance, and finally, the glory of heaven, through the merits of Jesus Christ and the intercession of Mary.

Third, give me a great love of you, which shall detach me from the love of this world and of myself, so that I may love none other but you and may neither do nor desire anything else but what is for your glory.

Fourth, I beg of you a perfect resignation to your will, in accepting with tranquillity sorrows, infirmities, contempt, persecutions, aridity of spirit, loss of property, of esteem, of relations, and every other cross which shall come to me from your hands. I offer myself entirely to you, that you may do with me and all that belongs to me what you please. Only give me light and strength to do your will, and especially at the hour of death help me to sacrifice my life to you with all the affection I am capable of, in union with the sacrifice which your Son Jesus Christ made of his life on the cross on Calvary.

Fifth, I beg of you a great sorrow for my sins, which may make me grieve over them as long as I live and weep for the insults I have offered you, the sovereign good who art worthy of infinite love and who hast loved me so much.

Sixth, I pray you to give me the spirit of true humility and meekness, that I may accept with peace and even with joy all the contempt, ingratitude and ill-treatment I may receive. At the same time I also pray you to give me perfect charity, which shall make me wish well to those who have done evil to me, and to do what good I can, at least by praying, for those who have in any way injured me.

Seventh, I beg you to give me love for the virtue of holy mortification, by which I may chastise my rebellious senses and cross my self-love; at the same time I beg you to give me holy purity of body and the grace to resist all bad temptations, by always having recourse to you and your most holy mother. Give me grace faithfully to obey my spiritual father and all my superiors in all things. Give me an upright intention, that in all I desire and do I may seek only your glory and to please you alone. Give me a great confidence in the Passion of Jesus Christ and in the intercession of Mary immaculate. Give me a great love for the sacrament of the altar and a tender devotion and love to your holy mother. Give me, I pray you, above all, holy perseverance and the grace always to pray for it, especially in time of temptation and at the hour of death.

Last, I recommend to you the holy souls of purgatory, my relations and benefactors, and in a special manner I recommend to you all those who hate me or who have in any way offended me; I beg you to render them good for the evil they have done or may wish to do me. I recommend to you all infidels, heretics, and all poor sinners; give them light and strength to deliver themselves from sin. Most loving God, make yourself known and loved by all, but especially by those who have been more ungrateful to you than others, so that by your goodness I may come one day to sing your mercies in heaven, for my hope is in the merits of your blood and in the patronage of Mary. Mary, Mother of God, pray to Jesus for me. So I hope. So may it be.

Prayer to Obtain All Holy Virtues:

My Lord and my God, by the merits of Jesus Christ, I ask you first to enlighten me. Make me know the vanity of the goods of this world, that there is no other good but to love you, the supreme and infinite good. Make me know my unworthiness and how worthy you are of being loved by all and especially by me because of the love you have borne me. Give me holy humility to embrace with cheerfulness all the contempt I may receive from men. Give me a great sorrow for my sins. Give me love of holy mortification, that by it I may curb my passions and punish my rebellious senses. Give me love for the obedience I owe to my superiors. Give me grace to direct all I do to the sole end of pleasing you. Give me holy purity of mind and body and a detachment from everything that does not tend to the love of you. Give me great confidence in the passion of Jesus Christ and in the intercession of Mary. Give me above all a great love for you and perfect conformity to your divine will. I recommend to you also the souls in purgatory, my relations, benefactors, and friends, and all those from whom I have received any affront or injury. I pray you shower down upon them all blessings. Finally, I recommend to you infidels, heretics, and all those who are in a state of sin. Since you, my God, are worthy of infinite love, make yourself known and loved by all, but especially by me who have been most ungrateful to you. I have offended you enough. Make me love you exceedingly, and bring me to heaven where I shall sing your mercies for all eternity. Blessed Mary, pray to Jesus for me! Amen.

Prayer for a Good Death:

My God, being certain that I shall die and not knowing when it will be, I intend now to prepare myself for death, and I therefore declare that I believe all that the Church believes and especially the mystery of the most holy Trinity, the Incarnation and death of Jesus Christ, heaven and hell, because you who are truth itself have revealed all these truths.

I deserve a thousand hells, but I hope in your mercy, through the merits of Jesus Christ, to obtain pardon, final perseverance, and the glory of paradise.

I protest that I love you above all things. Because you are infinite good and because I love you, I am sorrier that I have so often offended you than for any other evil, and I resolve rather to die than offend you again. I pray you rather to take away my life than to permit me to lose you by another sin.

I thank you, Jesus, for all the sufferings you have undergone for me and for the many mercies you have shown me after I had so greatly offended you.

My beloved Lord, I rejoice that you are infinitely happy and that you are loved by so many souls in heaven and on earth. I desire that everyone should know and love you.

I protest that if anyone has offended me, I pardon him for the love of you, my Jesus, and I beg of you to do good to him!

I declare that I desire to receive the sacraments, both in life and death; and I intend now to ask for absolution of my sins, in case I should not be able to give any sign of it at my death.

I accept my death and all the pains which shall accompany it, in union with the death and sorrows which Jesus suffered on the cross. And I accept, my God, all the pains and tribulations which you shall send me before my death. Do with me and with all that belongs to me what you please. Give me your love and holy perseverance and I ask nothing more.

My mother Mary, assist me always, but especially at my death; in the meantime, help me and keep me in the grace of God. You are my hope. Under your mantle I will live and die. Saint Joseph,

Saint Michael the Archangel, and my guardian angel, help me always, but especially in the hour of my death!

And you, my dear Jesus, who to obtain for me a good death did give yourself to suffer such a bitter death, do not abandon me in my last hour. From this time I embrace you, that I may die in your arms. I deserve hell but I throw myself on your mercy, hoping to die in your friendship and to receive your blessing when I shall see you first as my judge. Into your hands, wounded for my love, I commend my soul. I hope in you, that you will not then condemn me to hell. Help me always, but especially at my death; grant me to die loving you, so that the last sigh of my life may be an act of love which shall transport me from this earth to love you forever in paradise.

Jesus, Mary, and Joseph, assist me in my last agony! Jesus, Mary, and Joseph, I give myself to you; receive my soul at that moment.

A Short Prayer to Jesus Crucified:

My Lord Jesus Christ, by that bitterness which you did endure on the cross when your blessed soul was separated from your most sacred body, have pity on my sinful soul when it shall leave my body to enter into eternity.

Oh Mary, by that grief which you experienced on Calvary at seeing Jesus expire on the cross in front of your eyes, obtain for me a good death, that loving Jesus and you, my mother, in this life, I may attain heaven where I shall love you both for all eternity.

The Practice of Purity of Intention

Purity of intention consists in doing everything with the one aim of pleasing God. The good or bad intention with which an action is performed renders it good or bad before God. Saint Mary

Magdalene of Pazzi said: "God rewards actions according to the amount of purity of intention with which they are done." Let us examine the practice of it.

In the first place, in all our exercises of devotion, let us seek God and not ourselves; if we seek our own satisfaction we cannot expect to receive any reward from God. And this holds good for all spiritual works. How many labor and exhaust themselves in preaching, hearing confessions, serving at the altar, and in doing other pious works, but because they seek themselves and not God in these things, they lose all! When we seek neither approval nor thanks from others for what we do, it is a sign that we are working for God's sake, as also when we are not vexed at the failure of the good we undertake or when we rejoice as much at any good that is done by others as if it had been done by ourselves. However, when we have done some good in order to please God, let us not torment ourselves in trying to drive away vainglory. If we are praised for it, it is enough to say: "To God be the honor and glory." And let us never omit doing any good action which may be edifying to our neighbor, through the fear of vainglory. Therefore when you do good, have first the intention of pleasing God, and secondly that also of giving a good example to your neighbor.

In the second place, in our bodily actions, whether we work or eat or drink or amuse ourselves with propriety, let us do all in order to please God. Purity of intention may be called the heavenly alchemy, which changes iron into gold; by which is meant that the most trivial and ordinary actions when done to please God become acts of divine love. Saint Mary Magdalene of Pazzi used to say: "A person who performs all his actions with a pure intention will go straight to heaven." A holy hermit, before putting his hand to any work, used to raise his eyes to heaven and keep them fixed there for a short time; and when he was asked what he was doing, he replied: "I am taking my aim, so that I may not miss the mark." Let us do in like manner: before beginning any action let us make sure of our aim, and say: "Lord, I am doing this to please you."

Rules for Avoiding Tepidity

Souls that make no account of venial sins and give themselves up to tepidity, without a thought of freeing themselves from it, live in great danger. We do not here speak of those venial sins which are committed by mere frailty, such as useless or idle words, interior disturbances, or negligence in small matters, but we speak of venial sins committed with full deliberation, above all when they are habitual. Saint Teresa writes: "From all deliberate sin, however small it may be, oh Lord, deliver us!" The Venerable Alvarez used to say: "Those little backbitings, dislikes, culpable curiosity, acts of impatience and intemperance, do not indeed kill the soul, but they weaken it so that when any great temptation takes it unexpectedly it will not have strength enough to resist and will consequently fall." On the one hand deliberate venial sins weaken the soul, and on the other they deprive us of the divine assistance, for it is only just that God should be sparing with those who are sparing toward him: "He who sows sparingly, shall also reap sparingly" (2 Cor 9:6). And that is what a soul that has received special graces from God has the most reason to fear. Still more ought it to fear lest such faults should be caused by some passionate attachment, as of ambition or avarice, or of aversion, or inordinate affection toward any person. It often happens to souls that are enslaved by some passion as it does to gamblers who, after losing many times, at the last throw say, "Let us risk everything," and so finish by losing all they have. In what a miserable state is that soul which is the slave of any passion; for passion blinds us and does not allow us any longer to see what we are doing.

Let us now come to the practice of what we must do in order to be able to deliver ourselves from the wretched state of tepidity. In the first place, it is necessary to have a firm desire to get out of this state. The good desire lightens our labor and gives us strength to go forward. And let us rest assured that he who makes no progress in the way of God will always be going back; and he will go back so far that at last he will fall over some precipice. Second, let us try to find out our predominant fault to which we are most attached, whether it be anger, ambition, or inordinate affection to persons or things; with the help of God, a resolute will overcomes all. Third, we must avoid wherever possible the occasion, otherwise all our resolutions will fall to the ground. And last, we must above all be distrustful of our own strength and pray continually with all confidence to God, begging him to help us in the danger we are in and to deliver us from those temptations by which we shall fall into sin, which is the meaning of the petition—"Lead us not into temptation." Therefore we must always pray, "My God, help me, and soon!"

Advice for All That They May Secure Salvation

God wishes us all to be saved (1 Tim 2:4). He is ready to give to all the help necessary for salvation, but as Saint Augustine says: "He gives only to those who ask." Hence, it is a common opinion that prayer is necessary for adults as a means of salvation; that is to say, that a person who does not pray, and who neglects to ask of God the help required for overcoming temptations and for preserving grace already received, cannot be saved.

On the other hand, our Lord cannot refuse to give graces to those who ask for them, because he has promised to do so: "Cry to me and I will hear you" (Jer 33:3). This promise is not to be understood with reference to temporal goods, because God only gives these when they are for the good of the soul; but he has promised absolutely to give spiritual graces to anyone who asks him, and having promised it is obliged to give them: "By his promise he has made himself our debtor," says Saint Augustine.

It should also be observed that, while on God's part prayer is a promise, on our part it is a binding precept: "Ask, and it shall be given you" (Mt 7:7); "We ought always to pray" (Lk 18:1). These words, "ask" and "we ought," convey, as Saint Thomas teaches, a grave precept which is binding for our whole life, but especially when a person is in danger of death or of falling into sin, because if he does not then have recourse to God he will certainly be overcome. And he who has already fallen under God's displeasure commits a fresh sin when he does not turn to God for help to rise out of his miserable state. But will God hear him while he is yet his enemy? Yes, he does hear, if the sinner humbles himself and prays for pardon from his heart, since it is written, "Call upon me in the day of trouble: I will deliver you" (Ps 49:15). Call on me and I will deliver you from hell, to which you stand condemned.

There will be no excuse on the day of judgment for anyone who dies in mortal sin. It will be of no use for him to say that he did not have the strength to resist the temptation which troubled him, because Jesus Christ will answer: If you had not the strength, why did you not ask it of me, and I should certainly have given it you? If you fell into sin, why did you not have recourse to me, that I might have delivered you from it?

You see, then, that if you desire to be saved and would keep yourself in the grace of God, you must often pray to him, that he would keep his hand over you. For a person to persevere in God's grace, it is not enough that he should have only that general aid which God gives to all, but he must also have that special assistance which can only be obtained by prayer. For this reason all the Doctors of the Church say that everyone is bound, under serious sin, to recommend himself often to God, and to ask for the grace of holy perseverance. And anyone who finds himself in the midst of many dangerous occasions is under the obligation of asking more frequently for the grace of perseverance.

It is also most useful to keep up some particular devotion to the Mother of God, who is called the mother of perseverance, in order to obtain this grace, and a person who has not this special devotion to the Blessed Virgin will find it very difficult to persevere, for as Saint Bernard says, all divine graces, and especially this one of perseverance which is the greatest of all, come to us by means of Mary.

Would preachers were more thoughtful about putting before their hearers this great means of prayer! Some scarcely mention it more than once or twice in passing even in the whole course of their Lenten sermons, while they ought often to make it their main subject, besides speaking of it in every sermon; if they omit to do so, they will have to render a heavy account for it to God. Thus also many confessors are particular merely about the resolutions their penitents make not to offend God again, and few take the trouble to inculcate the idea that they must pray when tempted again to fall; but when a temptation is violent, if the penitent does not beg for God's assistance, all his resolutions will avail him little; prayer alone can save him.

Therefore, I repeat, if you wish to be saved, pray continually to the Lord to give you light and strength not to fall into sin. We must be importunate with God, in asking him for his grace. "This importunity with God is our opportunity," says Saint Jerome. Every morning we should beseech him to keep us from sin during that day. And when any bad thought or occasion of sin presents itself to your mind (or if you are tempted by some dangerous occasion), immediately have recourse to Jesus Christ and the Blessed Virgin, and say, "Jesus, help me! Most Blessed Virgin, come to my aid!" It is enough at such a time to pronounce the names of Jesus and Mary, and the temptation may vanish; but should the temptation continue, persevere in invoking the assistance of Jesus and Mary, and you will be victorious.

Reflections to Excite in Us the Holy Love of God

Here are short meditations to remind us of the holy love of God:

God is a treasury of all grace, of all good, of all perfection.

God is infinite, God is eternal, God is immense, God is unchangeable.

God is powerful, God is wise, God is provident, God is just.

God is merciful, God is holy, God is beautiful, God is brightness itself, God is rich, God is all things, and he is therefore worthy of love—and of how much love!

God is infinite; he gives to all and receives nothing from anyone. All that we have comes to us from God, but God has nothing from us: "you are my God, for you have no need of my goods" (Ps 15:2).

God is eternal; he has always been eternal and always shall be. We can count the years and the days of our existence, but God knows no beginning and will never have an end: "you are always the selfsame, and your years shall not fail" (Ps 101:28).

God is immense, and is essentially present in every place. We, when we are in one place, cannot be in another. But God is in all places, in heaven, on earth, in the sea, in the depths, without us, and within us. "Whither shall I go from your spirit? or whither shall I flee from your face? If I ascend into heaven, you are there; if I descend into hell, you are present" (Ps 138:7–8).

God is unchangeable, and all that he has ordained by his holy will from eternity he wills now and will do so forever. "For I am the Lord, and I change not" (Mal 3:6).

God is powerful; and in comparison with God, all the power of creatures is but weakness.

God is wise; and in comparison with God, all human wisdom is ignorance.

God is provident; and in comparison with God, all human foresight is ridiculous.

God is just; and in comparison with God all human justice is defective.

God is merciful; and in comparison with God, all human clemency is imperfect.

God is holy; in comparison with God, all human sanctity, though it be heroic, falls short in an infinite degree: "None is good but God alone" (Lk 18:19).

God is beauty itself—yes, how beautiful is God!—and in comparison with God, all human beauty is deformity.

God is brightness itself; and in comparison with God, all other brightness, even that of the sun, is darkness.

God is rich; and in comparison with God, all human wealth is poverty.

God is all things; and in comparison with God, the highest, most sublime, most admirable of created things, even if they were all united in one, are as nothing. He is, therefore, worthy of love; and oh, of how much! God is worthy of so much love that all the angels and all the saints of heaven do nothing but love God and will throughout all eternity be occupied only in loving him, and in this love of God, they are and will be always happy.

God is so worthy of love that he is obliged to love himself

with an infinite love; and in this same love, so necessary, but at the same time so delightful, which God bears to himself, consists his infinite happiness! And shall we not love him?

Saint Mary Magdalene of Pazzi, not satisfied with loving him so much herself, sometimes went about her convent, crying with a loud voice, "Love is not loved; Love is not loved!" And shall we then not love him?

Do you know why we do not love him? Because we know him so little. The saints, who knew him better than we do, loved him so much. Let us then also try to know him a little more.

Let us meditate from time to time on his divine attributes, on his divine perfections. Let us at least from time to time raise our minds by a simple glance to him, in the way I have here proposed, and our hearts will also become inflamed with this holy love.

It is condescension in so great a God that he should permit himself to be loved by such vile creatures as we are; and it is also his sweet commandment.

Signs by Which We Know Whether We Have Divine Love in Us

Our Lord, in declaring to us in the Gospel that he had come on earth to bring down the divine love, expresses himself by saying that he had come on earth to bring fire: "I am come to cast fire on the earth" (Lk 12:49). And God himself, in Revelation, counsels a soul to provide itself with burned gold: "I counsel you to buy of me gold fire tried" (Rev 3:18), that is, divine love.

Now fire has these two properties: it resists what is contrary to itself—I mean to say, that instead of being put out by winds and gusts, it is thereby augmented; and it is operative—if it is fire, it will act. Here are, therefore, two sure signs by which we may find out if we have in ourselves the holy love of God—works and patience.

Do we always work for our God, at least by means of a pure right intention of doing his divine will in all things, of finding his divine good pleasure in all things? Do we voluntarily suffer for his sake everything that is against our inclination, poverty, tribulations, sickness, and everything else? And instead of such things making us go far from him, do they bring us nearer to him? If they do, then we possess the holy love of God. Our love is a fire which acts, which opposes what is contrary to itself. Otherwise we do not have it; our love for God will be not true but false; it will be a love of the lips but not of the heart. Saint John also warns us: "Let us not love in word nor in tongue, but in deed and in truth" (Jn 3:18).

Saint Gregory says, "If there is no work, there is no love." And Jesus Christ says: He who has my commandments and keeps them, "he it is that loves me" (Jn 14:21). And Saint Augustine adds: "The bitterest and most disagreeable things are rendered comparatively easy, and almost of no account, by love." So that if we always act for our God—if we keep his divine commandments, if we observe them faithfully (and with the divine commandments come also those of the Church, the obligations of our state, and each one's own duty), if we overcome with generosity and even with cheerfulness, for our God, everything that is contrary to our nature, though it be most distasteful to us, we have in us the holy love of God. Our love is then a fire which acts, which resists what is contrary to itself. Otherwise, we do not have it; our love for God will certainly not be true, but false; it will be a love of the lips, not a love of the heart.

Let us give some more practical examples. Suppose you have

an opportunity to make such and such profit, but it is dishonest to do so; or an opportunity occurs for you to indulge yourself in some pleasure, but that pleasure is unlawful; the duties of your state trouble you, or the labors of your employment weary you; and for the sake of your God you do not care to make that profit, you renounce that pleasure, do your duty, and continue your work. Then you do have the holy love of God, your love is a fire which operates. Otherwise, you have it not, your love toward God will not be true love, but false; it will be a love of the lips, and not a love of the heart: let us not love in word, nor in tongue, but in deed and in truth.

Further, suppose some tribulation comes upon you suddenly—an action is brought against you unexpectedly, on which all you have depends, and you suddenly lose some person in whom you placed all your hopes and who was your whole support. Do you with promptness offer it all to our Lord? Do you even bear it all with joy? If so, you have the holy love of God. Your love is a fire which resists what is contrary to itself. Otherwise, you have it not; your love will not be true, it will be false—a love of the lips, not a love of the heart.

But it is a still surer sign of love to suffer than to act—because in acting a person employs himself in favor of the person loved and thus gives a sign of love, but in suffering a person has no care for himself and thinks of nothing but the person loved, and therefore gives a sign of greater love. And by this mark God was pleased to test the great love of Job for him. The holy man Job was certainly a great lover of God, but when did he show himself most truly to be so? Was it when he was surrounded by a large family? When he was enjoying an abundance of earthly goods? When he was in perfect health? Yes, even then; for even then he acknowledged that all came from God, he thanked God for all these things, offered sacrifices, and fulfilled his duty, giving good advice to his sons, and continually praying for them, that they might never sin and offend their Lord: "Lest perhaps my sons have sinned" (Job 1:5).

But his love of God showed itself really great when God, on purpose, to test his great love for him, stripped him of all his possessions at once, caused all his sons to die at the same time, and deprived him entirely in one moment of his health so that he was reduced to such a state that, covered with ulcers from head to foot, he sat on a dunghill and scraped with a potsherd the corrupt matter from all his limbs—with all these horrible misfortunes, and in the midst of all these unheard-of afflictions, he did nothing but repeat continually, with invincible and more than wonderful patience, "The Lord gave, and the Lord has taken away: as it has pleased the Lord so is it done: blessed be the name of the Lord" (Job 1:21).

But why speak of Job? Jesus Christ himself said to his apostles, as he was going to his Passion: "That the world may know, that I love the Father....Arise, let us go hence" (Jn 14:31). Here, then, we have the surest and most incontestable proof of the true love of God—patience, patience: the voluntary suffering of anything for him.

A Short Act of Love Toward God

My God, I love you above all things, and in all things, with my whole soul, because you are worthy of all love!

Twelve Short Ejaculations for the Twelve Greatest Solemnities in the Year

For the Nativity of Our Lord:

Come, my Jesus, and be born in my heart!

For the Circumcision of Our Lord:

May your name, Jesus, be my joy!

For Epiphany:

With your Magi, Jesus, I adore you, and love you!

For Easter:

My Jesus, let me first suffer, and then rejoice with you.

For the Ascension of Our Lord:

Take my heart also with you into heaven.

For Pentecost:

Holy Spirit, grant me Light, Fervor, and Perseverance!

For the Feast of Corpus Christi:

Jesus, our food! Jesus, our sweetness! Jesus, our joy!

For the Immaculate Conception:

Most holy Virgin, free from sin and full of grace at the first moment of your existence, may I be free from sin and in the grace of God at the last moment of my life!

For the Nativity of the Ever-Blessed Virgin:

Your birth, oh Blessed Virgin, was holy; may my death be holy!

For the Annunciation:

Virgin, ever blessed, you are raised to the sublime dignity of Mother of God; may I remain always faithful in his service!

For the Purification:

Most holy Virgin, purer than the angels after you had brought forth your Son, may I be purified at least after I have sinned!

For the Assumption:

Most holy Virgin, who died out of pure love, may I at least die with contrition!

On Prayer

Part I: The Necessity, Power, and Conditions of Prayer

I do not think I have written a more useful work than this one, in which I speak of prayer as a necessary and certain means of obtaining salvation and all the graces we require for that end. I say this because on the one hand I see that the absolute necessity of prayer is taught throughout the Holy Scriptures and by all the holy Fathers, while on the other hand I see that Christians are very careless in their practice of this great means of salvation. And, sadly, I see that preachers take little care to speak of it to their flocks, and confessors to their penitents.

I see, moreover, that even the spiritual books now popular do not speak sufficiently of it, for there is nothing which preachers, confessors, and spiritual books should insist upon with more warmth and energy than prayer. They teach many excellent means of keeping ourselves in the grace of God, such as avoiding occasions of sin, frequenting the sacraments, resisting temptations, hearing the Word of God, meditating on the eternal truths, and other means, all of them, I admit, most useful. But, I say, what profit is there in sermons, meditations, and all the other means pointed out by the masters of the spiritual life, if we forget to pray, since our Lord has declared that he will grant his graces to no one who does not pray?

Without prayer, in the ordinary course of providence, all the meditations we make, all our resolutions, all our promises, will be useless. If we do not pray, we shall be always unfaithful to the inspirations of God and to the promises we make him. Because, in order actually to do good, to conquer temptations, to practice virtues, and to observe God's law, it is not enough to receive illumination from God and to meditate and make resolutions. We require the actual assistance of God, and as we shall soon see he does not give this assistance except to those who pray, and pray with perseverance. The light we receive and the considerations and good resolutions that we make are of use to incite us to the act of prayer when we are in danger and tempted to transgress God's law; for then prayer will obtain for us God's help and we shall be preserved from sin. But if in such moments we do not pray, we shall be lost.

Now let us begin in the name of the Lord. The Apostle writes to Timothy: "I desire, therefore, first of all, that supplications, prayers, intercessions, and thanksgivings be made" (1 Tim 2:1). Saint Thomas explains that prayer is the lifting up of the soul to God. Petition is that kind of prayer which begs for determinate objects. When the thing sought is indeterminate (as when we say, "Incline to my aid, oh God!"), it is called supplication. Obsecration is a solemn adjuration, or representation of the grounds on which we dare to ask a favor, as when we say, "By your cross and passion, oh Lord, deliver us!" Thanksgiving is the returning of thanks for benefits received, whereby, says Saint Thomas, we merit to receive greater favors. Prayer, in a strict sense, says the holy Doctor, means recourse to God, but in its general meaning it includes all the kinds just enumerated. It is in this latter sense that the word is used in this book.

Chapter 1: The Necessity of Prayer

One author says that God has given to some animals swiftness, to others claws, to still others wings, for the preservation of their life, but he has so formed human beings that God himself is his only strength. They are completely unable to provide for their own safety, since God has willed that whatever they have, or can have, should come entirely from the assistance of his grace.

But this grace is not given in God's ordinary providence, except to those who pray for it, according to the celebrated dictum of Gennadius: "We believe that no one approaches to be saved, except at the invitation of God; that no one who is invited works out his salvation except by the help of God; that no one merits this help, unless he prays." From these two premises, on the one hand that we can do nothing without the assistance of grace, and on the other that this assistance is ordinarily only given by God to the person that prays, who does not see that as a consequence prayer is absolutely necessary to us for salvation? And although the first graces which come to us without any cooperation on our part, such as the call to faith or to penance, as Saint Augustine says, are granted by God even to those who do not pray, yet the saint considers it certain that the other graces, and especially the gift of perseverance, are not granted except in answer to prayer.

Hence it is that most theologians, following Saint Basil, Saint John Chrysostom, Clement of Alexandria, Saint Augustine, and others, teach that prayer is necessary to adults, not only because of the obligation of the precept, but because it is necessary as a means of salvation. That is to say, in the ordinary course of providence it is impossible that a Christian should be saved without recommending himself to God and asking for the graces necessary to salvation. Saint Thomas teaches the same: "After baptism, continual prayer is necessary, in order that we may enter heaven; for although our sins are remitted by baptism, there still remains concupiscence to assail us from within and the world and the devil to assail us from without." The reason then which makes us certain of the necessity of prayer is, in short, this: In order to be saved we must contend and conquer: "he…that strives for the mastery, is not crowned, except he strive lawfully" (2 Tim 2:5). But without the divine assistance we cannot resist the might of so many and so powerful enemies. Now this assistance is only granted to prayer. Therefore, without prayer there is no salvation.

That prayer is the only ordinary means of receiving the divine gifts is even more distinctly proved by Saint Thomas in another place, where he says that whatever graces God has from all eternity determined to give us, he will only give them if we pray for them. Saint Gregory says the same: "By prayer human beings merit to receive that which God had before the worlds determined to give him." Not, says Saint Thomas, that prayer is necessary so that God may know our necessities, but so that we may know the necessity of having recourse to God to obtain the help necessary for our salvation, and may thus acknowledge him to be the author of all our good. As, therefore, it is God's law that we should provide ourselves with bread by sowing corn and with wine by planting vines, so has he ordained that we should receive the graces necessary to salvation by means of prayer: "Ask, and it shall be given you: seek, and you shall find" (Mt 7:7).

We, in sum, are merely beggars, who have nothing but what God bestows on us: "But I am a beggar and poor" (Ps 39:18). The Lord, says Saint Augustine, desires to pour forth his graces upon us, but will not give them except to one who prays. This is declared in the words "Seek, and it shall be given you." Whence it follows, says Saint Teresa, that he who does not seek, does not receive. As moisture is necessary for the life of plants, to prevent their drying up, so, says Saint John Chrysostom, is prayer necessary for our salvation. Or, as he says in another place, prayer vivifies the soul as the soul vivifies the body: "As the body without soul cannot live, so the soul without prayer is dead and stinking." He says "stinking" because the person who omits to recommend himself to God at once begins to be defiled with sins. Prayer is also called the food of the soul because the body cannot be supported without food nor can the soul, says Saint Augustine, be kept alive without prayer.

Prayer is the most necessary weapon of defense against our enemies. He who does not avail himself of it, says Saint Thomas, is lost. He does not doubt that the reason for Adam's fall was that he did not recommend himself to God when he was tempted. Saint Gelasius said the same of the rebel angels: "Receiving the grace of God in vain, they could not persevere because they did not pray." Saint Charles Borromeo, in a pastoral letter, observes that among all the means of salvation recommended by Jesus Christ in the Gospel the first place is given to prayer. Saint Charles concludes that prayer is "the beginning, the progress, and the completion of all virtues." So that in darkness, distress, and danger, we have no other hope than to raise our eyes to God and with fervent prayers to beseech his mercy to save us: "as we know not," said King Josaphat, "what to do, we can only turn our eyes to you" (2 Chr 20:12). This also was David's practice, who could find no other means of safety from his enemies than continual prayer to God to deliver him from their snares: "My eyes are ever towards the Lord: for he shall pluck my feet out of the snare" (Ps 24:15). So he did nothing but pray: "I cried unto you, save me: that I may keep your commandments" (Ps 118:146). Lord, turn your eyes to me, have pity on me, and save me; for I can do nothing, and beside you there is none that can help me.

And, indeed, how could we ever resist our enemies and observe God's precepts—especially since Adam's sin, which has rendered us so weak and infirm—unless we had prayer as a means whereby we can obtain from God sufficient light and strength to enable us to observe them? It is true, says Saint Augustine, that human beings, because of their weakness, are unable to fulfill some of God's commands with their present strength and the ordinary grace given to all. But they can easily, by prayer, obtain such further aid as they require for salvation: "God commands not impossibilities; but by commanding he suggests to you to do what you can, to ask for what is beyond your strength; and he helps you, that you may be able. The holy Doctor immediately adds, "Let us see how" (that is, how we are enabled to do that which we cannot)—"By medicine we can do that which our natural sickliness renders impossible." That is, by prayer we obtain a remedy for our weakness. For when we pray, God gives us strength to do that which we cannot do of ourselves. We cannot believe, continues Saint Augustine, that God would have imposed on us the observance of a law and then made the law impossible. When, therefore, he shows us that of ourselves we are unable to observe all his commands, it is simply to admonish us to do the easier things by means of the ordinary grace which he bestows on us, and then to do the more difficult things by means of the greater help which we can obtain by prayer.

Why, it will be asked, has God commanded us to do things impossible to our natural strength? Precisely for this, says Saint Augustine, that we may be incited to pray for help to do that which of ourselves we cannot do: "He commands some things which we cannot do, so that we may know what we ought to ask of him." And in another place: "The law was given, so that grace might be sought for; grace was given so that the law might be fulfilled." The law cannot be kept without grace, and God has given the law with this aim, that we may always ask him for grace to observe it. In another place he says: "The law is good, if it be used lawfully; what, then, is the lawful use of the law?" He replies: "When by the law we perceive our own weakness, and ask of God the grace to heal us."

Saint Bernard's teaching is the same: "What are we, or what is our strength, that we should be able to resist so many temptations? This is certainly what God intended, that we, seeing our deficiencies and that we have no other help, should with all humility have recourse to his mercy." God knows how useful it is to us to be obliged to pray, in order to keep us humble and to exercise our confidence. He therefore permits us to be assaulted by enemies too mighty to be overcome by our own strength, so that by prayer we may obtain from his mercy aid to resist them. It is especially to be remarked that no one can resist the impure temptations of the flesh without recommending himself to God when he is tempted. This foe is so terrible that when he fights with us he, as it were, takes away all light; he makes us forget all our meditations, all our good resolutions; he makes us disregard the truths of faith, and even almost lose fear of the divine punishments. For he conspires with our natural inclinations, which drive us with the greatest violence to the indulgence of sensual pleasures. He who in such a moment does not have recourse to God is lost. As Saint Gregory of Nyssa says, "Prayer is the bulwark of chastity," and before him Solomon, "And as I knew that I could not otherwise be continent, except God gave it…I went to the Lord, and sought him" (Wis 8:21).

Chastity is a virtue which we do not have strength to practice unless God gives it to us, and God does not give this strength except to someone who asks for it. But whoever prays for it will certainly obtain it. Nor let it be said that it seems an injustice to order a cripple to walk straight. No, says Saint Augustine, it is not an injustice, provided always that means are given him to find the remedy for his lameness. For after this, if he continues to go crooked, the fault is his own: "It is most wisely commanded that human beings should walk uprightly, so that when they see that they cannot do so themselves, they may seek a remedy to heal the lameness of sin." In sum, the same holy Doctor says that they will never know how to live well who do not know how to pray well. On the other hand, Saint Francis of Assisi says that without prayer you can never hope to find good fruit in a soul. Wrongly, therefore, do those sinners excuse themselves who say that they have no strength to resist temptation. If you do not have this strength, why do you not ask for it? That is the reproof which Saint James gives them: "You have not, because you ask not" (Jas 4:2).

There is no doubt that we are too weak to resist the attacks of our enemies. But on the other hand it is certain that God will not permit us to be tempted beyond our strength. We are weak, but God is strong. As the Apostle reasonably assured himself: "I can do all things in him who strengthens me" (Phil 4:13). He, therefore, who falls has no excuse (says Saint John Chrysostom), because he has neglected to pray. For if he had prayed, he would not have been overcome by his enemies.

Is it necessary also to have recourse to the intercession of the saints to obtain the grace of God? Not quite. But it is a lawful and useful thing to invoke the saints as intercessors to obtain for us by the merits of Jesus Christ that which we by our demerits are not worthy to receive.

If it is lawful and profitable to invoke living saints to assist us with their prayers—as the prophet Baruch did, "And pray you for us to the Lord our God" (Bar 1:13), and as God himself commanded the friends of Job to recommend themselves to his prayers, that by the merits of Job God might look favorably on them—if, then, it is lawful to recommend ourselves to the living, how can it be unlawful to invoke the saints who in heaven enjoy God face to face? This is not derogating from the honor due to God, but doubling it, for it is honoring the king not only in his person but in his servants. Therefore, says Saint Thomas, it is good to have recourse to many saints, "because by the prayers of many we can sometimes obtain that which we cannot by the prayers of one." And if anyone object—But why have recourse to the saints to pray for us, when they are already praying for all who are worthy of it?—the same Doctor answers that no one can be said to be worthy that the saints should pray for him, but "he becomes worthy by having recourse to the saint with devotion."

Again, it is questioned whether there is any use in recommending oneself to the souls in purgatory. Some say that the souls in that state cannot pray for us, and rely on the authority of Saint Thomas who says that those souls while they are being purged by pain are inferior to us and therefore "are not in a state to pray for us, but rather require our prayers." But many other Doctors, as, for example, Bellarmine, Sylvius, Cardinal Gotti, and others, affirm with great probability that we should piously believe God reveals our prayer to those holy souls so that they may pray for us, and so that the charitable interchange of mutual prayer may be kept up between them and us. It is true that those souls are not in a state to pray because, as Saint Thomas says, while suffering they are inferior to us and rather require our prayers. Nevertheless, in this state they are well able to pray, as they are friends of God. If a father keeps a son whom he tenderly loves in confinement for some fault, if the son then is not in a state to pray for himself, is that any reason why he cannot pray for others? And may he not expect to obtain what he asks, knowing as he does his father's affection for him? So the souls in purgatory, being beloved of God and confirmed in grace, have absolutely no impediment to prevent their praying for us. Still the Church does not invoke them or implore their intercession, because ordinarily they have no knowledge of our prayers. But we may piously believe that God makes our prayers known to them, and then they, full of charity as they are, most assuredly do not omit to pray for us. Saint Catherine of Bologna, whenever she desired any favor, had recourse to the souls in purgatory and was immediately heard.

But here let me digress in favor of those holy souls. If we desire the help of their prayers, it is only fair that we should remember to help them with our prayers and good works. I said it is fair, but I should have said it is a Christian duty. For charity obliges us to help our neighbor when he requires our aid. Now it is certain that among our neighbors are to be counted the souls in purgatory, who though no longer living in this world have not yet left the communion of saints. "The souls of the pious dead," says Saint Augustine, "are not separated from the Church." And Saint Thomas says that the charity which is due to the dead who died in the grace of God is only an extension of the same charity which we owe to our neighbor while living. Therefore we ought to help, according to our ability, those holy souls as our neighbors, and as their needs are greater than those of our other neighbors, our duty to help them also seems greater.

But what are the needs of those holy prisoners? It is certain that their pains are immense. The fire that tortures them, says Saint Augustine, is more excruciating than any pain a person can endure in this life. Saint Thomas moreover supposes it to be identical with the fire of hell: "The damned are tormented and the elect purified in the same fire." And this only relates to the pains of sense. But the pain of loss (that is, the privation of the sight of God) which those holy souls suffer is much greater, because not only their natural affection, but also the supernatural love of God with which they burn draws them with such violence to be united with their sovereign good that, when they see the barrier their sins have put in the way, they feel a pain so acute that if they were capable of death they could not live a moment. So that, as Saint John Chrysostom says, this pain of the privation of God tortures them more than the pain of sense: "The flames of a thousand hells together could not inflict such torments as the pain of loss by itself." Those holy souls, then, would rather suffer every other possible torture than be deprived for a single instant of the union with God for which they long. Therefore, Saint Thomas says, the pain of purgatory exceeds anything that can be endured in this life. Saint Cyril wrote to Saint Augustine: "As far as regards the infliction of suffering, these pains are the same as those of hell—their only difference being that they are not eternal." Hence we see that the pains of these holy souls are excessive. They are destined to reign with Christ, but they are withheld from taking possession of their kingdom until the time of their purgation is accomplished. And they cannot help themselves (at least not sufficiently) to throw off their chains until they have entirely satisfied the justice of God.

On the other hand, since it is certain that by our sacrifices and prayers we can relieve those holy souls, I do not know how to excuse from sin those neglect to give some assistance by prayer. If a sense of duty will not persuade us to help, let us think of the pleasure it will give Jesus Christ to see us trying to deliver his beloved spouses from prison, so that he may have them with him in paradise. Let us think of the store of merits which we can lay up by practicing this great act of charity. Let us think, too, that those souls are not ungrateful and will never forget the great benefit we do them in relieving them of their pains and obtaining for them, by our prayers, an anticipation of their entrance into glory, so that when they are there they will never neglect to pray for us. And if God promises mercy to him who practices mercy toward his neighbor, he may reasonably expect to be saved who remembers to assist those souls, so afflicted and yet so dear to God. So we may expect that if any of us ever obtains by his prayers the liberation of a soul from purgatory, that soul will say to God: "Lord, suffer not him who has delivered me from my torments to be lost." Moreover, Saint Augustine says God will cause those who in this life have most helped those holy souls, when they come to purgatory themselves, to be most helped by others. I may here observe that in practice one of the best supplications is to hear Mass for them, and during the holy Sacrifice to recommend them to God by the merits and Passion of Jesus Christ. And it is a very charitable act to recommend at the same time the souls of all those who are at the point of death.

Whatever doubt there may be as to whether or not the souls in purgatory can pray for us, and therefore whether or not it is of any use to recommend ourselves to their prayers, there can be no doubt whatever with regard to the saints. For it is certain that it is most useful to have recourse to the intercession of saints canonized by the Church, who are already enjoying the vision of God.

But to return to the question just proposed: Are we obliged to have recourse to the intercession of the saints? Saint Thomas lays it down thusly: "Every person is bound to pray, from the fact that he is bound to procure spiritual good for himself, which can only be got from God; so it can only be obtained by asking it of God." Then, he proposes the exact question, "Whether we are bound to pray to the saints to intercede for us?" And he answers as follows—in order to catch his real meaning we will quote the entire passage—"According to Dionysius, the order which God has instituted for his creatures requires that things which are remote may be brought to God by means of things which are nearer to him. Hence, as the saints in heaven are nearest of all to him, the order of his law requires that we who 'remaining in the Body are absent from the Lord' should be brought to him by means of the saints; and this is effected by the divine goodness pouring forth his gifts through them. And as the path of our return to God should correspond to the path of the good things which proceed from him to us, it follows that, as the benefits of God come down to us by means of the supplications of the saints, we ought to be brought to God by the same way, so that a second time we may receive his benefits by the mediation of the saints. Hence it is that we make them our intercessors with God, and as it were our mediators, when we ask them to pray for us."

Note well the words, "The order of God's law requires," and especially note the last words, "As the benefits of God come down to us by means of the supplications of the saints, in the same way we must be brought back to God, so that a second time we may receive his benefits by the mediation of the saints." So that, according to Saint Thomas, the order of the divine law requires that we mortals should be saved by means of the saints, in that we receive by their intercession the help necessary for our salvation. He then puts the objection that it appears superfluous to have recourse to the saints, since God is infinitely more merciful than they and more ready to hear us. To which he answers: "God has so ordered things, not on account of any lack of mercy on his part, but to keep the right order, which he has universally established, of working by means of secondary causes. It is not for lack of his mercy, but to preserve the order in the creation."

And if this is true of the saints, how much more is it true of the intercession of the Mother of God. Saint Thomas says that the saints, in proportion to the merits by which they have obtained grace for themselves, are able also to save others, but that Jesus Christ and so also his mother have merited so much grace that they can save all men. "It is a great thing in any saint that he should have grace enough for the salvation of many besides himself; but if he had enough for the salvation of all men, this would be the greatest of all; and this is the case with Christ, and with the Blessed Virgin."

Saint Bernard speaks thus to Mary: "Through you we have access to your Son, oh discoverer of grace and mother of salvation, that through you he may receive us, who through you was given to us." These words signify that as we only have access to the Father by means of the Son, who is the mediator of justice, so we only have access to the Son by means of the mother, who is mediator of grace and who obtains for us by her intercession the gifts which Jesus Christ has merited for us. And therefore, Saint Bernard says in another place, Mary has received a twofold fullness of grace. The first was the Incarnation of the Word, who was made man in her most holy womb. The second is that fullness of grace which we receive from God by means of her prayers. Hence the saint adds: "God has placed the fullness of all good in Mary, that if we have any hope, any grace, any salvation, we may know that it overflows from her who ascends abounding with delights. She is a garden of delights, whose odors spread abroad and abound—that is, the gifts of graces."

So whatever good we have from God we receive by the intercession of Mary. Why is this so? Because, says Saint Bernard, it is God's will. But the more precise reason is deduced from the expression of Saint Augustine that Mary is justly called our mother because she cooperated by her charity in the birth of the faithful to the life of grace, by which we become members of Jesus Christ, our head. Therefore, as Mary cooperated by her charity in the spiritual birth of the faithful, so also God willed that she should cooperate by her intercession to make them enjoy the life of grace in this world and the life of glory in the next. And therefore the Church makes us call her and salute her, without any circumlocution, by the names "our life, our sweetness, and our hope." Hence Saint Bernard exhorts: "Go to Mary, I say, without hesitation; the Son will hear the mother."

Let us conclude this first point with the gist of all that has been said hitherto. He who prays is certainly saved. He who does not is certainly damned. All the blessed (except infants) have been saved by prayer. All the damned have been lost through not praying. If they had prayed, they would not have been lost. And this is, and will be, their greatest torment in hell: to think how easily they might have been saved, just by asking God for his grace, but that now it is too late—the time of prayer is gone.

Chapter 2: The Value of Prayer

Our prayers are so dear to God that he has appointed the angels to present them to him as soon as they come forth from our mouths. "The angels," says Saint Hilary, "preside over the prayers of the faithful and offer them daily to God." This is that smoke of the incense, the prayers of saints, which Saint John saw ascending to God from the hand of the angel (Rev 8:4) and which he saw elsewhere represented by golden vials full of sweet odors and acceptable to God. But in order to understand better the value of prayers in God's sight, it is enough to read the innumerable promises God makes to those who pray, both in the Old and New Testaments. "Cry to me and I will hear you" (Jer 33:3). "Call upon me in the day of trouble: I will deliver you" (Ps 49:15). "Ask, and it shall be given you: seek, and you shall find: knock, and it shall be opened to you" (Mt 7:7). "Your Father who is in heaven will give good things to them that ask him" (Mt 7:11). There are a thousand similar texts, but it would take too long to quote them.

God wills us to be saved. But for our greater good he wills us to be saved as conquerors. While, therefore, we remain here we have to live in continual warfare. Says Saint John Chrysostom, "No one can be crowned without victory." We are very feeble, and our enemies are many and mighty. How shall we be able to defeat them? Let us take courage and say with the Apostle, "I can do all things in him who strengthens me" (Phil 4:13). By prayer we can do all things, for by this means God will give us that strength which we need.

God knows the great good it does us to be obliged to pray and therefore permits us to be assaulted by our enemies in order that we may ask him for the help which he offers and promises to us. But as he is pleased when we run to him in our dangers, so is he displeased when he sees us neglectful of prayer. God thinks himself betrayed by those whom when they find themselves surrounded by temptations do not run to him for assistance. For he desires to help us and only waits to be asked and then gives abundant help. This is strikingly shown by Isaiah when on God's behalf he told King Achaz to ask for some sign to prove to himself God's readiness to help him: "Ask you a sign of the Lord your God" (Isa 7:11). The faithless king answered: "I will not ask, and I will not tempt [test] the Lord," for he trusted in his own power to overcome his enemies without God's aid. And for this the prophet reproved him: "Hear you therefore, O house of David: Is it a small thing for you to be grievous to men, that you are grievous to my God also?" (Isa 7:13). For that person is offensive to God who will not ask him for the graces which he offers.

If God were to allow us to present our petitions to him once a month, even this would be a great favor. The kings of the earth give audiences a few times a year, but God gives a continual audience. Saint John Chrysostom writes that God is always waiting to hear our prayers and that a case never occurred when he neglected to hear a petition offered to him properly. And in another place he says that when we pray to God, before we have finished recounting to him our requests he has already heard us. We even have the promise of God to do this: "as they are yet speaking, I will hear" (Isa 65:24).

We are so poor that we have nothing. But if we pray we are no longer poor. If we are poor, God is rich, and God, as the Apostle says, is "rich unto all that call upon him" (Rom 10:12). Since, therefore we have a Lord of infinite power and infinite riches, let us not go to him for little valueless things, but let us ask some great thing of him. If a person went to a king to ask some petty coin, like a penny, that man would only insult his king. On the other hand, we honor God, his mercy and his generosity, when, though we see how miserable we are and how unworthy of any kindness, we still ask for great graces, trusting in the goodness of God and in his faithfulness to his promises to grant the one who prays whatever grace he asks: "Ask whatever you will, and it shall be done unto you" (Jn 15:7).

On this point, then, we have to fix all our attention, namely, to pray with confidence, feeling sure that by prayer all the treasures of heaven are thrown open to us. "Let us attend to this," says Saint John Chrysostom, "and we shall open heaven to ourselves." Prayer is a treasure; he who prays most receives most. Saint Bonaventure says that every time a person has recourse to God by fervent prayer he gains good things that are of more value than the whole world. Some devout souls spend a great deal of time in reading and in meditating, but pay little attention to prayer. There is no doubt that spiritual reading and meditation on the eternal truths are very useful things, "but," says Saint Augustine, "it is of much more use to pray." By reading and meditation we learn our duty, but by prayer we obtain the grace to do it: "It is better to pray than to read: by reading we know what we ought to do; by prayer we receive what we ask."

And, therefore, as Saint Isidore observes, the devil is never busier trying to distract us with the thoughts of worldly cares than when he perceives us praying and asking God for grace. Why? Because the enemy sees that at no other time do we gain so many treasures of heavenly goods as when we pray. This is the chief fruit of mental prayer, to ask God for the graces we need for perseverance and eternal salvation, and it is chiefly for this reason that mental prayer is morally necessary for the soul, to enable it to preserve itself in the grace of God. For if a person does not remember in the time of meditation to ask for the help necessary for his perseverance, he will not do so at any other time, because without meditation he will not think of asking for it and will not even think of the need to ask for it. On the other hand, he who meditates every day will easily see the needs of his soul, its dangers, and the necessity of his prayer, and so he will pray and will obtain the graces which will enable him to persevere and save his soul. Father Segneri said of himself that when he began to meditate he aimed rather at exciting affections than at making prayers. But when he came to know the necessity and the immense utility of prayer, he more and more applied himself in his long mental prayer to making petitions.

"I will cry like a young swallow," said the devout King Hezekiah (Isa 38:14). The young of the swallow does nothing but cry to its mother for help and for food. So should we all do if we would preserve our life of grace. We should be always crying to God for aid to avoid the death of sin and to advance in his holy love. The ancient Fathers, who were our first instructors in the spiritual life, held a conference to determine which was the exercise most useful and most necessary for eternal salvation. They agreed that it was to repeat over and over again the short prayer of David, "Incline unto my aid, oh God!" "This," says Cassian, "is what everyone ought to do who wishes to be saved: He ought always to be saying, My God, help me! My God, help me!" We ought to do this the first thing when we wake up in the morning and then to continue doing it in all our needs and in setting about all our business, whether spiritual or temporal, and most especially when we find ourselves troubled by any temptation or passion. Saint Bonaventure says that at times we obtain a grace sooner by a short prayer than by many other good works. Saint Ambrose says that those who pray obtain what they ask while they are praying, because the very act of prayer is the same as receiving. Hence Saint John Chrysostom wrote that "there is nothing more powerful than one who prays," because such a person is made partaker of the power of God. To arrive at perfection, said Saint Bernard, we must meditate and pray. By meditation we see what we want; by prayer we receive what we want.

In sum, to save one's soul without prayer is most difficult, and perhaps even impossible, according to the ordinary course of God's providence. But by praying our salvation is made secure and very easy. It is not necessary for salvation to go among the heathen and give up our life. It is not necessary to retire into the desert and eat nothing but herbs. What does it cost us to say, My God, help me! Lord, assist me! Have mercy on me! Is there anything easier than this? And this little will suffice to save us if we will be diligent in doing it. Saint Laurence Justinian especially exhorts us to oblige ourselves to say a prayer when we begin any work. Cassian attests that the principal advice of the ancient Fathers was to have recourse to God with short but frequent prayers. Let no one, says Saint Bernard, think lightly of prayer, because God values it, and then gives us either what we ask or what is even more useful to us. And let us understand that if we do not pray we have no excuse, because the grace of prayer is given to everyone. It is in our power to pray whenever we will, as David said of himself: "With me is prayer to the God of my life. I will say to God: You are my support" (Ps 41:9–10).

Chapter 3: Conditions of Prayer

Jesus Christ has promised that whatever we ask his Father in his name his Father will give us. But always with the understanding that we ask under the proper conditions. Many seek, says Saint James, and obtain not because they seek improperly: "You ask, and receive not; because you ask amiss" (Jas 4:3). So Saint Basil, following out the argument of the Apostle, says, "you sometimes ask and receive not, because you have asked badly, either without faith or with levity; or you have requested things not fit for you, or you have not persevered." "Faithlessly," that is, with little faith or confidence; "Lightly," with little desire for the grace you request; "Things not fit for you," when you seek good things that will not be conducive to your salvation. Or you have left off praying and have lost "perseverance." Hence Saint Thomas reduces to four the conditions required in prayer in order that it may procure its effect. These four conditions require that a person pray: (1) *for himself*; (2) *for things necessary for salvation*; (3) *piously*; and (4) *with perseverance.*

Actually, no souls that really love God neglect to pray for poor sinners. For how is it possible for a person who loves God and knows what love he has for our souls and how our Savior desires us to pray for sinners—how is it possible, I say, that he should be able to look with indifference on the poor souls living as slaves of hell, without being moved to importune God with frequent prayers to give light and strength to these wretched beings, so that they may emerge from their miserable state of living death? It is true that God has not promised to grant our requests when those for whom we pray put a positive impediment in the way of their conversion. But still, God has often deigned, at the prayer of his servants, to bring back the most blinded and obstinate sinners to a state of salvation by means of extraordinary graces. Therefore let us never omit to recommend poor sinners to God for one who prays for others will find that his prayers for himself are heard much sooner.

Saint Augustine, explaining the words of the Gospel, "whatever ye shall ask in my name," says that "nothing which is asked in a way detrimental to salvation is asked in the name of the Savior." Sometimes, says the same Father, we seek some temporal favors and God does not hear us. But he does not hear us because he loves us and wants to be merciful to us. "A person may pray faithfully for the necessities of this life, and God may mercifully refuse to hear him; because the physician knows better than the patient what is good for the sick." The physician who loves his patient will not allow him to have those things which he sees would do him harm. Therefore, when men ask God for health or riches he often denies them because he loves them, knowing that these things would be to them an occasion of losing his grace, or at any rate of growing tepid in the spiritual life. Not that we mean to say that it is any defect to pray to God for necessaries of this present life, so far as they are not inconsistent with our eternal salvation. Nor is it a defect, says Saint Thomas, to have anxiety about such goods if it is not inordinate. The defect consists in desiring and seeking these temporal goods and in having an inordinate anxiety about them, as if they were our highest good. Therefore when we ask of God these temporal favors, we ought always to ask them with resignation and with the condition that they will be useful to our souls.

It often happens that we pray God to deliver us from some dangerous temptation, and yet God does not hear us but permits the temptation to continue troubling us. In such a case, let us understand that God permits even this for our greater good. It is not temptation or bad thoughts that separate us from God, but our consent to the evil. When a soul in temptation recommends herself to God and by his aid resists, how she then advances in perfection, and unites herself more closely to God! This is the reason why God does not hear her. Even in temptations we ought to pray with resignation, saying, Lord, deliver me from this trouble, if it is expedient to deliver me; and if not, at least give me help to resist. And here is what Saint Bernard says, that when we beg any grace of God he either gives us that which we ask or some other more useful to us. He often leaves us to be buffeted by the waves in order to test our faithfulness for our greater profit. It seems then that he is deaf to our prayers. But no, let us be sure that God then really hears us and is secretly aiding us and strengthening us by his grace to resist all the assaults of our enemies. See how he himself assures us of this by the mouth of the Psalmist: "You called upon me in affliction, and I delivered you: I heard you in the secret place of tempest: I proved you at the waters of contradiction" (Ps 80:8).

The Humility With Which We Should Pray

We all ought to feel that we are standing on the edge of a precipice, suspended over the abyss of all sins and supported only by the thread of God's grace. If this thread fails us we shall certainly fall into the gulf "unless the Lord had been my helper, my soul had almost dwelt in hell" (Ps 93:17).

Without the aid of grace we cannot do any good work nor even think a good thought. As the eye cannot see without light, so, said Saint Augustine, we can do no good without grace. The Apostle had said the same thing before him: "Not that we are sufficient to think anything of ourselves, as of ourselves; but our sufficiency is from God" (2 Cor 3:5). And David had said it before Saint Paul: "Unless the Lord build the house, they labor in vain that build it" (Ps 126:1). In vain do we weary ourselves to become saints, unless God lends a helping hand: "Unless the Lord keep the city, he watches in vain that keep it" (Ps 126:1). If God did not preserve the soul from sins, in vain would she try to preserve herself by her own strength.

If a person says he has no fear, it is a sign that he trusts in himself and in his good resolutions. But such a one deceives himself, because through trust in his own strength he neglects to fear, and through not fearing he neglects to recommend himself to God, and then he certainly will fall. And so, for like reasons, we should all abstain from noticing with any vainglory the sins of other people. Rather we should then esteem ourselves as worse in ourselves than they are and should say, "Lord, if you had not helped me, I should have done worse." Otherwise, to punish us for our pride God will permit us to fall into worse and more shameful sins. For this reason Saint Paul instructs us to labor for our salvation in fear and trembling (Phil 2:12). For he who has a great fear of falling distrusts his own strength and therefore places his confidence in God and will have recourse to him in dangers, and God will aid him and thus he will vanquish his temptations and be saved. Saint Philip Neri, walking one day through Rome, kept saying, "I am in despair!" A certain religious chided him for this. The saint thereupon said, "My father, I am in despair for myself; but I trust in God." So must we do if we would be saved. We must always live in despair of doing anything by our own strength. In so doing we shall imitate Saint Philip, who used to say to God the first moment he woke in the morning, "Lord, keep your hands over Philip this day; for if not, Philip will betray you."

This, then, we may conclude with Saint Augustine, is all the great science of a Christian—to know that he is nothing and can do nothing. For then he will never neglect to furnish himself by prayer to God with that strength which he has not of himself and which he needs in order to resist temptations and to do good. And so, with the help of God, who never refuses anything to the one who prays to him with humility, he will be able to do all things. The prayer of a humble soul penetrates the heavens and presents itself before the throne of God and does not leave without God's looking on it and hearing it. And though the soul be guilty of any amount of sin, God never despises a heart that humbles itself: "A contrite and humbled heart, O God, you will not despise" (Ps 50:19).

It will be useful to introduce here the advice which the pious Palafox, Bishop of Osma, gives to spiritual persons who desire to become saints. It occurs in a note to the eighteenth letter of Saint Teresa, which she wrote to her confessor to give him an account of all the grades of supernatural prayer with which God had favored her. Therefore, he says, it is superfluous and even presumptuous to desire and ask for these supernatural gifts, when the true and only way to become a saint is to exercise oneself in virtue and in the love of God. This is done by means of prayer and by corresponding to the inspirations and assistance of God, who wishes nothing so much as to see us saints: "For this is the will of God, your sanctification" (1 Thess 4:3).

Hence Bishop Palafox, speaking of the grades of supernatural prayer mentioned in Saint Teresa's letter—namely, the prayer of quiet, the sleep or suspension of the faculties, the prayer of union, ecstasy or rapture, flight and impetus of the spirit, and the wound of love—says very wisely that as regards the *prayer of quiet*, what we ought to ask of God is that he would free us from attachment to, and desire for, worldly goods which give no peace but bring disquiet and affliction to the soul, "Vanity of vanities," as Solomon well called them, "and vexation of spirit" (Eccl 1:2,14). The heart will never find true peace if it does not empty itself of all that is not God, so as to leave itself entirely free for his love that he alone may possess the whole of it. But this the soul cannot do of itself. It must obtain it of God by repeated prayers. As regards the *sleep and suspension of the faculties*, we ought to ask God for grace to keep them asleep regarding all that is temporal and only awake to consider God's goodness and to set our hearts upon his love and eternal happiness. As regards the *union of the faculties*, let us pray him to give us grace not to think nor to seek nor to wish anything but what God wills, since all sanctity and the perfection of love consist in uniting our will with the will of God. As regards *ecstasy and rapture*, let us pray God to draw us out of the inordinate love of ourselves and of creatures and to draw us entirely to himself. As regards *the flight of the spirit*, let us pray him to give us grace to live altogether detached from this world and to do as the swallows, which do not settle on the ground even to feed, but take their food flying; so should we use our temporal goods for all that is necessary for the support of life, but always flying, without settling on the ground to look for earthly pleasures. As regards *impulse of spirit*, let us pray him to give us courage and strength to do violence to ourselves whenever it is necessary, for resisting the assaults of our enemies, for conquering our passions, and for accepting sufferings even in the midst of desolation and dryness of spirit. Finally, as regards *the wound of love*, as a wound by its pain perpetually renews the remembrance of what we suffer, so ought we to pray God to wound our hearts with his holy love in such a way that we shall always be reminded of his goodness and the love which he has borne us. And thus we should live in continual love of him and be always pleasing him with our works and our affections. But none of these graces can be obtained without prayer. With prayer, provided it be humble, confident, and persevering, all are obtained.

The Confidence With Which We Should Pray

When did it ever happen that a person had confidence in God and was lost? Says Saint Augustine: "God is not a deceiver, that he should offer to support us, and then when we lean upon him should slip away from us." David calls that one happy who trusts in God: "Blessed is the man that trusts in you" (Ps 83:13). And why? Because he who trusts in God will always find himself surrounded by God's mercy (Ps 31:10), so that he shall be surrounded and guarded by God on every side in such a way that he shall be prevented from losing his soul.

David said that our confidence in God ought to be firm as a mountain, which is not moved by each gust of wind. It is this which our Lord recommends to us if we wish to obtain the graces which we ask: "Whatsoever you ask when ye pray, believe that you shall receive; and they shall come unto you" (Mk 11:24). Whatever grace you require, be sure of having it, and so you shall obtain it.

But on what am I, a miserable sinner, to found this certain confidence of obtaining what I ask? On what? On the promise made by Jesus Christ, "Ask, and you shall receive" (Jn 16:24). "Who will fear to be deceived, when the truth promises?" says Saint Augustine. How can we doubt our being heard, when God, who is truth itself, promises to give us what we ask of him in prayer? "We should not be exhorted to ask," says the same Father, "unless he meant to give." Certainly God would not have exhorted us to ask him for favors, if he had not determined to grant them. But this is the very thing to which he exhorts us so strongly and which is repeated so often in the Scriptures—pray, ask, seek, and you shall obtain what you desire. In order that we may pray to him with due confidence, our Savior has taught us in the Our Father that when we have recourse to him for the graces necessary to salvation (all of which are included in the petitions of the Lord's Prayer) we should call him not Lord but Father because it is his will that we should ask God for grace with the same confidence with which a son, when in want or sick, asks food or medicine from his own father. If a son is dying of hunger, he has only to make his case known to his father and his father will forthwith provide him with food. If he has received a bite from a venomous serpent, he has only to show his father the wound and the father will immediately apply whatever remedy he has.

Trusting, therefore, in God's promises, let us always pray with confidence. "Let us hold fast the confession of our hope without wavering, for he is faithful that has promised" (Heb 10:23). As it is perfectly certain that God is faithful in his promises, so ought our faith also to be perfectly certain that he will hear us when we pray. And although sometimes, when we are in a state of aridity or disturbed by some fault we have committed, we perhaps do not feel while praying that sensible confidence which we would wish to experience, yet for all this let us force ourselves to pray and to pray without ceasing, for God will not neglect to hear us. No, rather will he hear us more readily, because we shall then pray with more distrust of ourselves and confiding only in the goodness and faithfulness of God who has promised to hear those who pray to him.

Saint John says that he who reposes a sure trust in God certainly becomes a saint (1 Jn 3:3). For God gives abundant graces to them that trust in him. By this confidence the host of martyrs, of virgins, even of children, in spite of the dread of the torments which their persecutors prepared for them, overcame both their tortures and their persecutors. Sometimes we pray, but it seems to us that God will not hear us. Let us not then neglect to persevere in prayer and in hope. Let us then say with Job, "Although he should kill me, I will trust in him" (Job 13:15). Oh my God, though you have driven me from your presence, I will not cease to pray and to hope in your mercy. A woman had a daughter possessed by a devil, and prayed our Savior to deliver her: "Have mercy on me, O Lord…my daughter is grievously troubled by a devil" (Mt 15:22). Our Lord answered that he was not sent for the gentiles, of whom she was one, but for the Jews. She, however, did not lose heart, but renewed her prayer with confidence: "Lord, help me!" Jesus replied, "It is not good to take the bread of the children, and to cast it to the dogs." But, my Lord, she answered, even the dogs are allowed to have the fragments of bread which fall from the table. Then our Savior, seeing the great confidence of this woman, praised her, saying, "O woman, great is your faith: be it done to you as you will." For who, says Ecclesiasticus, has ever called on God for aid, who has been neglected and left unaided by him? (2:12).

When we find ourselves weak and unable to overcome any passion or any great difficulty so as to fulfill that which God requires of us, let us take courage. Let us not say, as some do: I cannot, I distrust myself. With our own strength certainly we can do nothing, but with God's help we can do everything. If God said to anyone, Take this mountain on your back, and carry it, for I am helping you, would not the person be a mistrustful fool if he answered, I will not take it for I have not strength to carry it? And thus, when we know how miserable and weak we are, and when we find ourselves most encompassed with temptations, let us not lose heart, but let us lift up our eyes to God and say with David, "The Lord is my helper: I will not fear what can be done unto me" (Ps 117:6). With the help of my Lord, I shall overcome and laugh to scorn all the assaults of my foes. And when we find ourselves in danger of offending God, or in any other critical position, and are too confused to know what is best to be done, let us recommend ourselves to God, saying, "The Lord is my light and my salvation, whom shall I fear?" (Ps 26:1).

But I am a sinner, you will say; and in the Scripture I read, "God doth not hear sinners" (Jn 9:31). Saint Thomas answers that this was said by the blind man, who when he spoke had not as yet been enlightened. Though, adds Saint Thomas, it is true that God does not hear the petition which the sinner makes when he asks from a desire of continuing to sin, as for instance if he were to ask help to enable him to take revenge on his enemy or to execute any other bad intention. The same holds good for the sinner who prays God to save him but has no desire to quit the state of sin. There are some unhappy persons who love the chains with which the devil keeps them bound like slaves. The prayers of such men are not heard by God. For what greater presumption can there be than to ask favors of a prince whom he not only often has offended but whom he intends to offend still more? This is the meaning of the Holy Spirit when he says that the prayer of one who turns away his ears so as not to hear what God commands is odious to God (Prov 28:9). To these people God says, It is of no use your praying to me, for I will turn my eyes from you and will not hear you (Isa 1:15). Such precisely was the prayer of the King Antiochus, who prayed to God and made great promises, but insincerely and with a heart obstinate in sin, the sole object of his prayer being to escape the punishment that hung over him. Therefore God did not hear his prayer, but caused him to die devoured by worms (2 Macc 9:13).

But others, who sin through frailty or by the violence of some great passion, and who groan under the yoke of the enemy and desire to break these chains of death and therefore ask the assistance of God—the prayer of these, if it is persevering, will certainly be heard by him, who says that everyone who asks receives and that he who seeks grace finds it (Mt 7:8). And in Saint Luke, our Lord, when speaking of the man who gave all the loaves he had to his friend, not so much because of his friendship as because of the other's strong request, says, "If he shall continue knocking, I say to you, although he will not rise and give him, because he is his friend, yet because of his importunity, he will rise, and give him as many as he needs. So that persevering prayer obtains mercy from God, even for those who are not his friends. That which is not obtained through friendship, says Saint John Chrysostom, is obtained by prayer. And Saint Basil does not doubt that even sinners obtain what they ask, if they persevere in praying. Saint Gregory said the same: "The sinner also shall cry, and his prayer shall reach to God." So Saint Jerome, who says that even the sinner can call God his Father if he prays him to receive him anew as a son, after the example of the prodigal son who called him Father ("Father, I have sinned") even though he had not as yet been pardoned.

Saint John Chrysostom says that the only time God is angry with us is when we neglect to ask him for his gifts: "He is only angry when we do not pray." And how can it ever happen that God will not hear a soul who asks him for favors all according to his pleasure? When the soul says to him, Lord, I do not ask you for goods of this world, riches, pleasures, honors; I only ask you for your grace: deliver me from sin, grant me a good death, give me paradise, give me your holy love (which is that grace which Saint Francis de Sales says we should seek more than all others), give me resignation to your will—how is it possible that God should not hear? What petitions will you, oh my God, ever hear (says Saint Augustine), if you do not hear those which are made after your own heart? But, above all, our confidence ought to revive when we pray to God for spiritual graces, as Jesus Christ says, "If you then, being evil, know how to give good gifts to your children, how much more will your Father from heaven give the good Spirit to them that ask him!" (Lk 11:13).

The Perseverance Required in Prayer

Our prayers, then, must be humble and confident. But this is not enough to obtain final perseverance and thereby eternal life. Individual prayers will obtain the individual graces which they ask of God, but unless they are persevering they will not obtain final perseverance which, as it is the accumulation of many graces, requires many prayers, right up until death. The grace of salvation is not a single grace but a chain of graces, all of which are at last linked with the grace of final perseverance. Now to this chain of graces there ought to correspond another chain of our prayers. If we, by neglecting to pray, break the chain of our prayers, the chain of graces will be broken too, and as it is by this that we have to obtain salvation we shall not be saved.

It is true that we cannot merit final perseverance. Nevertheless, says Saint Augustine, this great gift of perseverance can in a manner be merited by our prayers. And Suarez adds that those who pray infallibly obtain it. But to obtain it and to save ourselves, says Saint Thomas, a persevering and continual prayer is necessary: "After baptism continual prayer is necessary in order that a person may enter heaven." And before this, our Savior himself had said it over and over: "we ought always to pray, and not to faint"; "Watch ye, therefore, praying at all times, that you may be accounted worthy to escape all these things that are to come, and to stand before the Son of Man" (Lk 18:1; 21:36). The same had been previously said in the Old Testament: "Let nothing hinder you from praying always" (Eccl 18:22); "Bless God at all times: and desire of him to direct your ways"

(Tob 4:20). And Saint Jerome said that the more persevering and importunate our prayers are, so much the more are they acceptable to God.

Happy are they, says God, who listen to me and watch continually with holy prayers at the gates of my mercy; and Isaiah says, "blessed are all they that wait for him" (Isa 30:18). Blessed are they who until the end wait in prayer for their salvation from God. Therefore in the Gospel Jesus Christ exhorts us to prayer. But how? "Ask, and it shall be given you: seek, and you shall find: knock, and it shall be opened to you" (Lk 11:9). Would it not have been enough to have said, "ask"? Why add "seek" and "knock"? No, it was not superfluous to add them. For thereby our Savior wished us to understand that we ought to do as the poor who go begging. If they do not receive the alms they ask, they do not cease asking.

But someone will say, since God can give me the grace of perseverance, and indeed wishes to, why does he not give it to me all at once, when I ask him? The holy Fathers assign many reasons. God does not grant it at once but delays it, first, so that he may better prove our confidence, and further, says Saint Augustine, so that we may long for it more vehemently. Great gifts, he says, should be greatly desired, for good things soon obtained are not held in the same estimation as those which have been long looked for. Again, he does so that we may not forget him. If we were already sure of persevering and of being saved, and if we did not have continual need of God's help to preserve us in his grace and to save us, we should soon forget God. Want makes the poor keep resorting to the houses of the rich. So God, to draw us to himself, as Saint John Chrysostom says, and to see us often at his feet, in order that he may thus be able to do us greater good, delays giving us the complete grace of salvation until the hour of our death: "It is not because he rejects our prayers that he delays, but by this contrivance he wishes to make us careful and to draw us to himself." Again, he does so in order that we, by persevering in prayer, may unite ourselves more closely to him with the sweet bonds of love: "Prayer," says the same Saint John Chrysostom, "which is accustomed to converse with God, is no slight bond of love to him."

But, until when must we pray? Always, says the same saint, until we receive favorable sentence of eternal life, that is to say, until our death. And he goes on to say that those who resolve, I will never to leave off praying until they are saved, will most certainly be saved. The Apostle writes that many run for the prize but that he only receives it who runs until he wins (1 Cor 9:24). It is not then enough for salvation simply to pray, but we must pray always in order to receive the crown which God promises but promises only to those who are constant in prayer to the end.

Part II: The Grace of Prayer Is Given to All

Taking for granted, then, that prayer is necessary for the attainment of eternal life, we ought also to take for granted that everyone has sufficient aid from God to enable him actually to pray, without need of any further special grace, and that by prayer he may obtain all other graces necessary to enable him to persevere in keeping the commandments and so gain eternal life. No one who is lost can ever excuse himself by saying that it was through lack of the aid necessary for his salvation. For as God in the natural order has ordained that we should be born naked and in want of several things necessary for life, but then has given us hands and intelligence to clothe ourselves and provide for our other needs, so in the supernatural order we are born unable to obtain salvation by our own strength, but God in his goodness grants to everyone the grace of prayer by which they are able to obtain all other graces which they need in order to keep the commandments and be saved.

But before I explain this point, I must prove two preliminary propositions: first, that God wills all men to be saved and therefore that Jesus Christ died for all; secondly, that God on his part gives to all men the graces necessary for salvation, by which everyone may be saved if he corresponds to them.

Chapter 1: God Wills All People to Be Saved

God loves all things that he has created: "For you love all things that are, and hate none of the things which you have made" (Wis 11:25). Now love cannot be idle. Love necessarily implies benevolence, so that the person who loves cannot help doing good to the person beloved whenever there is an opportunity: "Love persuades us to do those things which we believe to be good for us whom we love," says Aristotle. If, then, God loves all men, he must in consequence will that all should obtain eternal salvation, which is the one and sovereign good of human beings, seeing that it is the one end for which they are created: "you have your fruit unto sanctification; and the end is life everlasting" (Rom 6:22).

Saint Thomas asserts in several places that God truly wills all men and each individual to be saved. On the text "Him that comes to me I will not cast out," he quotes Saint John Chrysostom, who makes our Lord say, "If then I was incarnate for the salvation of men, how can I cast them out? And this is what he means when he says, Therefore I cast them not out, because I came down from heaven to do my Father's will, who wills all men to be saved." God by his most liberal will gives grace to everyone who prepares himself. He "will have all men to be saved" (1 Tim 2:4).

Therefore the grace of God is wanting to no one, but as far as he is concerned he communicates it to everyone. Again, Chrysostom declares the same thing more expressly in his explanation of the text of Saint Paul, "God wills all men to be saved." "In God," he says, "the salvation of all men, considered in itself, belongs to that class of things which he wishes, and this is his antecedent will; but when the good of justice is taken into consideration, and the rightness of punishing sin, in this sense he does not will the salvation of all, and this is his consequent will." He adds the comparison of a merchant, who antecedently wills to save all his merchandise; but if a tempest comes on, he willingly throws it overboard in order to preserve his own life. In like manner, he says, God, considering the iniquity of some persons, wills them to be punished in satisfaction of his justice and consequently does not will them to be saved; but antecedently, and considered in itself, he wills with a true desire the salvation of all men. So that God's will to save all people is on his part absolute; it is only conditional on the part of the object willed, that is, if we will correspond to what the right order demands, in order to be saved. "Nor yet," he says, "is there imperfection on the part of God's will, but on the part of the thing willed; because it is not accepted with all the circumstances which are required, in order to be saved in the proper manner." And he again and more distinctly declares what he means by antecedent and consequent will: "A judge antecedently wishes every man to live, but he consequently wishes a murderer to be hanged; so God antecedently wills every person to be saved, but he consequently wills some to be damned; in consequence, that is, of the exigencies of his justice."

David says: "For wrath is in his indignation; and life in his good will" (Ps 29:6). If God chastises us, he does it because our sins provoke him to indignation; but as to his will, he wills not our death, but our life, finding "Life in his will." Saint Basil says on this text that God wills all to be made partakers of life. David says elsewhere: "Our God is the God of salvation: and of the Lord, of the Lord are the issues from death" (Ps 67:21). On this Bellarmine says: "This is proper to him, this is his nature, our God is a saving God, and his are the issues from death—that is, liberation from it." So that it is God's proper nature to save all, and to deliver all from eternal death.

Again, our Lord says: "I stand at the gate, and knock. If any one shall…open…I will come in to him" (Rev 3:20). "What is there that I ought to do more to my vineyard, that I have not done to it?" (Isa 5:4). "How often would I have gathered together your children, as the hen doth gather her chickens under her wings, and you would not!" (Mt 23:37). How could our Lord have said that he stands knocking at the heart of us sinners? How exhort us so strongly to return to his arms? How reproach us by asking what more he could have done for our salvation? How say that he has willed to receive us as children if he had not a true will to save all men?

All the holy Fathers agree in saying that Jesus Christ died to obtain eternal salvation for all men. Saint Jerome: "Christ died for all; he was the only one who could be offered for all, because all were dead in sins." Saint Ambrose: "Christ came to cure our wounds; but since all do not search for the remedy…therefore he cures those who are willing; he does not force the unwilling." In another place: "He has provided for all men the means of cure, so that whoever perishes may lay the blame of his death on himself, because he would not be cured when he had a remedy; and so that, on the other hand, to all may be openly proclaimed the mercy of Christ who wills that all men should be saved." And more clearly still in another place: "Jesus did not write his will for the benefit of one, or of few, but of all; we are all inscribed therein as his heirs; the legacy is in common and belongs by right to all, the universal heritage, belonging wholly to each." Mark the words, "we are all inscribed as heirs": the Redeemer has written us all down as heirs of heaven. Saint Leo: "As Christ found no one free from guilt, so he came to deliver all." Saint Augustine, on the words of John 3:17, "God sent not his Son into the world, to judge the world, but that the world may be saved by him," says: "So, as far as it lies with the physician, he came to heal the sick." Mark the words, "as far as it lies with the physician." For God, as far as he is concerned, effectually wills the salvation of all, but (as Saint Augustine goes on to say) cannot heal the person who will not be healed: "He heals universally, but he does not heal the unwilling. For what can be happier for you than, as you have your life in your hands, so to have your health depend on your will?" When he says "He heals," he speaks of sinners who are sick and unable to get well by their own strength; when he says "universally," he declares that nothing is lacking on God's part for sinners to be healed and saved. Then when he says, "as you have your life in your hands, so your health depends on your will," he shows that God for his part really wills us all to be saved; otherwise, it would not be in our power to obtain health and eternal life.

That God truly on his part wills all men to be saved and that Jesus Christ died for the salvation of all, is certified to us by the fact that God imposes on us all the precept of hope. The reason is clear. Saint Paul calls Christian hope the anchor of the soul (Heb 6:19). Now in what could we fix this sure and firm anchor of our hope except in the truth that God wills all to be saved? "With what confidence," says Petrocorensis, "will men be able to hope for God's mercy, if it is not certain that God wills the salvation of all of them? With what confidence will they offer the death of Christ to God, in order to obtain pardon, if it is uncertain whether he was offered up for them?" And Cardinal Sfondrati says that if God had elected some to eternal life and excluded others, we should have a greater motive to despair than to hope, seeing that in fact the elect are much fewer than the damned: "No one could have a firm hope, since he would have more grounds of despair than of hope; for the reprobate are much more numerous than the elect." And if Jesus Christ had not died for the salvation of all, how could we have a sure ground to hope for salvation through the merits of Jesus Christ, without a special revelation? But Saint Augustine had no doubt when he said, "All my hope, and the certainty of my faith, is in the precious blood of Christ, which was shed for us and for our salvation." Thus the saint placed all his hope in the blood of Jesus Christ, because the faith assured him that Christ died for all.

Chapter 2: God Commonly Gives Grace to All

If God wills all to be saved, it follows that he gives to all that grace and those aids which are necessary for attaining salvation. Otherwise it could never be said that he has a true will to save all. "The effect of the antecedent will," says Saint Thomas, "by which God wills the salvation of all men, is that order of nature whose purpose is our salvation, and likewise those things which conduce to that end and which are offered to all in common, whether by nature or by grace." It is certain that God does not impose a law that it is impossible to observe. On the other hand, it is certain that without the assistance of grace the observance of the law is impossible, as Innocent I declared against the Pelagians when he said, "It is certain that as we overcome by the help of God, so without his help we must be overcome." Therefore, if God gives to all men a possible law, it follows that he also gives to all men the grace necessary to observe it, whether immediately or mediately by means of prayer. Otherwise, if God refused us both the proximate and remote grace to enable us to fulfill the law, either the law would have been given in vain or sin would be necessary, and if necessary would no longer be sin, as we shall shortly demonstrate. This is the general opinion of the Fathers. For instance, Saint Cyril of Alexandria says, "If a person endowed as others, and equally with them, with the gifts of divine grace, has fallen by his own free will, how shall Christ not be said to have saved even him since he delivered the man so far as relates to the aids granted him in order to avoid sin?" How, says the saint, can that sinner who has received the assistance of grace equally with those who remained faithful, and who has of his own accord chosen to sin, how can he blame Jesus Christ who has, as far as he is concerned, delivered him by means of the assistance granted him? Saint John Chrysostom asks, "How is it that some are vessels of wrath, others vessels of mercy?" And he answers, "Because of each person's free will, for since God is very good he manifests equal kindness to all." Then, speaking of Pharaoh whose heart is said in Scripture to have been hardened, he adds, "If Pharaoh was not saved, it must all be attributed to his own will, since no less was given to him than to those who were saved."

Saint Jerome says, "We can do no good work without him who, in giving free will, did not refuse his grace to aid every single work." Mark the words "did not refuse his grace for every single work." Saint Ambrose says, "He would never come and knock at the door unless he wished to enter; it is our fault that he does not always enter." Saint Leo: "Justly does he insist on the command, since he furnishes beforehand aid to keep it." Saint Hilary: "Now the grace of justification has abounded through one gift to all men." Innocent I: "He gives daily remedies and unless we put confidence in them and depend on them we shall never be able to overcome human errors." Saint Augustine: "It is not imputed to you as a sin if you are ignorant against your will, but only if you neglect to inquire into that about which you are ignorant. Nor is it imputed as a sin that you do not cure your wounded limbs, but that you despise him who is willing to cure you. These are your own sins, for no one is deprived of the knowledge of how to seek with advantage." So everyone receives at least the remote grace to seek, and if he makes good use of this he will receive the proximate grace to perform what at first he could not do. Saint Augustine founds all this on the principle that no person sins in doing what he cannot help; therefore if a person sins in anything he sins in what he might have avoided by the grace of God, which is lacking to no one: "No one sins in that which cannot anyhow be helped. But a person does sin, therefore it might have been helped; but only by his aid, who cannot be deceived." An evident reason by which it becomes quite clear that if the grace necessary to observe the commandments were wanting, there would be no sin.

Saint Thomas teaches the same in several places. In explaining the text, "Who will have everyone be saved" (1 Tim 2:4) he says, "and therefore grace is wanting to no one, but (as far as God is concerned) is communicated to all, as the sun is present even to the blind." As the sun sheds its light upon all, and only those are deprived of it who voluntarily blind themselves to its rays, so God communicates to all men grace to observe the law, and men are lost simply because they will not avail themselves of it. In another place: "It belongs to divine providence to provide all people with what is necessary to salvation, if only there be no impediment on our part." If, then, God gives all of us the graces necessary for salvation, and if actual grace is necessary to overcome temptations and to observe the commandments, we must necessarily conclude that he gives all of us either immediately or mediately actual grace to do good; and when mediately, no further grace is necessary to enable us to put into practice the means, such as prayer, of obtaining actual proximate grace. In another place, in the words of Saint John's Gospel, "No one comes to me, etc.," he says, "If the heart is not lifted up, this is from no defect on the part of him who draws it, who as far as he is concerned never fails, but from an impediment caused by him who is being drawn." Scotus says the same thing: "He wills to save all persons so far as rest with him and with his antecedent will by which he has given them the ordinary gifts necessary to salvation." And the Council of Cologne: "Although no one is converted unless he is drawn by the Father, yet let no one pretend to excuse himself on the plea of not being drawn. He stands at the gate and knocks by the internal and the external Word."

Nor did the Fathers speak without warrant of Scripture, for God in several places most clearly assures us that he does not neglect to assist us with his grace if we are willing to avail ourselves of it, either for perseverance if we are in a state of justification or for conversion if we are in sin. "I stand at the gate, and knock. If anyone shall hear my voice, and open to me the door, I will come in to him" (Rev 3:20). Bellarmine reasons well on this text that our Lord, who knows that we cannot open without his grace, would knock in vain at the door of his heart unless he had first conferred on us the grace to open when he will. This is exactly what Saint Thomas teaches in explaining the text. He says that God gives everyone the grace necessary for salvation, so that he may correspond to it if he will. "God by his most liberal will gives grace to everyone who prepares himself: 'Behold, I stand at the door and knock.' And therefore the grace of God is lacking to no one, but communicates itself to all men as far as it is concerned." In another place he says, "It is the business of God's providence to provide everyone with what is necessary to salvation." So that, as Saint Ambrose said, the Lord knocks at the gate because he truly wishes to enter; if he does not enter or if after entering he does not remain in our souls, it is because we prevent his entering or drive him out when he has entered.

"We have received your mercy, O God, in the midst of your temple" (Ps 47:10). On this Saint Bernard observes, "Mercy is in the midst of the temple, not in any hole and corner; it is placed in public, it is offered to all, and no one is without it except he who refuses it."

"Or despise you the riches of his goodness, and patience, and long-suffering? Know you not, that the benignity of God leads you to penance?" (Rom 2:4). You see that it is through his own malice that the sinner is not converted, because he despises the riches of the divine goodness which calls him and never ceases to move him to conversion by grace. God hates sin but at the same time never ceases loving the sinful soul while it remains on earth, and always gives it the assistance it requires for salvation: "But you spare all; because they are yours, O Lord, who love souls" (Wis 11:26). Hence we see, says Bellarmine, that God does not refuse grace to resist temptations to any sinner, however obstinate and blinded he may be. "Assistance to avoid new sin is always at hand, either immediately or mediately" (that is, by means of prayer), "so that they may ask further aid from God, by the help of which they will avoid sin." Here we may quote what God says by Ezekiel: "As I live, saith the Lord God, I desire not the death of the wicked, but that the wicked turn from his way, and live" (Ezek 33:11). Saint Peter says the same, "The Lord…deals patiently for your sake, not willing that any should perish, but that all should return to penance" (2 Pet 3:9). If therefore God wishes that all should actually be converted, it must necessarily be held that he gives to all the grace they need for actual conversion.

And so say the theologians who follow Saint Thomas—thus Soto: "I am absolutely certain and I believe that all the holy Doctors who are worthy of the name were always most positive that no one was ever deserted by God in this mortal life." And the reason is evident, for if the sinner was quite abandoned by grace, either his sins afterward committed could no longer be imputed to him or he would be under an obligation to do what he had no power to do. But it is a positive rule of Saint Augustine that there is never sin in what cannot be avoided. And this agrees with the teaching of the Apostle: "God is faithful, who will not suffer you to be tempted above that which you are able: but will make also with temptation issue, that you may be able to bear it" (1 Cor 10:13). Which "issue" means the divine assistance that God always gives to the tempted in order to enable them to resist, as Saint Cyprian explains it: "He will make with the temptation a way of escape." And Primasius more clearly: "He will so order the issue that we shall be able to endure; that is, in temptation he will strengthen you with the help of his grace, so that you may be able to bear it." Saint Augustine and Saint Thomas go so far as to say that God would be unjust and cruel if he obliged anyone to a command which he could not keep. Saint Augustine says, "It is the deepest injustice to reckon anyone guilty of sin for not doing that which he could not do." And Saint Thomas says, "God is not more cruel than human beings, but it is reckoned cruelty to oblige a person by law to do that which he cannot do; therefore we must by no means imagine this of God." "It is, however, different," he says, "when it is through his own neglect that he does not have the grace to be able to keep the commandments." In other words, when we neglect to avail ourselves of the remote grace of prayer, in order to obtain the proximate grace to enable us to keep the law.

Chapter 3: God Gives All the Grace to Pray

Assuming, then, that God wills all to be saved and that as far as he is concerned he gives to all the graces necessary for their salvation, we must say that all persons have given to them the grace to enable them actually to pray (without needing a further grace) and by prayer to obtain all further aid needed for observing the commandments and for salvation.

No Father is clearer on this point than Saint Augustine. According to him, no one is deprived of the grace of prayer whereby he may obtain help for his conversion. Otherwise, if this grace were lacking, it could not be his fault if he were not converted. "What else," he says, "is shown us but that it is he who gives us power to ask and to seek and to knock who commands us to do these things?" Again: "Once and for all receive this and understand it. Are you not yet drawn? Then pray that you may be drawn." Everyone, then, has the grace necessary for prayer. And if he makes a good use of this, he will receive grace to do what before he was unable to do. Again: "Let those who are willing but who cannot do what he wills pray that they may have such a measure as suffices for fulfilling the commandments."

Again: "Free will is admonished by command to seek the gift of God, but it would be admonished without fruit to itself unless it had first received some little love to induce it to seek such aid as would enable it to fulfill what was commanded." Mark the words, "some little love." This means "sufficient grace" whereby we are able to obtain by prayer actual grace to keep the commandments. Again: "He gives us commandments for this reason, that when we have tried to do what we are commanded and are wearied through our weakness, we may know how to ask the help of grace." Here the saint supposes that with ordinary grace we are not able to do difficult things, but that by means of prayer we can obtain the aid necessary to do them. He therefore goes on to say, "The law entered that sin might abound," when men do not implore the help of God's grace. But when, by God's invitation, they understand to whom they must appeal and thereupon invoke him, the succeeding words will be fulfilled: "Where sin abounded, grace superabounded." Here we see in express terms the lack of abundant grace and, on the other hand, the presence of ordinary and common grace which enables men to pray, and which Saint Augustine here calls "God's invitation."

In another place he says, "Free will is left to human beings in this mortal life, not to enable him to fulfill justice when he pleases but to enable him to turn with pious supplications to him by whose gift he can fulfill it." When, therefore, Augustine says that we are unable to fulfill the whole law and that prayer is the only means given to obtain help to fulfill it, he certainly supposes that God gives everyone the grace of actual prayer, without need of a further extraordinary aid not common to all. Otherwise, where this special aid was lacking, "nothing would be left to the will" to observe all the commandments, or at least the more difficult of them. And when the saint speaks like this, he certainly cannot mean that "sufficient grace" gives only the power, not the act, of prayer; for so far as relates to power, it is certain that "sufficient grace" gives power for even the most difficult works. So the holy Father evidently means (as he teaches elsewhere) that easy things, such as prayer, may well be actually accomplished by any man with "sufficient grace" and difficult things with the help obtained by prayer.

Saint Augustine elsewhere says, "Let them not deceive themselves who say, why are we commanded to abstain from evil and to do good if it is God who works in us both to will and to do it?" And he answers that when men do good they should thank God who gives them the strength to do it, and when they do not do it, they should pray to have the strength they lack. Now if people did not even have the grace for the act of prayer, they might answer, "Why are we commanded to pray, if God does not work in us to make us pray? How are we to will to pray, if we do not receive the grace necessary for actual prayer?"

Saint Thomas assumes the certainty of our proposition when he says, "It belongs to God's providence to provide every individual with what is necessary for salvation, provided he puts no impediment in the way." Since, then, it is true on the one hand that God gives to all people the graces necessary for salvation and on the other for prayer, we require the grace which enables us actually to pray and thereby to obtain further and greater assistance to enable us to do what we cannot accomplish with ordinary grace. It follows necessarily that God gives all people sufficient grace actually to pray if they will, without need of efficacious grace.

The virtue of hope is so pleasing to God that he has said he delights in those who trust in him: "The Lord takes pleasure in them that...hope in his mercy" (Ps 146:11). And he promises victory over his enemies, perseverance in grace and eternal glory to those who hope: "Because he hoped in me I will deliver him: I will protect him....I will deliver him, and I will glorify him" (Ps 90:14,15). "Preserve me, O Lord, for I have put my trust in you" (Ps 15:1). "He will...save them, because they have hoped in him" (Ps 36:40). "No one has hoped in the Lord, and has been confounded" (Eccl 2:11). And let us be sure that "heaven and earth shall pass, but my words shall not pass" (Mt 24:35). Saint Bernard therefore says that all our merit consists in resting all our confidence in God: "This is the whole merit of a person, if he places all his hope in Him." The reason is that he who hopes in God honors him much: "call upon me in the day of trouble: I will deliver you, and you shall glorify me" (Ps 49:15). He honors the power, the mercy, and the faithfulness of God, since he believes that God can and will save him and that God cannot fail in his promises to save the one who trusts in him. And the prophet assures us that the greater our confidence is the greater will be the measure of God's mercy poured out upon us: "Let your mercy, O Lord, be upon us, as we have hoped in you" (Ps 32:22).

Now, as this virtue of hope is so pleasing to God, he has willed to impose it on us by a precept that binds under mortal sin, as is evident from many texts of Scripture. "Trust in him, all ye congregation of people" (Ps 61:9). "You that fear the Lord, hope in him" (Sir 2:9). "Hope in your God always" (Hos 12:6). "Trust perfectly in the grace which is offered you" (1 Pet 1:13). Then hope of eternal life ought to be sure and firm in us, according to the definition of Saint Thomas: "Hope is the certain expectation of beatitude." And long before, Saint Paul had said of himself, "I know whom I have believed, and I am certain that he is able to keep that which I have committed unto him" (2 Tim 1:12). And herein is the difference between Christian and worldly hope. Worldly hope need only be an uncertain expectation. Nor can it be otherwise, for it is always doubtful whether or not a one who has promised a favor may not later change his mind. But the Christian hope of eternal salvation is certain on God's part, for he can and will save us and has promised to save those who obey his law, and to this end has promised us all necessary graces to enable us to obey this law, if we ask for them. It is true that hope is accompanied by fear, as Saint Thomas says, but this fear does not arise from God's part but from our own, since we may at any time fail by not corresponding as we ought and by putting an impediment in the way of grace by our sins. Saint Thomas says we ought to look with certainty to receive eternal happiness from God, trusting in his power and mercy and believing that he can and will save us. "Whoever has faith is certain of God's power and mercy."

And therefore the Apostle Saint James declares that the person who desires God's grace must ask for it not with hesitation but with the confident certainty of obtaining it. "Let him ask in faith, nothing wavering" (Jas 1:6). For if he asks with hesitation, he shall obtain nothing: "For he that wavers is like a wave of the sea, which is moved and carried about by the wind. Therefore let not that person think that he shall receive anything of the Lord" (Jas 1:6–7). And Saint Paul praises Abraham for not doubting God's promise as he knew that when God promises he cannot fail to perform: "In the promise also of God he staggered not by distrust; but was strengthened in faith, giving glory to God: Most fully knowing, that whatsoever he has promised, he is able also to perform" (Rom 4:20–21). Hence, also, Jesus Christ tells us that we shall then receive all the graces we desire, when we ask for them with a sure belief of receiving them.

Now let us come to the point. Our hope of salvation and of receiving the means necessary for attaining it must be certain on God's part. The motives on which this certainty is founded, as we have seen, are the power, mercy, and truth of God. And of these the strongest and most certain motive is God's infallible faithfulness to the promise he has made us through the merits of Jesus Christ, to save us and to give us the graces needed for our salvation because, although we might believe God to be infinite in power and mercy, nevertheless we could not feel confident expectation of God's saving us unless he had surely promised to do so. But this promise is conditional, if we actively correspond to God's grace and pray, as is clear from Scripture: Ask, and ye shall receive; if ye ask the Father any thing in my name, he will give it you. He will give good things to those that ask him. We ought always to pray. Ye have not, because ye ask not. If anyone wants wisdom, let him ask it of God.

I say and repeat and will keep repeating as long as I live that all our salvation depends on prayer and therefore that all writers in their books, all preachers in their sermons, all confessors in their instructions to their penitents, should not urge anything more strongly than continual prayer. They should always admonish, exclaim, and continually repeat, Pray, pray, never cease to pray; for if you pray your salvation will be secure, but if you stop praying, your damnation will be certain.

Counsels From Which a Soul May Derive Comfort and Confidence

A Spiritual Conference Between the Author and One Who Seeks His Advice When Subjected by God to Spiritual Tribulations

Question. Let me hear what these troubles of conscience are which you tell me keep you in a state of such affliction.

Answer. Father, it is now about three years since I began to suffer such dryness and desolation of spirit as to prevent my finding God either in prayer, before the sacrament of the altar, or in my Communions. I seem to be a soul without love, without hope, and without faith, one abandoned, in short, by God. Neither the Passion of Jesus Christ nor the Holy Eucharist any longer affects me; I have become insensible to devotions of every kind. I confess that it is all on account of my sins, for which I deserve nothing short of hell.

Q. You tell me, in short, that you have now been for a long time in a state of aridity. In order to give you an answer adequate to your need, it is necessary that I should know whether this aridity of yours is voluntary or involuntary. Let me explain myself. It is "voluntary aridity" when a person commits voluntary and deliberate faults, and takes no pains to amend. This is not properly speaking to be called aridity but tepidity, from which, if the soul does not exert itself to get free, it will always be going from bad to worse. Aridity of this kind is a slow fever which does not cause death immediately but certainly brings it on. On the other hand, aridity is "involuntary" when a person tries to walk in the way of perfection, keeps on his guard against deliberate faults, frequently prays and goes to the sacraments, and with all this feels himself dry of spirit. To come to our present case: you have mentioned the sins of your past life; I ask, have you not made these sins the subject of confession?

A. Yes, Father. I have not only made a general confession of them, but I have confessed them many times over.

Q. And what does your director say?

A. He has forbidden me to make further mention of what belongs to my past life. But I always feel disquieted, continually fearing that I may not have explained myself sufficiently. I am, moreover, tormented by thousands of temptations to unbelief, impurity, and pride. I drive them away, but I still am always fearful that I may in some way have tacitly consented to them.

Q. And what does your director say with regard to these bad thoughts?

A. He wishes me not to confess them, except when I can swear that at first sight I had consented to them. What do you tell me, Father? Give me some instruction for my comfort.

Q. What do I tell you? I tell you that you ought more implicitly to trust in obedience to your director. Have you read that instruction of Saint Philip Neri, that he who acts in obedience to his confessor may rest assured that he will not have to render an account to God of the things he does? The saint used also to say that "one should have faith in one's confessor, for there is nothing more certain to defeat the designs of the devil than obedience to one's spiritual father as regards what relates to God; whereas, on the contrary, there is nothing more dangerous than the will to be guided by one's own opinion." And have you read what Saint Francis de Sales says, when speaking on the subject of obedience to one's director? "Of all counsels this is the chief." "Search as much as you will," says the devout Juan of Avila, "and you will never so surely find out the will of God as by way of this humble obedience, which was so much recommended and practiced by all the devout in the early ages." We find the same also in the writings of Saint Teresa, who says: "Let the soul choose its confessor with the determination to take no further thought for itself, but to place its trust in the words of the Lord, 'He that hears you hears me.' So great is the value which God sets on this submission that, whether it costs us suffering or not, let us act according to it and thus fulfill the divine will." Saint John of the Cross, too, says: "Not to rest satisfied with what one's confessor says is pride and lack of faith." The saint speaks this way because of those words of Jesus Christ which have been quoted above, "He that hears you, hears me."

This is also why Saint Francis de Sales set down these other most useful maxims: "(1) One who is truly obedient is never lost; (2) We should rest satisfied with knowing from our spiritual father that we are going on well, without searching for the reasons on which that judgment of his is formed." Saint Francis adds another excellent maxim, as a consequence of the foregoing, saying, "(3) It is best for us in this life to go on blindly, under divine providence, in a state of darkness and perplexity." This instruction to be obedient to one's spiritual father in doubts of conscience is, moreover, given by all the Doctors of the Church, and by all the holy Fathers; for all the rest of whom let Saint

Bernard suffice, saying, as he does, that whatever is imposed by human beings acting on behalf of God, provided only that it is clearly not a sin, should not be regarded otherwise than as the command of God himself. In short, obedience to his consecrated ministers is the one safest remedy which Jesus Christ has left us for quieting the doubts of conscience, and we ought to return him the greatest thanks for it. This tribulation of scruples—and for those who love God it has far greater torments than all other afflictions—is what all the saints have had to suffer. Saint Teresa, Saint Mary Magdalene of Pazzi, Saint Jane de Chantal, and many others besides suffered from scruples and how did they obtain tranquillity, except by obedience? Now, what do you say? Are you satisfied that, in obeying your director, you are going on safely?

A. Yes, Father, I am persuaded of it. But how does it happen that, in the course of obedience persevered in for two whole years, I have experienced nothing in the way of devotion?

Q. Now, then, I understand what your defect is, and why it is that, as you say, you do not find peace. Is the will of God the object of your search, or are you seeking consolations and spiritual sweetnesses? If you wish to sanctify yourself, seek only from this day forth the will of God, whose will it is that you become a saint, but who will not keep you in this life in a state of consolation. If you do not have consolation, console yourself with the hope of having with you him who is the Consoler. Do you complain of having suffered two years of dryness? Saint Jane de Chantal endured forty years of dryness. Saint Mary Magdalene of Pazzi suffered five years of pains and temptations without the smallest alleviation; and at the end of those five years she herself prayed to God that he would not grant her, in this world, any other sensible consolations. Saint Philip Neri was inflamed with divine love, but he used to say: "My Jesus, I have never yet loved you, and I would like to love you." At another time he would say: "As yet I do not know you, Jesus, for I am seeking you." This is how the saints speak; why are you so alarmed, then, because you are in a state of dryness and do not find God as you would like to find him?

A. But these were saints, but I do not know whether God has yet pardoned the many sins by which I have offended him, since I cannot be sure of having had a true sorrow for them.

Q. But what is the matter now? Perhaps you take complacency in the thought of the sins you have committed?

A. No. I detest them! I hate them more than death.

Q. Then why do you fear that God may not have pardoned you? The holy Fathers say that he who hates the sins he has committed is sure of forgiveness from God. And besides, it is certain, as Saint Teresa says, that "he who is resolved to die rather than offend God, is without a doubt penitent for his past offenses against him." Tell me, are you resolved to endure sufferings of every description rather than lose divine grace?

A. Yes, Father. By the grace of God, I am resolved to let myself be torn to pieces sooner than commit, with my eyes open, a single sin, even a venial one.

Q. Well, then, what reason is there why God should hate you? You are afraid God hates you. Oh, if you only saw the love which he is now bearing toward you, you would this very moment drop down dead here where you are standing out of mere consolation! Do you not know that Jesus Christ is that good Shepherd who has come into the world to give life, and to save every poor sheep of his flock, even though voluntarily lost? How, then, is it his will to abandon one of those sheep of his who is ready to die sooner than deliberately cause him the least possible displeasure?

A. But who knows whether I may not have consented to some grievous sin, and God have abandoned me on this account?

Q. No, you are not speaking well. Mortal sin is so horrible a monster that it is impossible for a sin of this kind to be in the soul without the soul's being aware of it. No sinner who is out of God's grace has any doubts about it, but is certain that he has lost it. Therefore it is an established maxim with all the masters of the spiritual life that when a person who fears God wonders whether he has lost divine grace, it is certain that he has not lost it, for the very reason that no one loses God without knowing it for certain. Thus, whenever you are in doubt about having lost God, be sure that you have not lost him.

A. But why is it that I feel so devoid of confidence?

Q. Listen. You know that true confidence consists not in feeling it, but in willing it. Have you the will to put your trust in God? If you have the will to confide in him, you have already confidence itself.

A. But where is my love for God?

Q. As regards love for God, the same rule holds good which holds with regard to confidence. Love, too, is in the will. Have you the will to love God? If it is your will to love him, understand that you already love him. You would like to have the consolation of feeling the confidence and the love; but God, for your greater good, does not will that you should be consoled by feeling this confidence and this love of yours. Be content, therefore, to possess it without feeling it. I tell you the same thing with regard to faith also: it is enough that you have the will to believe whatever the Church teaches you, without feeling that you believe. There will come a time when the clouds will clear away, and the light will brighten, which will make your consolation twofold. Meanwhile, be content to remain in the dark and to abandon yourself to the hand of God's divine will and mercy. Let us take Scripture for our comfort during this interval. In one place God says: "Turn ye to me, says the Lord of hosts: and I will turn to you" (Zech 1:3). If, then, we wish for God; let us turn with love to him, and he will straightway turn with love to us. To all he says: "Come to me, all you that labor, and are burdened, and I will refresh you" (Mt 11:28). You who are afflicted, come to me, and it shall be my care to raise you up. In another passage he says: "Come, and accuse me, saith the Lord: if your sins be as scarlet, they shall be made as white as snow" (Isa 1:18). He goes after sinners as one weeping out of compassion over their ruin, saying: "And why will you die, O house of Israel?" (Ezek 33:11). As though he said: "And why will you involve yourselves in damnation, my children, when you have in me one who is ready to save you, if you will have recourse to me?" Now, if he speaks in this way to those who are obstinate, how is it possible that he should drive away a soul that wishes to love him? Tell me honestly, are you attached to any earthly affection, to any person, to anything in the shape of property, to the ambition of excelling,

of being preferred before others? Take heed of what is said by Saint John of the Cross, that "every attachment, however trifling, every thread, has power to prevent you from winging your way to God and from being all his own."
A. No, by the grace of God, I think that I have no attachment to anything in this world, so as to be willing to commit for it any deliberate fault; but I see, nevertheless, that I am full of defects. I dislike being despised, and on such occasions I sometimes show resentment.

Q. And, after this resentment, what do you do?
A. I humble myself, I pray to God to forgive me, and I resolve not to fall into the same error again, trusting in Jesus Christ to give me strength; but notwithstanding this, I remain in a state of fear and disquiet. Then it seems as though it were impossible for me to possess the power of sanctifying myself; in fact, the very pretending to it seems to me to be pride.

Q. All is well; keep on acting this way. Only it is not good to remain in a state of disquiet. If you fall a hundred times in a day, always do the same things—make an act of contrition and a resolution, through God's assistance, not to fall again, together with an act of confidence in Jesus Christ; and then remain in peace. You must know that it is not pride, even after a fault, for us to hope to sanctify ourselves. Rather it would be pride to be despondent after the fault and to be troubled, as though the resolutions we had made had secured us against any subsequent fall. Humble yourself, then, and have confidence in God. Enough now. I already understand the substance of all your fears, which come from not knowing whether or not you will obtain your salvation, and whether or not you are now in the grace of God. What you have told me is enough; do not propose to me any more doubts and questions about these troubles of yours. I know your conscience already; and I wish to leave with you some reflections, which I hope will give you peace whenever you are troubled—peace, I say, but not that peace which is free from every shadow of fear, for that is the peace which God reserves for us in heaven. While we are in this world, it is his will that we should always have a certain degree of fear, so that we may not stop waiting upon and praying for divine assistance and confiding in divine mercy. Otherwise we would often forget to have recourse to God, and that is why he permits us to be harassed by fears, so that we may not give up having recourse to him.

Reasons to Have Confidence in Divine Mercy Through the Merits of Jesus Christ

There are, according to what you have told me, two great fears by which you are distressed principally: the first, that salvation may not be yours; the second, that God may not have pardoned your sins. With regard to the former—whether your name is or is not inscribed in the Book of Life—this is a secret which it is not the will of God that any should know; so that through fear of damnation, everyone should be diligent, by means of good works, to secure his salvation. Thus Saint Peter writes: "Wherefore, brethren, labor the more, that by good works you may make sure your calling and election" (2 Pet 1:10). It is true that our conversion and salvation must be the work of God; but it is requisite for us, too, to strive on our own part to convert ourselves to God, and then he will not fail to save us: "Be converted to me, and you shall be saved" (Isa 45:22).

God declares, even with regard to the wicked, who richly deserve everlasting death, that he would wish them too to be converted and saved: "As I live, saith the Lord God, I desire not the death of the wicked, but that the wicked turn from his way, and live" (Ezek 33:11). It is observed by Tertullian that the words which stand first in this sentence ("As I live") are an oath which is taken by God in order that we may believe him without hesitation: "Swearing even saying 'As I live,' desiring to be believed." Hence that most learned writer, Petavius, expresses himself in terms of great astonishment that anyone should doubt the truth that God's will is for all to be saved. And why is it that God has so great a desire to save all humankind? Because he himself created them, because of the love which he has had for them from all eternity. "I have loved you with an everlasting love"—this is what the Lord says to every person—"therefore have I drawn you, taking pity on you" (Jer 31:3). Moreover, the Lord, knowing our weakness, has patience with sinners, as Saint Peter tells us, because he wills not that they should perish, but that they should do penance for their sins and obtain salvation: "The Lord delays not his promise, as some imagine, but deals patiently for your sake, not willing that any should perish, but that all should return to penance" (2 Pet 3:9). That Redeemer who has ransomed us from eternal death at the price of his own blood, says Saint Augustine, does not desire to see lost those souls of ours which have cost him so much: "He who has redeemed us at so great a price does not wish those whom he has purchased to perish." In short, God would like to save all; and when he sees any who are constraining him by their sins to sentence them to hell, he, as it were, weeps in compassion over them and says: "And why will you die, O house of Israel?...Return ye and live" (Ezek 18:31,32). As though he were to say: "But, my children, why will you destroy and damn yourselves in eternity, when I have died upon the cross in order to save you? If you have gone astray from me, return to me as penitents, and I will restore to you the life you have lost."

Now from this you may infer whether or not it is God's desire to see you saved. And therefore, from this day forth, never again say, "But who knows whether God wills that I be saved? Who knows whether he does not will that I be damned for the offenses which I have given him?" Drive all thoughts like these utterly away, seeing, as you do, that God is assisting you with his grace and calling you by so many motives to his love.

Moreover, as regards your other fear—that the Lord may not yet have pardoned the sins of your past life—I have already told you that, in regard to this, you ought to quiet yourself by the obedience which your confessor has given you, to think no further about confessing what has happened during your past life, after the confessions which you have already made. Recollect, as I told you, what Saint Teresa says, that one who obeys his confessor, "whether with suffering or without it," may rest assured that he is doing God's will. And I would also put you in mind of what Saint John of the Cross says, "that not to rest satisfied with what one's confessor says is a lack of faith," since, in truth, Jesus Christ has said that he who is obedient to his ministers is obedient to himself, and he who despises his ministers despises him.

And so, from this day forth, let us place every thought about our salvation in the hands of our Lord, and leave it there; for (as Saint Peter says) he has taken us into his care: "Casting all your care upon him, for he has care of you" (1 Pet 5:7).

Moreover, in order to keep ourselves in God's grace, we must have an utter distrust of our own strength, since, without the aid of grace, we could not do anything that is good and, on the contrary, might fall into all that is evil; and therefore our entire safety lies in recommending ourselves continually unto

God, because since we are in continual danger of falling, we continually need to procure the assistance of God through prayer. This assistance, says Saint Bernard, is offered to all, and no one remains without it except one who despises it. Divine aid, then, is offered to all, but it is God's will that he who desires it should ask him for it—"Ask, and you shall receive" (Jn 16:24)—and he who is careless about asking for it will remain without it and will involve himself in destruction. When the devil, then, is frightening us by the thought of our weakness, let us not give ourselves up to despair, but hope to receive the power from God to resist all temptations, for God strengthens us to hope, saying, with the Apostle, "I can do all things in him who strengthens me" (Phil 4:13). If we place our confidence in God, how shall it be possible for us to be put to confusion? The mere name of Jesus is sufficient to vanquish all the powers of hell. Saint Paul says that God has given to Jesus Christ a name which is above every name, since at that name everything is made to humble itself: He "has given him a name which is above all names: That in the name of Jesus every knee should bow, of those that are in heaven, on earth, and under the earth" (Phil 2:9–10). In contending with the enemies of our salvation, we will often find victory more likely if we call the name of Jesus to our aid than if we say many long prayers.

Further, while on this point, I wish to leave with you for consolation some other instructions as to particulars which, I think, may prove of great use to your conscience.

1 • I repeat my recommendation to you to be obedient to your confessor, because, by what I have been able to learn about this obedience, you have not up to this time had a complete and entire faith, and therefore have often been disturbed. What I have said to you above on this matter is sufficient. Hold it as certain that one who goes on under obedience is journeying safely to heaven.

2 ◆ Then, when things go contrary, be careful to receive it all as from the hands of God; and especially in times of sickness be scrupulously obedient to your medical adviser, in taking the remedies he prescribes, making known to him without exaggeration anything that you are suffering, and then remain in peace. Forbear to ask for sympathy from those who come to see you; and whenever anyone expresses more than a moderate amount of sympathy for you, let your reply be made in the words of Jesus Christ: "The chalice which my Father has given me, shall I not drink it?" (Jn 18:11). Say: "God sends me this evil, not because he wishes me evil but because he wishes me well; and shall I not accept it peacefully?" In time of sickness it is seen whether a person is spiritual or not. There are some devout people who, when they are in health, are all sweetness and humility; but if they are in any way invalided, they straightway become impatient and proud, complaining of everyone around them, especially if they have not, right at the minute, the medicine or attendance they need. In sickness, then, suffer everything without complaining, and also in all circumstances which savor of adversity, say with Job, "as it has pleased the Lord so is it done: blessed be the name of the Lord" (Job 1:21). Be careful, too, to endure scorn without resentment; this is how one knows whether a person is humble—if he receives contempt patiently.

3 ◆ God is all goodness to one who seeks him. No one has ever put his trust in God, and has remained abandoned by him: "No one has hoped in the Lord, and has been confounded" (Eccl 2:11). God lets himself be found even by those who do not seek him, as Saint Paul observes, echoing Isaiah: "I was found by them that did not seek me" (Rom 10:20; Isa 65:1). With how much greater ease will he not allow himself to be found by one who does seek him! From this day on, then, refrain from saying God has abandoned you. The Lord abandons none but the obstinate who desire to live in sin; neither does he altogether abandon even these, but is forever going after them up to the time of their death, giving them portions of light for their guidance, so that he may not see them lost.

4 • When a soul is seeking to love him, he cannot but love it, as he has himself declared: "I love them that love me" (Prov 8:17). And whenever he hides himself from these loving souls, he does so only for their advantage, that he may see them still more desirous of finding his grace, and more closely united with himself. See what Saint Catherine of Genoa used to say, when suffering aridity to such a degree that it seemed to her as if God had abandoned her and that nothing remained to her as a ground for hope; it was then that she would say: "How happy I am in this state, deplorable as it is! May my heart be broken down into ruins, provided that my Love be glorified! My dearest Love, if from this unhappy state of mine is produced just a single atom of glory for you, I pray that you would leave me thus for all eternity!"

5 • You must know that souls which love the Crucified enter in time of desolation into a closer union with God in the interior of their hearts. There is nothing which occasions so diligent a search for God as desolation does; neither is there anything which attracts God to the heart so much as desolation, since the acts of uniformity to the divine will which are made in desolation are more pure and perfect than others. Therefore, the greater the desolation, the greater is the humility, the purer is the resignation, the purer is the confidence, the purer are the prayers, and so the more abundant are the divine graces and assistances.

6 • In order to arrive at perfection, pay attention above all things to the exercise of divine love. The love of God, when he makes your heart his abode, by itself despoils the heart of every irregular affection; nevertheless, let it also be your endeavor to make frequent acts of divine love, saying: "My God, I love you, I love you; and I hope to die with these words on my lips." The saints tell us that a perfect soul should make as many acts of love as it does of respiration!

7 • In time of prayer, make an unreserved offering of yourself to God many times over. Say to him in all sincerity: "My Jesus, I give myself up to you without reserve. I wish to be all thine own, all thine own; and if I do not know how to give myself up as I ought, do you, my Jesus, take me, and make me all your own." Saint Teresa made an entire offering of herself to God fifty times every day. This is a practice which even you can follow. Therefore make a continual offering to him of your will, in the words of Saint Paul: "Lord, what will you have me do?" (Acts 9:6). This one act was enough to transform Saint Paul from a persecutor of the Church into a vessel of election. For this purpose, too, pray to God frequently in the words of David: "Teach me to do your will" (Ps 142:10). To this end should be directed all the prayers which you offer to God and to the Mother of God, to your guardian angel, and to all your patron saints, that they may obtain for you the grace to do God's will perfectly.

8 • And when you experience more aridity than usual, exercise yourself by delighting in the infinite joy which your God, whom you love, is enjoying. This is the most perfect act of love, exercised by the saints in heaven, who rejoice not so much for their own happiness as for that of God, loving him all the while, as they do, immeasurably beyond themselves.

9 • Then, with reference to the subject of prayer, always meditate on the Passion of Jesus Christ suffering out of his love for us is the object which most forcibly attracts our hearts. If, while meditating on the mysteries of the Passion, the Lord grants you any feeling of tenderness, receive it with thankfulness; but even when you do not experience this, you must know that you will always derive from the practice great strength for your soul. Go often to the garden of Gethsemane, following the example of Saint Teresa who used to say that she found him there alone; and on considering him when he is in such affliction that he falls into an agony, sweats blood, and declares his sorrow to be great enough to cause him to die, you will readily find comfort in any afflictions of your own, seeing that he endures all this out of his love for you. At the sight of Jesus preparing himself to die for you, prepare yourself to die for him; and when you experience in your distresses more affliction than usual, then say what Saint Thomas the Apostle said to the other disciples: "Let us also go, that we may die with him" (Jn 11:16). Let us die with Jesus.

10 • Go likewise to Calvary, where you will find him expiring on the cross, consumed by suffering; and on seeing him in that condition, it will be impossible for you not to remain content to suffer willingly pain of every kind for a God who is dying of sufferings undertaken because of his love for you. Saint Paul protested that he neither knew nor wished to know anything in this life except Jesus crucified: "For I judged not myself to know anything among you, but Jesus Christ, and him crucified" (1 Cor 2:2). Saint Bonaventure says that one who would maintain a continued devotion toward Jesus Christ ought, with the eye of his understanding, to be forever contemplating him dying upon the cross: "Let him who would preserve devotion within his soul, ever keep the eyes of his heart fixed upon Christ dying upon the cross." Thus, in all your fears, look at Jesus crucified and take courage, and brace yourself to suffer through your love for him.

11 • Above everything, prayer is what I recommend to you. When you cannot tell what else to say, it is enough for you to say, Lord, help me, and help me quickly: "Lord, come to my assistance; make haste, O Lord, to help me." You are already aware how often the Church repeats this prayer in the office which priests and religious recite. Saint Philip Neri made the recital of this same prayer, sixty-three times, in the manner of a rosary, a subject of his instruction. The Lord has promised to grant us whatever we ask him: "Ask, and it shall be given you." Saint Bernard went off into an ecstasy while thinking upon the words of Jesus Christ to the two sons of Zebedee, who said to him: "Master, we desire that whatsoever we shall ask, you would do it for us," and the reply of Jesus was: "What would you that I should do for you?" (Mk 10:35,36).

12 • And all the graces which you ask of God, ask for them always in the name of Jesus Christ. Everything we receive from God, we receive through the merits of Jesus Christ; and our Redeemer himself has promised us that whatever we ask of the Father in his name, the Father will give: "Amen, amen I say to you: If you ask the Father anything in my name, he will give it to you" (Jn 16:23).

13 • And why, then, when you are in a state of desolation, are you disposed to entertain the suspicion that God hates you? You ought not to grieve, but rather to be greatly consoled to see God dealing with you as he deals with the souls of those of his servants who are the most dear to him. And how has he not dealt with his own Son, of whom it is written in Scripture: "The Lord was pleased to bruise him in infirmity" (Isa 53:10). It was his will to see him consumed and crushed under sufferings and torments.

14 • When you are frightened by the thought that it may be God's will to abandon you because of your ingratitude, do what was done by the two disciples who, as they were going to Emmaus, were accompanied by Jesus in the guise of a pilgrim. When they were near the place, Jesus gave signs of its being his will to go farther ("He made as though he would go farther"); but they, the Gospel tells us, urged him, saying: "Stay with us, because it is towards evening." And then he was pleased to enter their house and to remain with them: "And he went in with them." All this is told us by Saint Luke (24:28,29). Thus, when it seems to you as if it were the Lord's will to leave you, urge him to remain with you, saying to him: "My Jesus, stay with me, remain with me, I wish that you would not leave me; if you do leave me, to whom shall I have to go for consolation and salvation?" "Lord, to whom shall we go?" as was said by Saint Peter (Jn 6:69). So go on praying to him lovingly and tenderly. And do not fear that he will leave you. Then say with the Apostle: "Neither death, nor life…nor any other creature shall be able to separate us from the love of God, which is in Christ Jesus our Lord" (Rom 8:38,39). Say to him: "My Savior, show yourself as much displeased with me as you will; but know that neither the fear of death, nor a desire for life, nor any other of this world's creatures, shall ever have power to separate me from my love for you." Or, again, say what Saint Francis de Sales, when he was a young man and in a state of aridity, said in answer to the devil, who suggested to him that he was destined to go to hell: "Then since I shall not be able to love my God in eternity, I wish to love him, at least in this life, as much as lies in my power." And so he recovered his cheerfulness.

15 ◆ Again: when you feel yourself more than usually oppressed by fears or dryness, do not fail to have recourse to Mary, whom God has given as a consoler for those who are in affliction. Jesus Christ is the foundation of all our hopes, but the Church desires us to call Mary our hope. All graces, in their origin, come to us from God, but Saint Bernard says that they all pass through Mary's hands. Consequently, he who does not recommend himself to the Blessed Virgin closes against himself the channel of grace, while on her part she does not neglect to give aid to everyone who calls upon her to aid him. And therefore all the saints have been careful to recommend themselves continually to this divine mother, who has such power with God.

16 ◆ Moreover, all the time that you have the intention of loving God, keep your heart open: "Open your mouth wide, and I will fill it" (Ps 80:11). The meaning of what is here said by God is that the more we hope for from God, the more we shall receive from him. He has declared that he shows favor toward those who place confidence in him: "He is the protector of all that trust in him" (Ps 17:31). Whenever you feel doubts about the Lord's hearing you, remember that he is chiding you as he did Saint Peter, and saying to you: "O you of little faith, why did you doubt?" (Mt 14:31). Why do you doubt my hearing you, knowing as you do the promise which I have made, to grant the requests of everyone that prays to me? And because he is willing to grant us our requests, it is his will that we believe that he certainly does grant them whenever we ask him for graces: "All things whatsoever you ask when ye pray, believe that you shall receive; and they shall come unto you" (Mk 11:24). Observe the words, "believe that you shall receive"; for they show that we must ask God for graces with a sure, unhesitating confidence that we shall receive them, as Saint James also exhorts us: "But let him ask in faith, nothing wavering" (Jas 1:6). In dealing with this God, who is all goodness, have great confidence, and rid yourself of everything like sadness. He who serves God and is sad, instead of honoring him, rather treats him with dishonor. Saint Bernard tells us that he wrongs God who thinks of him as cross and severe, since he is really goodness and mercy itself. "How can you entertain a doubt," says the saint, "of Jesus pardoning your sins, when he has affixed them to the cross, whereon he died for you, with the very nails by which his own hands were pierced?"

17 ◆ God declares that it is his delight to be with us: "My delights were to be with the children of men" (Prov 8:31). If, then, it is God's delight to be with us, it is only just that all our delights should consist in being with him; and this thought should give us courage to treat God with every confidence, endeavoring to spend all that remains of life to us with this God of ours, who loves us so much, and with whom we hope to be in company in heaven for all eternity.

18 ◆ Let us, then, treat him with all confidence and love, as our most dear and affectionate friend, who loves us more than anyone else does. Unfortunately, souls that are scrupulous treat God as a tyrant from whose subjects only reserve and fear are required, and consequently they are apprehensive that, at every word inconsiderately spoken, at every thought which crosses their mind, he may enter into his wrath with them, and be disposed to cast them into destruction in hell. No, God does not take his grace away from us except when we consciously and deliberately despise him and will to turn our backs upon him. When by some venial fault we slightly offend him, he is certainly displeased by it, but he does not therefore deprive us of the love which he bears toward us, and then, by an act of contrition or of love, he is at once appeased.

19 • His infinite majesty may justly claim all reverence and self-abasement from us; but he is better pleased that the souls which love him should treat him with loving confidence than with timid servility. So do not treat God as a tyrant any more. Recall to your mind the graces which he has bestowed upon you, even after the offenses and acts of ingratitude which you have committed against him. Recollect the loving treatment with which he has dealt with you, in order to extricate you from the disorders of your past life, and the extraordinary lights which he has given you, by means of which he has so often called you to his holy love. And so treat him from this day forth with great confidence and affection, as your dearest friend.

20 • It is unnecessary for me here to recommend to you the sacraments, frequenting them as you do already. Go to confession at least once or twice a week. With regard to Communion, act in obedience to your director. When you do not make an actual Communion, at least make a spiritual one, which you are able to do at any time, and make it frequently in the course of the day.

21 • Let the dearest objects of your affection be these two great mysteries—the sacrament of the altar and the Passion of Jesus Christ. If the love of all hearts were to gather itself together into one heart only, this would certainly not be able to correspond, even in the smallest measure, to the love which Jesus Christ has shown us in these two mysteries of the Passion and the Blessed Sacrament. Let it, then, be your endeavor, during the remainder of your life, to love and have confidence in him, and do not become sad when you find yourself in afflictions and tribulations, for this is a sign not of his hatred but of the love which God bears toward you. And therefore, in reference to this point, and as a conclusion to this little treatise, I will here cite for you the example of Saint Lidwina. I do not know whether there is to be met with among the annals of saints an instance of any other soul suffering as much affliction and desolation as did this holy virgin.

She was born of poor parents, in a town of Holland called Schiedam. One day, while she was still a little girl, in walking on the ice, she fell and broke a rib; and as, in consequence of their poverty, it was not afterward cured, there was formed upon the broken rib an abscess, which of itself broke and infected her whole body, so that it became paralyzed. Her parents left her to herself without taking any care of her, while she continued full of pain, with all the limbs of her body, excepting only her head and left arm, contracted. Her right arm was, consequently, utterly useless; and at the same time she was seized with Saint Antony's fire to such a degree that her very bones were gradually eaten away. During all this she did not venture even to speak of the evils from which she was suffering, lest her parents might do something to increase them.

22 ◆ She suffered continual and excruciating pains in her head. On her forehead she had a large sore; and in her chin there was a wound extending to the mouth, full of congealed blood, which prevented her from speaking and eating. One of her eyes had retreated inward and become useless; the other was so infected that she could not bear the light of the sun, and scarcely even that of a lamp. She suffered so much from toothache that the pain brought her down even to death's door. She had a continual flow of blood either from the mouth, nostrils, eyes, or ears. In her throat she had a tumor, which prevented her even from breathing freely; she had to bear the torment of a perpetual fever; she suffered continually from vomiting, throwing up a great quantity of bloody water after taking even the smallest amount of food. She was at one and the same time dropsical, feverish, and consumptive, destitute of everything, and she received assistance from no one. There might sometimes be one who out of compassion would hand her some medicine, but that only made her sufferings twofold, and she would take it with all the obedience of a lamb, never making complaints about it. Her parents; being poor, and wearied by her calamities, which were so great, used to grumble at her, saying that she was born only to be a torment to them and to consume whatever little supplies their home might furnish, so that it would be better if death were to take her. She used to weep, not for her own afflictions but for the inconvenience which she caused others.

23 ◆ Being unable to move, she was obliged constantly to lie on her back, which was all in such a state of putrefaction that the skin stuck to the bed—that is to say, to that poor straw on which she lay abandoned—so that whenever anyone out of compassion raised her up, her skin would remain stuck to the straw, and her body became, as it were, excoriated. In short, the appearance of that poor fifteen-year-old girl, lying on her bed, was the same as that of a corpse lying all but breathless on a bier. And such was the state in which this holy virgin lived for thirty-eight years. It is also related that four soldiers entered her room one day, and after using much abusive language to her, calling her a hypocrite and a witch, the truth about whom would in due time be discovered, they took away from her the poor blanket which covered her half-dead body. And before taking their departure, they beat her and even wounded her with their swords.

24 ◆ There was added to all these external evils an interior desolation, an affliction from which she suffered for years, since God, for her greater purification, withdrew from her (as he often does with those souls which are most precious in his sight) his sensible assistance, so that she found herself without her usual loving confidence in God. And then the devil tormented her fiercely, suggesting to her that such great evils as those by which she was oppressed were a sure sign that the Lord had abandoned her, and that she would die in a state of despair. Nevertheless, assailed though she was by so much sickness and by such interior tribulations, she suffered it all with resignation, blessing God for dealing with her in that way, and in order to offer him still more, she tied around herself a horsehair belt, which cut into her sores.

25 ◆ Such was the state of desolation in which the saint lived for four years. But all her sufferings she bore with resignation to the divine will, ever blessing God for treating her in this manner. All that she had to undergo she united to the Passion of Jesus Christ. This was the way in which throughout the whole of that time she sustained that fearful storm. But then God began to give her great consolation, and however great the sufferings which she might experience, she would nevertheless say: "When I see my Jesus Christ hanging upon the cross, I feel my pains no longer. My sufferings urge me to cry out, but my heart urges me to say, Jesus, my love, increase my pains, but also increase my love." To others, when condoling with her, she would say: "All the evil from which I am suffering is a mere nothing, being, as I am, in the hands of a goodness which is infinite, such as my God is, whose bowels of compassion exceed those of either one's father or mother."

26 • Once more: if you love Jesus Christ, do not fail to make a daily recommendation of sinners to him. Saint Teresa and Saint Mary Magdalene of Pazzi paid great attention to prayer for sinners. It is a sign of little love for God when a soul which knows how many outrages God receives at the hands of infidels, heretics, and sinners of so many other descriptions, neglects to pray to the Lord for their conversion.

27 • Take courage, I pray you, from all that you have now heard, and bear your aridity with fortitude, and when you feel more than usually oppressed, offer up the following prayer:

Prayer for a Loving Soul When in Desolation

My crucified Jesus, you already know that out of love for you I have left all. But after you have caused me to leave my all, I find that you yourself have left me too. But what am I saying, oh my Love? Have pity upon me. It is not I who speak, it is my weakness that makes me speak thus. For myself, I deserve every kind of suffering, for such great sins as mine have been. You have left me, as I have deserved, and have withdrawn from me that loving assistance of yours with which you have so often consoled me. Nevertheless, however disconsolate and abandoned I may be by you, I protest that it is my will ever to love you and to bless you. Provided that you do not deprive me of the grace of being able to love you, deal with me as you please.

Lord, take not yourself from me; then take from me all besides, as may seem good in your sight. "Draw me after you." My

Love, draw me after you; then it matters not though you take from me the consolation of being conscious of it. But let it be forcibly that you draw me, dragging me out of the mire of my sins. Help your servants, whom you have redeemed with your precious blood. I wish to be all thine own, cost me what it may. I wish to love you with all my strength, but what can I do myself? Your blood is my hope. Mary, Mother of God, my refuge, do not neglect to pray for me in all my tribulations! First of all in the blood of Jesus Christ, and then in your prayers, I trust for my eternal salvation. "In you, Lady, have I hoped," I will say to you with Saint Bonaventure, "I shall not be confounded forever." Obtain for me the grace ever to love my God in this life and in eternity, and I ask for nothing more.

On Conformity to the Will of God

If we would give full satisfaction to the heart of God, we must bring our own will in everything into conformity with his, and not only into conformity, but into uniformity, too, as regards all that God ordains. Conformity signifies the conjoining of our own will to the will of God. Uniformity signifies, further, our making of the divine and our own will one will only, so that we desire nothing but what God desires, and his sole will becomes ours. This is the sum and substance of that perfection to which we ought ever to aspire; this is what must be the aim of all our works, and of all our desires, meditations, and prayers. For this we must invoke the assistance of all our patron saints and of our guardian angels, and above all of our mother Mary, who was the most perfect of all the saints, for this reason, that she most perfectly ever embraced the divine will.

But the chief point lies in our embracing the will of God in all things which befall us, not only when they are favorable, but when they are contrary to our desires. When things go well, even sinners find no difficulty in being in a state of uniformity to the divine will; but the saints are in uniformity also under circumstances which run counter and are mortifying to self-love. It is herein that the perfection of our love for God is shown.

We must bring ourselves into uniformity to the divine will, not only as regards those adverse circumstances which come to us directly from God—such as infirmities, desolations of spirit, poverty, the death of parents, and other things of a similar nature—but also as regards those which come to us through the instrumentality of men, such as reproaches, acts of injustice, thefts, and persecutions of every kind. On this point, we must understand that when we suffer injury from anyone in our reputation, our honor, or our property, although the Lord does not will the sin which such a one commits, he nevertheless does will our humiliation, our poverty, and our mortification. It is certain and of faith that every thing which comes to pass in the world comes to pass through the divine will: "I form the light and create darkness, I make peace, and create evil" (Isa 45:7). From God come all things that are good and all things that are evil, that is to say, all things which are contrary to our own likings, and which we falsely call evil, for in truth they are good when we receive them as coming from his hands: "Shall there be evil in a city, which the Lord has not done?" said the prophet Amos (3:6). And the Wise One said it before: "Good things and evil, life and death, poverty and riches, are from God" (Eccl 11:14).

It is true, as I observed above, that whenever anyone unjustly treats you in an injurious manner, God does not will the sin which such a person commits, nor concur in the malice of his intentions. But he concurs as regards the material action by which such a person wounds, plunders, or injures you, so that what you have to suffer is certainly willed by God, and comes to you from his hands. Hence it was that the Lord told David that he was the author of the injuries which Absalom would inflict upon him, even to the taking away of his wives in his very presence, in punishment for his sins: "Behold, I will raise up evil against you out of your own house, and I will take your wives before your eyes and give them to your neighbor" (2 Kings 12:11). Hence, too, he told the Jews that it would be as a punishment for their wickedness when he should have commanded the Assyrians to spoil and bring them to ruin: "The Assyrian, he is the rod and the staff of my anger...I will give him a charge...to take away the spoils, and to lay hold on the prey" (Isa 10:5,6). Saint Augustine explains it thus: "The wickedness of these men is made to be, as it were, an axe of God," to chastise the Jews. And Jesus himself said to Saint Peter that his Passion and Death did not come to him so much from men as from his Father himself: "The chalice which my Father has given me, shall I not drink it?" (Jn 18:11).

When the messenger came to Job to tell him that the Sabeans had taken all his goods away, and had put his sons to death, what was the saint's reply? "The Lord gave, and the Lord has taken away" (Job 1:21). He did not say, the Lord has given me sons and property, and the Sabeans have taken them away from me, but the Lord has given them to me and the Lord has taken them away, because he perfectly understood that his loss was willed by God; and therefore he added, "As it has pleased the Lord so is it done; blessed be the name of the Lord." We must not, then, look upon the troubles which befall us as happening by chance, or only through the fault of others. We must rest assured that everything which happens to us comes to pass through the divine will.

He who acts in this way does not only become a saint, but he enjoys, even in this world, a perpetual peace. Alphonsus the Great, King of Aragon and a most wise prince, on being one day asked whom he considered to be the happiest person in the world, replied, He who abandons himself to the will of God and receives all things, whether prosperous or adverse, as from his hands. "To them that love God, all things work together unto good" (Rom 8:28). Those who love God are ever content, because their whole pleasure lies in the accomplishment, even in things that run counter to themselves, of the divine will. Hence even afflictions are converted into contentment by the thought that in the acceptance of them they are giving pleasure to the Lord whom they love: "Whatsoever shall befall the just man, it shall not make him sad" (Prov 12:21). And, in truth, what greater contentment can a man ever experience than in seeing the accomplishment of all that he desires? Now whenever anyone desires nothing save what God desires, since everything that comes to pass in the world (sin only excepted) always comes to pass through the will of God, everything that such a one desires does consequently come to pass. There is a story in the lives of the Fathers of a certain countryman, whose land was more productive than that of others, and who, on being asked how it happened, replied, that no one should be surprised at it, because he always had such weather as he desired. "And how so?" it was asked. "Yes," replied he, "because I desire no weather but that which God desires; and as I desire what God desires, so does he give me the fruits of the earth as I desire them." Souls that are truly resigned, says Salvian, if they are in a state of humiliation, desire this; if they suffer poverty, they desire to be poor. Whatever happens to them, they desire it all; and therefore they are, in this life, happy. When cold or heat, rain or wind, prevails, he who is in a state of union with the divine will says: I wish it to be cold, I wish it to be hot; I wish the wind to blow, the rain to fall, because God wishes it so.

This is the beautiful liberty which the sons of God enjoy, worth more than all the kingdoms of this world. This is that great peace which the saints experience, which "surpasses all understanding" (Phil 4:7), with which all the pleasures of the senses, all festivities, distinctions, and all other worldly satisfactions cannot compete. For these, being as they are unsubstantial and transitory, although while they last they may be fascinating to the senses, nevertheless do not bring contentment but affliction to the spirit in which true contentment resides, so that Solomon, after having enjoyed such worldly pleasures to the full, cried out in his affliction, "But this also is vanity, and vexation of spirit" (Eccl 4:16). "A fool" (says the Holy Spirit) "is changed like the moon" but "a holy person continues in wisdom like the sun" (Sir 27:12). The fool, that is to say, the sinner, changes like the moon, which today grows, tomorrow wanes. Today you will see him laughing, tomorrow weeping; today all gentleness, tomorrow furious like the tiger. And why so? Because his contentment depends on the prosperity or the adversity which he meets with, and therefore he varies as the circumstances which befall him vary. Whereas the just person is like the sun, ever uniform in his serenity under whatever circumstances may come to pass, because his contentment lies in his uniformity to the divine will, and therefore he enjoys a peace which nothing can disturb: "and on earth peace to men of good will" (Lk 2:14), said the angel to the shepherds. And who can these men of good will ever be, but those who are at all times in unison with the will of God, which is supremely good and perfect? The will of God is good, delightful, and perfect, because he wills only that which is best and most perfect.

Great indeed is the folly of those who fight against the divine will! They have now to suffer troubles, because no one can ever prevent the accomplishment of the divine decrees. And, on the other hand, they have to suffer them without deriving benefit from them, even drawing down upon themselves greater chastisements in the next life and greater unhappiness in this: "Who has resisted him, and has had peace?" (Job 9:4). Let the sick cry as they will about their pains. Let those who are in poverty complain, rave, blaspheme against God as much as they please—what will they gain by it but the doubling of their affliction? "What are you in search of, foolish one," says Augustine, "when seeking good things? Seek that one good in whom are all things good." Find God, unite yourself to, bind yourself up with, his will, and you will be ever happy, both in this life and in the other.

In short, what is there that God wills but our good? Whom can we ever find to love us more than he? It is his will that all should save and sanctify themselves: "not willing that any should perish, but that all should return to penance" (2 Pet 3:9). "This is the will of God, your sanctification" (1 Thess 4:3). It is in our good that God has placed his own glory, being, as Saint Leo says, in his own nature goodness infinite. It being the nature of goodness to desire to spread itself abroad, God has a supreme desire to make our souls partakers of his own bliss and glory. And if, in this life, he sends us tribulations, they are all for our own good: "all things work together unto good" (Rom 8:28). Even chastisements, as was observed by the holy Judith, do not come to us from God for our destruction, but for our amendment and salvation (Jdt 8:27). In order to save us from eternal evils, the Lord throws his own good will around us: "O Lord, you have crowned us, as with a shield of your good will" (Ps 5:13). He not only desires but is anxious for our salvation. And what is there that God will ever refuse us, says Saint Paul, after having given us his own Son (Rom 8:32). This, then, is the confidence in which we ought to abandon ourselves to the divine dispensations, all of which have for their object our own good.

But let us now look at the matter from a more practical point of view, and consider what things there are in which we have to bring ourselves into uniformity with the will of God. In the first place, we must have this uniformity as regards those things of nature which come to us from without, as when there is great heat, great cold, rain, scarcity, pestilence, and the like. We must take care not to say, What intolerable heat! What a misfortune! How unlucky! What wretched weather! or other words expressive of repugnance to the will of God. We ought to will everything to be as it is, since God orders it all. Saint Francis Borgia, on going one night to a house of the Society of Jesus when the snow was falling, knocked at the door several times, but the fathers being asleep, he was not let in. They apologized greatly in the morning for having kept him so long waiting in the open air. But the saint said that during that time he had been greatly consoled by the thought that it was God who was sending down on him those flakes of snow.

In the second place, we must have this uniformity as regards things which happen to us from within, as in the sufferings that come from hunger, thirst, poverty, desolations, or disgrace. In all, we ought ever to say, "Lord, be it thine to make and to unmake: I am content; I will only what you will." And thus too we ought, as Father Rodriguez says, to reply to such imaginary cases as the devil occasionally suggests to the mind, in order to make us agree to something that is wrong. If such a person were to say so and so to you, if he were to do so and so to you, what would you say, what would you do? Let our answer always be, "I would say and do that which God wills." And by this means we shall keep ourselves free from all fault and agitation.

In the third place, if we have any natural defect either in mind or body—a bad memory, slowness of apprehension, small talents, a crippled limb, or weak health—let us not therefore lament. What did we deserve? What obligation had God to give us a mind more richly endowed, or a body more perfectly framed? Could he not have created us mere brute animals or have left us in our own nothingness? Who is there that ever receives a gift and tries to make bargains about it? Let us, then, return him thanks for what, through a pure act of his goodness, he has bestowed upon us, and let us rest content with the manner in which he has treated us. Who can tell whether, if we had had a larger share of ability, stronger health, or greater personal attractions, we should not have possessed them to our destruction? How many there are whose ruin has been occasioned by their talents and learning, of which they have grown proud, and in consequence of which they have looked upon others with contempt, a danger which is easily incurred by those who excel others in learning and ability. How many others there are whose personal beauty or bodily strength have furnished the occasions of plunging them into innumerable acts of wickedness. And, on the contrary, how many others there are who, in consequence of their poverty, or infirmity, or ugliness, have sanctified themselves and been saved; who, had they been rich, strong, or handsome, would have been damned. And thus let us ourselves rest content with that which God has given us: "But one thing is necessary" (Lk 10:42). Beauty is not necessary, nor health, nor keenness of intellect; what alone is necessary is our salvation.

In the fourth place, we must be particularly resigned under the pressure of corporal infirmities. We must embrace them willingly, both in such a manner and for such a time as God wills. Nevertheless, we ought to employ the usual remedies, for this is what the Lord wills too. But if they do us no good, let us unite ourselves with the will of God, and this will do us much more good than health. Lord, let us then say, I have no wish either to get well or to remain sick; I will only what you will. Certainly the virtue is greater if in times of sickness we do not complain of our sufferings. But when these press heavily upon us, it is not a fault to make them known to our friends, or even to pray God to free us from them. I am speaking now of sufferings that are severe; for, on the other hand, there are many who are very faulty in this, that on every trifling pain they would have the whole world come to shed tears around them. Even Jesus Christ, on seeing the near approach of his most bitter Passion, manifested to his disciples what he suffered: "My soul is sorrowful even unto death" (Mt 26:38), and he prayed the eternal Father to liberate him from it: "My Father, if it be possible, let this chalice pass from me" (Mt 26:39). But Jesus himself has taught us what we ought to do after praying in this manner, namely, straightway to resign ourselves to the divine will, adding, as he did, "Nevertheless not as I will, but as you will."

How foolish, too, are those who say that they wish for health, not indeed in order to suffer, but to render greater service to God by the observance of rules, by serving the community, by going to church, by receiving Holy Communion, by doing penance, by study, by employing themselves in saving souls. But, my good friend, I wish you would tell me why it is that you want to do these things? Is it to please God? And why go out of your way in order to do them, certain as you are that what pleases God is not that you pray, receive Communion, do acts of penance, study, or preach sermons, but that you suffer with patience the infirmity or the pains which he sees fit to send you? Unite your own sufferings, then, with those of Jesus Christ. But, you say, I am troubled that, because I am an invalid, I am burdensome to the community or to the house. But as you resign yourself to the will of God, so you ought to believe that your superiors, too, resign themselves, seeing as they do that it is not through any laziness of your own but through the will of God that you have laid this burden upon the house. No, these desires and regrets do not spring from the love of God, but from the love of self, hunting after excuses to depart from the will of God. Is it our wish to give pleasure to God? Let us say, then, whenever we happen to be confined to our beds, to the Lord this only, "Your will be done." By this alone we shall give more pleasure to God than we could give him by all the mortifications and devotions which we could perform. There is no better mode of serving God than by cheerfully embracing his will. Juan of Avila wrote to a priest who was an invalid: "My friend, do not stop to calculate what you might do if you were well, but be content to remain unwell as long as

God shall please. If your object is to do God's will, how is it of more consequence for you to be well than ill?" And certainly this was wisely said, for God is not glorified so much by our works as by our resignation and conformity to his holy will. And that is why Saint Francis de Sales used to say that we serve God more by suffering than by working.

I call the time of sickness the touchstone by which spirits are tried, because in it is ascertained the value of the virtue which anyone possesses. If he does not lose his tranquillity, if he makes no complaints, and is not overanxious, but obeys his medical advisers and his superiors, preserving throughout the same peacefulness of mind, in perfect resignation to the divine will, it is a sign that he possesses great virtue. But what, then, ought one to say of the sick person who laments over himself, and says that he receives but little help from others, that his sufferings are intolerable, that he can find no remedy to do him good, that his physician is ignorant, at times complaining even to God that his hand presses too heavily upon him? Saint Bonaventure relates, in his life of Saint Francis, that when the saint was suffering pains of an extraordinary severity, one of his religious, who was somewhat too simple, said to him: "Father, pray to God to treat you with a little more gentleness; for it seems that he lays his hand upon you too heavily." Saint Francis, on hearing this, cried aloud and said to him in reply: "Listen. If I did not know that these words of yours were the offspring of mere simplicity, I would never see you more, daring, as you have done, to find fault with the judgments of God." And after saying this, extremely enfeebled and emaciated through his sickness though he was, he threw himself from his bed upon the floor and, kissing it, he said: "Lord, I thank you for all the sufferings which you send me. I pray you send me more of them, if it so please you. It is my delight for you to afflict me, and not to spare me in the least degree, because the fulfillment of your will is the greatest consolation which in this life I can receive."

Under this head we must also class the loss which at times we may have to suffer of persons who, either temporally or spiritually, happen to be of service to us. This is a matter regarding which those who are devout are often very faulty, through their lack of resignation to the divine dispensations. Our sanctification must come to us not from spiritual directors but from God. It is indeed his will that we should avail ourselves of directors as spiritual guides, when he gives them to us. But when he takes them away, he wills that we should rest content with this, and increase our confidence in his goodness, saying at such times: Lord, it is you who have given me this assistance; now you have taken it from me. May your will be ever done, but I pray you now to supply my needs yourself and to teach me what I ought to do to serve you. And in the same way we ought to receive all other crosses from the hands of God. But so many troubles, you say, are chastisements. I ask in reply, are not the chastisements which God sends us in this life acts of kindness and benefits? If we have offended him, we have to satisfy the divine justice in some way or other, either in this life or in the next. Therefore we ought all of us to say with Saint Augustine, "Here burn, here cut, here do not spare; so that you may spare in eternity." It ought, too, to be a consolation to one who has deserved hell to see that God is punishing him in this world. This should give him good hope that it may be God's will to deliver him from eternal punishment. Let us, then, say when suffering the chastisements of God what was said by Heli the high priest: "It is the Lord: let him do what is good in his sight" (1 Kings 3:18).

In times of spiritual desolation also, we ought to be resigned. When a soul gives itself up to the spiritual life, the Lord is accustomed to heap consolations upon it, in order to wean it from the pleasures of the world. But afterward, when he sees it more settled in spiritual ways, he draws back his hand, in order to make proof of its love, and to see whether it serves and loves him unrecompensed, while in this world, with spiritual joys. "While we are living here," as Saint Teresa used to say, "our gain does not consist in any increase of our enjoyment of God, but in the performance of his will." And in another passage: "The love of God does not consist in tendernesses, but in serving him with firmness and humility." Let, then, the soul thank the Lord when he caresses it with sweetnesses, but not torment itself with acts of impatience when it sees itself left in a state of desolation. This is a point which should be well attended to, for some foolish persons, seeing themselves in a state of aridity, think that God may have abandoned them, or, again, that the spiritual life was not made for them, and so they leave off prayer and lose all that they have gained. There is no better time for exercising our resignation to the will of God than that of dryness. These spiritual desolations and abandonments are what all the saints have suffered. "What hardness of heart," said Saint Bernard, "do I not experience! I no longer find any delight in reading, no longer any pleasure in meditation or in prayer." The condition of the saints has been ordinarily one of dryness, not of sensible consolations. These are things which the Lord does not bestow, except on rare occasions, and to perhaps the weaker sort of spirits, in order to prevent their coming to a standstill in their spiritual course. The joys which he proposes as rewards, he prepares for us in heaven. This world is the place for meriting, where we merit by suffering; heaven is the place for rewards and enjoyments. Therefore, what the saints have desired and sought for in this world has been not a sensible fervor with rejoicing, but a spiritual fervor with suffering.

But, you will say, if I could only know that this desolation comes from God, I should be content. But what afflicts and disquiets me is the fear that it may have come through my own fault and as a punishment for my tepidity. Well, then, stop thinking about your tepidity and employ greater diligence. But will you, because you are perhaps under a cloud, will you therefore disquiet yourself, leave off prayer, and thus double the evil of which you complain? Let it be that, as you say, the dryness is come upon you as a chastisement. Then accept it as a chastisement on one who so much deserves to be chastised, and unite yourself with the divine will. Go and rest content with the manner in which God is dealing with you, persevere in prayer and in the way on which you have entered, and henceforth let it be your fear that your complaints may arise from your too slight humility and too slight resignation to the will of God. When a soul applies itself to prayer, it can derive no benefit from it that can be greater than the union of itself with the divine will. Therefore make an act of resignation, and say: Lord, I accept this pain from your hands, and I accept it for as long as may please you. And in this way your prayer, painful though it may be, will be a greater help to you than any consolation, however sweet.

We must, however, bear in mind that dryness is not always a punishment, but is occasionally ordained by God for our greater good, in order to keep us humble. That Saint Paul might not grow proud of the gifts which he had received, the Lord permitted him to be tormented by temptations of impurity: "Lest the greatness of the revelations should exalt me, there was given me a sting of my flesh, an angel of Satan, to buffet me" (2 Cor 12:7). He who prays in times of sweetness does no great thing: "There is a companion at the table, and he will not abide in the day of distress" (Sir 6:10). You would not think a true friend of yours the person who was with you only at your table, but rather the one who assisted you in times of trouble and without any advantage to himself. When God sends darkness and desolations, he is testing his true friends. Paladius suffered a great weariness in prayer; when he went to tell Saint Macarius, the latter said to him, "When the thought suggests itself to you that you should leave off prayer, let this be your reply: I am content, for the love of Jesus Christ, to remain here as guardian of the walls of this cell." This, then, is your answer, whenever you feel yourself tempted to leave off prayer, because it seems to you nothing more than a mere waste of time: "I am here in order to give pleasure to God." Saint Francis de Sales used to say that if in time of prayer we did no more than drive away distractions and temptations, our prayer would be well made.

What is said with regard to aridity, must also be said of temptations. We should try to avoid temptations; but if God wills or permits that we be tempted against the faith, against purity, or against any other virtue, we ought not to complain, but to resign ourselves in this also to the divine will. To Saint Paul, who prayed to be released from his temptation to impurity, the Lord answered: "My grace is sufficient for you." And so if we see that God does not listen to us by releasing us from some troublesome temptation, let us likewise say: Lord, do and permit whatever pleases you; your grace is sufficient for me; only grant me your assistance, that I may never lose it. It is not temptations, but the consenting to temptations, that is the cause of our losing divine grace. Temptations, when we overcome them, keep us more humble, gain for us greater merits, make us have recourse to God more frequently, and thus keep us further from offending him, and unite us more closely to his holy love.

Lastly, we must unite ourselves with the will of God in regard to our death, and as to the time and manner in which he will send it. Saint Gertrude one day, when climbing up a hill, slipped down and fell into a ravine. Her companions asked her afterward whether she would not have been afraid to die without the sacraments. The saint replied: "It is my great desire to die with the sacraments; but I consider that the will of God is more important, because I hold that the best disposition one could have for making a good death would be one's submission to that which God might will. Therefore, I desire whatever death my Lord shall be pleased to allot me." As to the manner, then, we ought to esteem that death to be the best for us which God may have determined shall be ours. Save us, Lord, let us ever say when thinking of our death, and then let us die in whatever manner seems good to you.

Thus, again, we ought to unite our will with his as to the time of our death. What is this world but a prison for us to suffer in, and to be in danger every moment of losing God? It was this fear which made Saint Teresa sigh for death; on hearing the clock strike, she felt the utmost consolation in the thought that an hour of her life had passed, an hour of her danger of losing God. What is more precious, or more to be desired, than by a good death to secure to ourselves the impossibility of losing the grace of our God? But, you say, "I have as yet done nothing; there is nothing that I have gained for my soul." But if it be the will of God for your life to terminate at this time, what would you do afterward, if you were to remain alive contrary to that will of his? And who knows whether in that case you would make such a death as you can have hope of making now? Who knows whether, through a change of will, you might not fall into other sins and involve yourself in damnation?

I say, moreover, that he who has but little desire for heaven shows that he has but little love for God. One who loves desires the presence of the object loved. But we cannot see God without leaving this world, and that is why all the saints have sighed for death, in order to go and see the Lord whom they have loved.

Thus did Augustine sigh, "Oh, may I die, that I may see you!" Thus, too, Saint Paul, "having a desire to be dissolved and to be with Christ" (Phil 1:23). And in like manner, also, all the souls that have been enamored of God. It is related by a certain writer that one day as a gentleman was out hunting in a forest he heard a man singing sweetly. On going in that direction, he found a poor leper in a state of semiputrefaction. He asked him if it was he who was singing. "Yes," replied he, "it was I." "And how can you ever be singing and contented under sufferings like these, which are taking your life away?" The leper replied: "There is nothing to stand between my Lord God and myself but this wall of clay which is my body. When this impediment is removed, I shall go to enjoy my God. And seeing, as I do, that it is falling into pieces every day, I therefore rejoice and sing."

Finally, even as regards our degrees in grace and glory, we must bring our own will into uniformity to the divine. Highly as we ought to value the things of the glory of God, we ought to value his will even more. It is right for us to desire to love him more than the seraphim do, but it is not right for us to go on to wish for any other degree of love than that which the Lord has determined on granting us. It all comes to this, as Rodriguez explains it, that although we should be diligent to attain the greatest perfection in our power; nevertheless, when we fall short, we ought not to lose our peace and conformity to the will of God, which has permitted the failing on our part, nor our courage either. Let us raise ourselves up immediately from our fall. Let us humble ourselves in acts of penance and, seeking for greater assistance from God, let us pursue our course. So in like manner, although we may rightly desire to be added in heaven to the choir of the seraphim—not, indeed, that we may have the more glory for ourselves, but in order to give more glory to God, and so that we may love him the more—we should, nevertheless, resign ourselves to his holy will, contenting ourselves with that degree which through his mercy he shall deign to grant us.

It would be too obvious a fault to desire to possess gifts of supernatural prayer, such as ecstasies, visions, and revelations. On the contrary, spiritual writers say that those souls on which God bestows the favor of such graces ought to pray him to deprive them of them, in order that they may love him by the way of pure faith, which is the safest way. There are many who have attained perfection without these supernatural graces. Those only are virtues which raise the soul to sanctity, and chief among their number stands uniformity to the will of God. If God does not choose to raise us to a high degree of perfection and of glory, let us conform ourselves in all respects to his holy will, praying to him that he would at least save us through his mercy.

In short, we ought to regard all things that do or will happen to us as proceeding from God's hands, and everything that we do we should direct to this one end, the fulfillment of his will, and to do it simply because God wills it to be done. And so that we may go on with greater security in this, we must follow the guidance of our superiors in regard to what is external and of our directors with regard to what is internal, so that we may through them understand what it is that God wants of us, having great faith in those words of Jesus Christ to us: "He that hears you, hears me" (Lk 10:16). And above all let it be our study to serve God in the way in which it is his will we should serve him. I say this so that we may shun the deception practiced upon himself by one who loses time amusing himself by saying: "If I were in a desert, if I were to enter a monastery, if I were to go somewhere so as not to remain in this house, to a distance from these relations or these companions of mine, I would sanctify myself; I would do such and such a penance; I would make such and such prayers." He says, "I would do, I would do." But in the meantime, by bearing with a bad will the cross which God sends him, he not only does not sanctify himself, but goes from bad to worse. These desires are temptations of the devil. We must therefore drive them away and embrace the service of God in that one way which he has chosen for us. By doing his will, we shall certainly sanctify ourselves in any state in which God places us. Let us, then, always will only that which God wills, so that he may take and press us to his heart. For this end, let us make ourselves familiar with some of those passages of Scripture which call upon us to unite ourselves ever more and more with the divine will: "I am thine, save thou me" (Ps 118:94). And especially at times when any very grievous calamity befalls us—as in the case of the death of parents, of the loss of property, and things of a similar kind—"Yea, Father" (let it ever be ours to say), "yea, Father; for so hath it seemed good in your sight" (Mt 11:26). The Lord told Saint Catherine of Genoa that whenever she said the "Our Father" she was to pay particular attention to these words and pray that his holy will might be fulfilled by her with the same perfection with which it is fulfilled by the saints in heaven. Let us, too, act in this manner and we shall certainly become saints ourselves.

Considerations on the Religious State

The Damage Done to Religious by Tepidity

Consider the misery of that religious who, after having left his home, his parents, and the world with all its pleasures, and after having given himself to Jesus Christ, consecrating to him his will and his liberty, exposes himself at last to the danger of being damned, by falling into a lukewarm and negligent life, and continuing therein. Oh, no, not far from perdition is a lukewarm religious who has been called into the house of God to become a saint. God threatens to reject such, and to abandon them, if they do not amend. "But because you are lukewarm, I will begin to vomit you out of my mouth" (Rev 3:16).

Saint Ignatius of Loyola, seeing a laybrother of his order become lukewarm in the service of God, called him one day and said to him: Tell me, brother, why did you come to religion? He answered: To serve God. O my brother! Replied the saint, what have you said? If you had answered that you came to serve a cardinal, or a prince of this earth, you would be more excusable; but you say that you came to serve God, and do you serve him thus?

Father Nieremberg says that some are called by God to be saved only as saints, so that, if they should not take care to live as that, if they should not take care to live as saints, thinking to be saved as imperfect Christians, they will not be saved at all. And Saint Augustine says that such are in most cases abandoned by God: "Negligent souls God is accustomed to abandon" (Ps 118:10).

And how does he abandon them? By permitting them from lighter faults, which they see, and do not mind, to fall into grievous ones, and lose divine grace and their vocations. Saint Teresa of Jesus saw the place prepared for her in hell, had she not detached herself from an earthly, though not a grievously culpable affection. "One who despises small things, shall fall by little and little" (Sir 19:1).

Many wish to follow Jesus Christ, but from afar as Saint Peter did, who, when his Master was arrested in the garden, says Saint Matthew, "followed him afar off" (Mt 26:58). But by doing so, that will easily happen to them which happened to Saint Peter, namely, that when the occasion came he denied Jesus Christ. A lukewarm religious will be contented with what little he does for God; but God, who called him to a perfect life, will not be contented, and in punishment for his ingratitude will not only deprive him of his special favors, but will sometimes permit his fall. "When you said, It is enough, then you perished" (Serm 169, E.B.). The fig tree of the Gospel was cast into the fire, only because it brought forth no fruit.

Father Louis de Ponte said: "I have committed many faults, but I have never made peace with them." Miserable is that religious who, being called to perfection, makes peace with his defects. As long as we detest our imperfections, there is hope that we may still become saints; but when we commit faults and make little of them, then, says Saint Bernard, the hope of becoming saints is lost. "He who sows sparingly, shall also reap sparingly" (2 Cor 9:6). Common graces do not suffice to make one a saint, extraordinary ones are necessary; but how will God be liberal with his favors towards the one that acts sparingly and with reserve in his love towards him?

Moreover, to become a saint one must have courage and strength to overcome all repugnances; and let no one ever believe, says Saint Bernard, that he will be able to attain to perfection if he does not render himself singular among others in the practice of virtue. "What is perfect cannot but be singular." Reflect, my brother, for what you left the world and all. To become a saint. But that lukewarm and imperfect life which you lead, is that the way of becoming a saint? Saint Teresa animated her daughters by saying to them: *My sisters, you have done the principal thing necessary to become saints; the least remains yet to be done.* The same I say to you; you have, perhaps, done the chief part already; you have left your country, your home, your parents, your goods, and your amusements; the least remains yet to be done, to become a saint; do it.

How Necessary It Is, in Order to Become a Saint, to Have a Great Desire for It

No saint has ever attained to sanctity without a great desire. As wings are necessary to fly, so holy desires are necessary to the soul in order to advance in the road to perfection. To become saints, we must detach ourselves from creatures, conquer our passions, overcome ourselves, and love crosses. But to do all this, much strength is required, and we must suffer much. But what is the effect of holy desire? Saint Laurence Justinian answers us: "It supplies strength, and makes the pain easier to be borne" (De Dis. mon. c. 6). Hence the same saint adds, that he has already vanquished who has a great desire of vanquishing: "A great part of the victory is the desire of vanquishing" (De Casto Conn. c. 3). He who wishes to reach the top of a high mountain will never reach it if he has not a great desire to do so. This will give him courage and strength to undergo the fatigue of ascending, otherwise he will stop at the foot wearied and discouraged.

Saint Bernard asserts that we acquire perfection in proportion to the desire for it which we preserve in our heart, and Saint Teresa said that God loves generous souls that have great desires, for which reason the saint exhorted all in this way: "Let our thoughts be high,...for thence will come our good. We must not have low and little desires, but have that confidence in God, that, if we make the proper efforts, we shall by little and little attain to that perfection which, with His grace, the saints attained in a short time, to a great degree of perfection, and were able to do great things for God." "Being made perfect in a short time, he fulfilled a long time" (Wis 4:13). Thus Saint Aloysius Gonzaga attained in a few years (he lived not over twenty-three years) to such a degree of sanctity, that Saint Mary Magdalene of Pazzi, in an ecstasy, seeing him in heaven, said, it seemed to her in a certain way that there was no saint in heaven who enjoyed a greater glory than Aloysius; and she understood at the same time that he had arrived at so high a degree by the great desire he had cherished of being able to love God as much as he deserved, and that seeing this beyond his reach, the holy youth had suffered on earth a martyrdom of love.

Saint Bernard, being in religion, in order to excite his fervor used to say to himself: "Bernard, for what did you come here?" I say the same to you: What have you come to do in the house of God? To become a saint? And what are you doing? Why do you lose the time? Tell me, do you desire to become a saint? If you do not, it is certain you will never become one. If, then, you have not this desire, ask Jesus Christ for it, ask Mary for it. And if you have it, take courage, says Saint Bernard, for many do not become saints, because they do not take courage. And so I repeat it, let us take courage, and great courage. What do we fear? What inspires this diffidence in us? That Lord who has given us strength to leave the world will give us also the grace to embrace the life of a saint. Everything comes to an end. Our life, be it a contented or a discontented one, will also come to an end, but eternity will never terminate. Only that little we have done for God will console us in death and throughout eternity. The fatigue will be short, eternal shall be the crown, which is already, so to speak, before our eyes. How satisfied are the saints now with all that they have suffered for God! If a sorrow could enter paradise, the blessed would be sorry for this alone, that they have neglected to do for God what they might have done more, but which now they are unable to do. Take courage then, and be prompt, for there is no time to lose; what can be done today, we may not be able to do tomorrow. Saint Bernardine of Siena said that one moment of time is of as great a value as God himself, for at every moment we may gain God, his divine grace, and higher degrees of merits.

A Dialogue Between a Pastor and Penitent

Consolation for a Soul in a State of Spiritual Desolation

Pastor: Tell me what these troubles of conscience are, which give you so much uneasiness.

Penitent: For about two years I have never found God, neither in meditation, nor before the Blessed Sacrament, nor in the Holy Communion. My soul seems to be devoid of love, of hope, and of faith; in a word, abandoned by almighty God. Neither the Passion of Jesus Christ, nor the most holy Eucharist, any longer affects me, and I am become quite insensible to all feelings of devotion. I acknowledge that I have merited all this, for by my sins I have deserved hell.

Pastor: Have you confessed your sins?

Penitent: Yes, Father, I confessed them when I made a general confession, and have many times since confessed them.

Pastor: Obedience to God's ministers is the only and most secure means of calming doubts of conscience left us by Jesus Christ; for which we ought to return him our sovereign thanks. Without it how could a scrupulous soul find in her doubts perfect security or rest? The trial of scrupulosity (which of all others is the most afflicting to those who love God, more so than sickness, or persecution, or any similar crosses) has been endured by almost all the saints. Saint Teresa, Saint Mary Magdalene of Pazzi, Saint Jane Frances de Chantal and many others, how were they pacified? By obedience. Now, what do you say? Are you convinced that you will be safe in obeying your director?

Penitent: Yes, Father, I am convinced; but why, after being obedient to my director for these two years, do I not experience more devotion?

Pastor: Now I know where your fault lies; why do you say that you cannot find peace of soul? Do you seek to discover the will of God, or do you look for consolations and spiritual sweetness; if you wish to become a saint, from this day forward seek only the will of God, who wills your sanctification, and not your consolation, be consoled with the hope that your comforter is with you. Do you complain of two years of aridity? Saint Mary Magdalene of Pazzi suffered five years of interior trials and temptations, without the least comfort, and, after these five years, she besought God not to grant her sensible consolations in this life. Saint Philip Neri was so inflamed with divine love, that he sometimes exclaimed: "O Jesus, never have I yet loved you; would that I did really love you!" On other occasions he would say: "As yet I do not know you, O Jesus, because I do not seek you." On others: "I would indeed love you, O Jesus, but I know not how to love you. I seek you, but I do not find you." Such are the sentiments of the saints: and are you so discouraged because you experience aridity and do not find God as you wish to find him?

Penitent: But they were saints, and I do not know whether God has forgiven me the many offenses which I have committed against him, for I am not sure that I have ever had true contrition for them.

I humble myself, I beg of God to forgive me, and purpose to do better for the future, relying on Jesus Christ for strength and assistance; but notwithstanding I feel dejected and disturbed, and it seems to me almost impossible ever to become a saint; it even seems pride to aspire to it.

Pastor: All is right; continue always to do so; but do not be disquieted, for this is not right; should you fall a hundred times in the day, do always the same, repent, purpose to do better for the future, with the divine assistance, place your trust in Jesus Christ, and be not any longer uneasy. Know that it is not pride, even after a fault, to hope to become a saint; but it would indeed be pride to lose courage, and to be disquieted, as though your resolutions had secured you from falling again. Humble yourself therefore and confide in God.

Penitent: Father, since you are so charitable to me, I beg of you to give me some instructions which may comfort me in my difficulties, when I shall not see you.

Pastor: Well then, I will give you some few things written confusedly, simply, and without order, which you may read when you find yourself more than usually depressed, and which may encourage you to endure the struggle which every one without exception must undergo in this valley of tears and death.

1 • The first thing I recommend to you is strict obedience to your director; be particular in obeying him in every thing; and by every thing I mean whatever you are certain is sinful. Recollect what Saint Teresa says, that by being obedient to our directors, whether painful to us or not, we are sure to do the will of God. Saint Bernard says, that the most certain remedy for scruples is to submit to the judgment of a guide, God himself having appointed this remedy, in order that those who cannot resolve their own doubts and scruples, may be able to do so by the advice of a director, who, although he may be deceived, as the scrupulous will have it, yet will not deceive them; they will be safe in obeying him as a guide divinely appointed them by God.

2 ◆ Be careful in all adverse circumstances to receive all as coming from the hands of God, and, especially in time of sickness, be strictly obedient to your physician in using the remedies which he prescribes; explain to him all your sufferings without exaggeration, and then be satisfied. Do not crave the compassion of those who visit you, and when any one immoderately commiserates you, say, with Jesus Christ: "The chalice, which the Father has given me, shall I not drink it?" (Jn 28:11). God sends me this sickness, not because he wishes me evil, but because he desires my good; and shall I not calmly accept of it? In sickness it is seen of what spirit a person really is. There are devout persons, who so long as they enjoy good health, are all sweetness and humility, but are no sooner attacked with indisposition than they immediately become impatient and proud, and complain of every body, especially if they have not some remedy or service exactly when they want it. When then you are unwell, endure all without any complaint. In all adversities say with holy Job: "As it has pleased the Lord, so it be done. Blessed be the name of the Lord" (1:21). Be careful also to bear with slights and contempt without resenting them: it is seen whether or no a person is humble, when he receives contempt with patience.

3 ◆ For the rest be cheerful and of good heart, placing great confidence in Jesus Christ, who is all goodness to them that seek him: "The Lord is good to the soul that seeks him. No one has hoped in the Lord and has been confounded" (Eccl 2:11). God allows himself to be found even by those who do not seek him, as Saint Paul says: "I was found by them that did not seek me" (Rom 10:20); reciting Isaiah 65:1. How much more readily will he present himself to them that do seek him? Be careful then henceforward how you say that God has abandoned you: the Lord abandons only such as are obstinate in their sins, and even these he does not abandon altogether, but is evernigh to them until their death, assisting them with certain lights that they may not be lost.

4 • When a soul endeavors to love God, he cannot help loving such a soul in return: "I love them that love me" (Prov 8:17). And when he hides himself from them that love him, he does it only for their good, to make them more desirous of his grace, and to unite them more closely to himself. Hear what Saint Catherine of Genoa said when she was suffering great spiritual dryness, so great that she seemed to herself to be abandoned by God, and that no hope was left her: "How happy am I in this deplorable state! Let my heart be desolate, provided my love be glorified. My dear love, if from this my unhappy state the least glory accrue to you, I beseech you to leave me in it for all eternity." And saying this she shed floods of tears in the midst of her desolation.

5 • Know that the lovers of the cross, in time of desolation, unite themselves more closely with God in their own interior. Nothing so much obliges the soul to seek God, and nothing brings God into the soul so much as desolation; because the acts of conformity with the divine will which are made in the time of desolation, are more pure and perfect; and because the greater the desolation, the greater is humility; resignation, confidence, and prayer, are more pure, and hence grace and the divine assistance are more abundant.

6 • In order to attain perfection, attend, above all, to the exercise of divine love: the love of God alone, when it becomes master of our hearts, destroys in us all inordinate affection. Therefore endeavor to make frequent acts of divine love, saying: My God, I love you, I love you, I love you, and hope to expire as I repeat; my God I love you. The saints say that the soul ought not less to love than to breathe.

7 ◆ Moreover in your meditations offer yourself frequently to God and without reserve. Say to him with your whole heart: O Jesus, I give myself to you without reserve. I desire to be all thine, and if I know not how to give myself to you as I ought, do you yourself, O Jesus, take possession of me and make me all thine own. Saint Teresa offered herself to God fifty times in the day. You may do the same. Hence always give him your will, repeating with Saint Paul: "Lord, what will you have me do?" (Acts 9:6). This act alone was sufficient to change Saint Paul from a persecutor of the Church into a vessel of election. Frequently pray with holy David: "Teach me to do your will." (Ps 132:10). Let all your prayers to God, to the Blessed Virgin, to your Angel Guardian and patron saints be directed to obtain the grace of perfectly accomplishing the will of God. In short, *your will be done* may serve you as a remedy for all your evils.

8 ◆ And when you experience greater aridity, exercise yourself in taking delight in the infinite happiness which God whom you love enjoys, which is the most perfect act of love of the blessed in heaven, who rejoice not so much in their own happiness as in that of God, since they love him immensely more than they love themselves.

9 ◆ As regards the subject of meditation, never cease from meditating on the Passion of Jesus Christ suffering for the love of us, is the object of all others to attract our hearts. In meditating on the mysteries of the Passion, if our Lord be pleased to affect you with tenderness, receive it with gratitude; but if you should experience none, you will at least always receive great comfort in the soul. Go frequently, in particular, to the garden of Gethsemane, as did Saint Teresa, saying that there she found him alone; and considering him in his great afflictions, in an agony, sweating blood, and declaring his soul to be sorrowful unto death, you will indeed find comfort in your afflictions, seeing that he suffers all for the love of you. And at the sight of Jesus thus preparing himself to die for you, you will prepare to die for him, and the more you are afflicted, the more will you say with Saint Thomas the Apostle: "Let us also go, that we may die with him" (Jn 11:16).

10 ◆ Go also to Calvary, where you will find him expiring upon the cross, exhausted with sufferings, and, seeing him in this state, it will be impossible for you not to be encouraged to suffer willingly all things for a God who dies in sorrow for the love of you. Saint Paul protested that he neither knew, nor desired to know, any thing in this life but Jesus Christ crucified: "For I judged myself to know any thing among you, but Jesus Christ and him crucified" (1 Cor 2:2). Saint Bonaventure says that he who desires to preserve a constant devotion to Jesus Christ, ought ever to look upon him with the eyes of the mind dying on the cross. And thus in all your fears look on the crucifix, take courage, and animate yourself to suffer for his love.

11 ◆ Above all, I recommend to you prayer. Although you should say nothing else, it would be sufficient to say: *Incline unto my aid, O God. O Lord, make haste to help me.* You know that the Church obliges her priests and religious to repeat this very often; and Saint Philip Neri advised this prayer to be said as a chaplet sixty-three times in the day. Our Lord has promised to grant us what we ask: *Ask and it shall be given to you.* Saint Bernard was in ecstasy when he thought of the words of Jesus Christ to the sons of Zebedee, who said to him: "Master, we desire that whatsoever we shall ask, you would do it for us.

But he said to them: What would you that I should do for you?" (Mk 10:35).

12 ◆ All the graces which you ask for of God, ask for them always in the name of Jesus Christ. Whatever we receive from God, we receive through the merits of Jesus Christ. And our blessed Redeemer has promised us, that whatever we ask of God in his name, the Father will give to us: "Amen, Amen, I say to you: if you ask the Father anything in my name, he will give it you" (Jn 16:23). Now, when you fear lest God should condemn you to hell, think if it be possible that he should say to you, ask what you please of me and I will give it you, and, at the same time, have the will to consign you to that place of torments.

13 ◆ But perhaps, because you are in desolation, you are willing to suppose that God hates you? You ought not thus to afflict yourself, but to be the more consoled, seeing that God treats you as he treats the souls of his dearest servants, and as he has treated his own Son, of whom the Scripture says: "And the Lord was pleased to bruise him in infirmity" (Isa 43:10). He was pleased that he should be consumed and broken to pieces with grief and torments.

14 ◆ When you are alarmed at the thought that God may wish to abandon you on account of your ingratitude, do as did the two disciples, who, while they were going to Emmaus, Jesus accompanied them in the form of a pilgrim, and when they drew near the place, our Lord appeared to wish to go forward, *and he made as though he would go farther, but they*, says the Evangelist, *constrained him saying: Stay with us because it is towards evening*. And he was pleased to enter into the house, and to remain with them: "And he went in with them" (Lk 24:28,29). And thus you also, when it appears to you that our Lord wishes to leave you, constrain him to remain with you, and say to him: My Jesus, *stay with me*, I am unwilling that you should leave me; if you leave me, to whom shall I go for comfort or safety? "Lord, to whom shall we go?" (Jn 6:69). And thus continuing to pray to him with love and tenderness, fear not, but be assured that he will not leave you. Say to him with the Apostle: "Neither death, nor life…nor any other creature, shall be able to separate us from the love of God" (Rom 8:38,39). Say to him: my Savior show yourself disdainful of me when you please, but neither the fear of death, nor the desire of life, nor any creature in the world, shall be able to separate me from your love. Say indeed what Saint Francis de Sales said when he was a young man, and, being in a state of aridity, the devil suggested to him that he was doomed to hell; he answered: "And since I shall not be able to love my God in eternity, I will love him at least in this life as much as I am able." Saying this he regained the tranquillity of his mind and the peace of his soul.

15 ◆ As often as you desire to love God, dilate your heart. "Open your mouth wide and I will fill it" (Ps 80:11). That is to say, that the more we hope in God, the more we shall receive from him. He himself has declared that he favors them that confide in him: "He is the protector of all that trust in him" (Ps 17:31). And when you doubt whether the Lord regards you, imagine that you hear him reprove you as he did Saint Peter, saying to you: "O you of little faith, why did you doubt?" (Mt 14:31). Why do you doubt whether I have regard to you, knowing my promise that I will listen to all who pray to me? And because he is willing to hear us, he desires that we should believe that he will certainly hear us, when we ask for graces from him: "All things whatsoever you ask, when ye pray, believe that you shall receive: and they shall come unto you" (Mk 11:24). Take notice of the words, *believe that you shall receive*. It is necessary then to ask graces of God with a firm confidence, without doubting whether we shall receive them, as Saint James exhorts us: "Let him ask in faith, nothing wavering" (Jas 1:6). Treating with a God who is all bounty, have full confidence in him, and drive away all melancholy. He who serves God and is sad, instead of honoring him, almost dishonors him. Saint Bernard says that he who represents to himself God as stern and severe, wrongs him, being as he is all goodness and mercy. How can you doubt, says the saint, whether Jesus will forgive you your sins, when he has nailed them to the cross, on which he died for you, with the nails which pierced his hands and feet?

16 ◆ God has declared that his delight is to be with us: "My delight is to be with the children of men" (Prov 8:31). If then it is God's delight to treat with us, it is just that all our delight should be to treat with him. And this thought ought to animate us to treat with God with the greatest confidence, and to take care to pass the remainder of our lives with this our God, who so loves us, and in whose blessed company we hope to live for eternity.

17 ◆ Let us then treat with him with the greatest confidence and love, as with our most dear and affectionate friend, who loves us more than any other. O God! Scrupulous souls treat you as a tyrant, who requires nothing else from his subjects but reserve and fear, and hence are afraid that at every word spoken inconsiderately, at every thought that passes through the mind, you become enraged against them, and wish to plunge them into hell. But no; God does not deprive us of his grace, unless we deliberately slight it and wilfully turn our backs upon him. And when we commit some light offense against him, by some venial sin, this certainly displeases him, but he does not on this account deprive us of the same love which he had for us, hence he is immediately appeased with an act of repentance and love.

18 ◆ His infinite majesty is deserving of all reverence and humility, but from souls that love him he is more pleased to be treated with loving confidence than with timid subjection; and hence treat not God any more as a tyrant. Remind yourself of the graces which he has bestowed upon you, even after the offenses and ingratitude which you have been guilty of against him. Call to your recollection the loving attractions by which he has withdrawn you from a disorderly life, the extraordinary lights which he has communicated to you, by which he has so often called you to his love, and hence from this day forward treat with God with great confidence and tenderness, as with the dearest object which you possess. Let us pass on.

19 ◆ It is not necessary to recommend you to approach the sacraments frequently, because you already do so. Go to confession twice in the week or at least once. As to Communion, obey your director, and although you feel dry, fail not to request it; because directors regulate the Communions of their penitents by the desire which they discover in them for Communion. When your director sees that you do not evince any desire for it, he will hardly of himself require you to receive it. And when you do not really communicate, make at least a spiritual communion; and this you may repeat several times in the day.

20 ◆ Let then these two great mysteries of the most holy Sacrament of the altar and of the Passion of Jesus Christ, be the dearest objects of your heart. If the love of all hearts were united in one, assuredly it would not be sufficient to correspond with the love which Jesus Christ has shown us in these mysteries. Continue then for the remainder of your life, to love and to confide in God, and be not grieved when you find yourself in afflictions and trials, for these are not a sign of the hatred but of the love of God towards you....

Poems

To the Instruments of the Passion of Jesus

O ruthless scourges, with what pain you tear
My Savior's flesh, so innocent and fair!
Oh, cease to rend that flesh divine,
    My loving Lord torment no more;
Wound rather, wound this heart of mine,
    The guilty cause of all He bore.

Ye cruel thorns, in mocking wreath entwin'd,
My Savior's brow in agony to bind,
Oh, cease to rend that flesh divine,
    My loving Lord torment no more;
Wound rather, wound this heart of mine,
    The guilty cause of all He bore.

Unpitying nails, whose points, with anguish fierce,
The hands and feet of my Redeemer pierce!
Oh, cease to rend that flesh divine,
    My loving Lord torment no more;
Wound rather, wound this heart of mine,
    The guilty cause of all he bore.

Unfeeling lance, that dar'st to open wide
The sacred temple of my Savior's side!
Oh, cease to wound that flesh divine,
    My loving Lord insult no more;

Pierce rather, pierce this heart of mine,
The guilty cause of all He bore.

On the Tomb of Alexander the Great

Behold the end of all the pomp of earth,—
All human greatness, beauty, noble birth!—
Worms, rottenness, a little dust, a stone,
Close the brief scene of life for ev'ry one.
Who gives his heart to God alone is wise,
Dead to the world already ere he dies.
O you that read this! You, too, one day
Must die;—which lot do you prefer, I pray,
To die a slave, and then in bliss to reign,—
Or die a king, and pass to endless pain?
Reflect, prepare; the present time flies fast;
Repentance comes too late when life is past.

A Soul Who Is the Lover of Mary

I am the lover of a Queen,
Whose heart so sweet and kind doth prove,
That seeing one who seeks her love,
She scouts him not though poor and mean.

She sits a Queen, with heavenly grace;
But from her throne her gentle eyes
Look down on him who humbly sighs
To see the beauty of her face.

This Virgin is so pure, that she
    Was chosen by the Eternal Word
    The Spouse, the Mother of our Lord;
And she has stol'n my heart from me.

Oh! could I but behold, one day,
    All hearts with love of her inflam'd,
    And hear her sweetest name proclaim'd
By every tongue in joyful lay!

Then in sweet harmony should flow,
    In every land through endless days:
    Praise be to Mary, ceaseless praise!
And praise to God who loved her so!

Let him who wills seek other love,
    If earthly beauty can rejoice
    His soul:—she only is my choice
Whose beauty ravished God above.

Then, Mary, stretch your hand to me,
    Sweet loving Robber! seize your prey:
    Take from my breast this heart away,
Which sighs and languishes for you.

That fire of love into it pour
    With which you cease not to burn,
    That my poor heart, like thine, may yearn
With love of Jesus evermore.

In Honor of Saint Teresa

Written on these words of hers:
"I am dying because I cannot die."

Ye angels most inflamed
    With fires of heavenly love,
Bright Seraphim! descend
    From your high thrones above;
To this most chosen soul
    Your loving succor bring,
To her, the spouse belov'd
    Of Christ your God and King.

Jesus, your Love, your Life,
    Who loves the pure of heart,
Has pierced Teresa's soul
    With love's own flaming dart,
And lo! she pines away,
    She languishes, she sighs;
For Him who gave the wound
    Of very love she dies.

Too bitter is the pang
    Of such a wounded heart,
That loves and pines away
    From her Belov'd apart.
Come, heavenly spirits, come;
    Console the wounded dove;
Teresa moans with grief
    Of absence from her Love.

To see her loving Spouse
So fierce is her desire,
That evermore she burns,
Consuming in its fire.
That sweet and longing wish
Into His arms to fly,
Is but a living death,
Because she cannot die.

No angels come to aid;
Come You, who in this breast
Have kindled flames so dear,
Come You, and give her rest.
Sick is her soul with love,
And wounded is her heart;
You did inflict the wound,
Then, Jesus, cure its smart.

Your spouse was ever true,
To please your heart divine,
All earth could give she left,
All she could give is Thine;
And now she loves You well,
And sighs to come to You;
She longs to take her flight,—
Ah! set her spirit free.